Today, 17 million women own guns. Yet widespread and persistent discomfort with this choice still begs the question— should they?

IN THEIR OWN WORDS

"There's a sense of danger now, an awareness that there may come a point where I am responsible for myself and other human beings. So, a lot of women are saying: Now is the time to go out to the range and learn how a gun functions. . . ."

"Why do we need to balance the 'needs and desires of gun enthusiasts' with anything at all? Why should we bow to the rage and hunger of a single-issue lobby? I am no longer an advocate of gun control. I am an advocate of gun elimination. . . ."

"The KKK was riding through the black community, burning churches, beating up people, killing people. . . . At one point it got so bad that my grandfather kept his gun—a double-barreled shotgun—close by at all times. . . . I remember thinking that whatever happened, I wanted to see it. I wanted to see him shoot that gun. . . ."

"My children are my life. . . . I don't want scars on their bodies or in their brains and hearts. The way parents were afraid of polio in the 1950s, scared of public pools and free-floating germs, I am afraid of guns. . . ."

American Women and Guns

BLOWN AWAY

CAITLIN KELLY

POCKET BOOKS
New York London Toronto Sydney

POCKET BOOKS, a division of Simon & Schuster, Inc.
1230 Avenue of the Americas, New York, NY 10020

ISBN: 0-7434-6418-4

First Pocket Books trade paperback edition April 2004

10 9 8 7 6 5 4 3 2 1

POCKET and colophon are registered trademarks of
Simon & Schuster, Inc.

Interior design by Davina Mock

Manufactured in the United States of America

For information regarding special discounts for bulk purchases,
please contact Simon & Schuster Special Sales at 1-800-456-6798
or business@simonandschuster.com

To the memory of Philippe Viannay
journalist, teacher, and friend,
whose courage, vision, and
joie de vivre touched so many

Contents

Acknowledgments

————◆·✕·◆————

THIS BOOK, LARGELY BASED ON ORIGINAL REPORTING THAT required direct access to a number of wary sources, would not have been possible without the help and encouragement of many people.

I first explored this subject in 1996 in an essay for *The Globe and Mail,* and I thank former Focus editor Sarah Murdoch for giving me that initial opportunity. Ray Sokolov, the former Arts and Leisure editor of the *Wall Street Journal,* sent me to the Smith & Wesson Academy for three days, where I began to appreciate firsthand more of the complexities of the gun world. Peter Bloch, editor of *Penthouse,* further encouraged my focus specifically on women and guns.

Fellow writers who generously offered insights, practical advice, and sources include Colin Beavan, David Porter, Kate Buford, Sam Tenenhaus, Jason Berry, Ellis Henican, Steve Slavin, Mathew Phelps, Madeline Bodin, Jeff Inglis, Chris Mele, and Salem Alaton. Nicole Curvin and Elaine Heinzman offered suggestions on early drafts, and Bill Porter helped ensure technical accuracy.

In Texas, managing editor John Cowan, and columnist and

author Ross McSwain, of the *San Angelo Standard Times,* were extremely generous with their local sources. Thanks to Mike and Millie Lopez in Fort Worth and Stacy Ruedebusch in San Antonio for their hospitality.

Others who graciously shared their knowledge and contacts with me include Bill Brown, Bill Porter, and Paul Cunningham of the Smith & Wesson Academy; Peter Coddington of the Bronx District Attorney's office; firearms historian Gary James; civil rights historian Tim Tyson; security expert John Timoney; film writer Cari Beauchamp; music historian John Rumble; Rolland Riggs; Calum Johnston; James Gray; Dennis Wygmans; Doris McClellan; and John McCann, director of COPE. Gary Mehalik and Paul Erhardt of the National Shooting Sports Foundation patiently fielded my dozens of queries, as did Mary Sue Faulkner of the National Rifle Association. Amy Heath of Women on Target allowed me unimpeded access to her Manhattan event.

Librarians Rusty Gamez and Dora Guerra at the Daughters of the Republic of Texas Library at the Alamo in San Antonio, and Tracey MacGowan at the Woman's Collection of Texas Woman's University in Denton, helped me make good use of their extensive collections.

I'm especially indebted to Jamilah Clark, director of the women's program, and to Clinton Lacey, executive director of the Friends of Island Academy in Manhattan, for helping me meet, and talk with, young women I could not otherwise have reached.

Research assistants Rachel Markowitz, Laura Ciechanowski, Elaine Heinzman, and Jessica Brown were a joy to work with. Their speed, diligence, skills, and enthusiasm were indispensable. Nothing fazed them, for which I'm grateful.

My fiancé Jose R. Lopez, a fellow journalist, offered extraordinary emotional and practical support.

In 1982, I won a European fellowship from Journalistes en Europe, an innovative program founded in 1981 by the late Philippe Viannay to educate young journalists from around the world. Already a legend in his native France as a Resistance hero, as founder of a respected Paris journalism school, and as cofounder of the daily *Le Matin,* among other ventures, Viannay became an indelible mentor, demanding of excellence while encouraging risk. I remain grateful for his enthusiasm and his friendship.

Lauren McKenna, my editor at Pocket Books, has this spirit of adventure and immediately understood and appreciated the larger goals of this project as did my agent, William Clark.

My father, Ron, a filmmaker, and my mother, Cynthia, a journalist, showed me the importance, and pleasure, of tackling difficult stories.

My greatest thanks are due the many women, and men, who trusted me with their stories. This book is theirs.

Introduction

————◆◆◆————

Iт was 4 a.m., and Theresa Kingsbury was driving north from Danbury, Connecticut, to Kingston, New York, a distance of about one hundred miles. Alone in her Honda, she had $5,000 cash, transferring it from one branch of her employer's ski shop to another. The highway was empty. Suddenly, two cars raced up behind her, forcing her onto the shoulder. A woman alone in a deserted location, she appeared an easy mark. The cars stopped and two men walked toward her car, one brandishing a hammer. She raised her loaded pistol to the window where they could easily see it. The men fled.

Peggy Landry, sixty-four, was out one summer's evening with her girlfriends in a residential part of New Orleans. They'd enjoyed dinner and had just gotten into their car when Landry heard a man's voice threatening the driver. Suddenly he jammed a revolver into the open window against the head of another of Landry's friends, sitting beside her in the backseat. "This is a robbery! Give me all your jewelry and your money!" he shouted. As her friend pulled out her cash and pulled off her jewelry, Landry reached for her Smith & Wesson .38, grabbed her friend's arm to stop her, and planted the gun against the man's heart. "It was like a standoff at the O.K. Corral," recalls Landry. "He was waiting to see what I would do and I was waiting to see what he would do." Terrified, he took off.

For Carrmon Whitehead, a thirty-three-year-old nurse in Colorado City, Texas, a protection order against her ex-husband was proving worthless. Ordered to stay away from her and their three young children, he had already poured sugar in her gas tank, punctured her tires, and cut her telephone lines. A friend encouraged her to get a gun and learn to use it. The next time he appeared at her door, drunk and eager for another round of cat and mouse, proved his last. Wearing her "little red nightgown," Whitehead raised a .357 Magnum, pointed it in his direction (aiming carefully for the empty field behind him), and fired it for the first time. He hasn't bothered her since.

The muzzle of a gun was the only part of "No!" these men understood.

Do women *really* want to arm themselves for self-defense? Probably not. In an ideal world, women would never have to fear attack. But that's not the world we live in, whether home lies at the end of a silent country road or the thirty-fifth floor of a city high-rise.

Many women abhor fighting violence with more violence, and so this book includes those who hate and fear guns as well as those who enjoy owning them. Women buy guns for the pleasures of sport and competition, for a sense of safety, independence, and competence. My aim here is not to judge them, but to present both sides: those who enjoy guns and those horrified by them.

One thing is true: none of us wants to become a victim. Yet when women decide to fight back, and when that choice involves acquiring a firearm, they often face considerable social disapproval, both privately and publicly. Even if her friends and family support her choice, politicians, journalists, feminists, and gun-control advocates—who may never even have touched or fired a gun—are eager to dissuade her. Those who most consistently favor women arming themselves for self-defense are police officers and private investigators (usually former police), who understand criminal behavior and have seen firsthand its devastating physical and psychological effects, short- and long-term.

Since the terrorist attacks of September 11, 2001, fighting terrorism has dominated the imagination, and manpower, of local, state, regional, and federal law enforcement, arguably placing women at greater risk as police forces are spread more thinly, their attention focused on issues of national security—not domestic violence, rape, or burglary. No matter how distasteful or frightening to consider, creating and practicing an effective form of self-defense may now be more crucial than ever for women.

Depending upon where you live and what social circles you move in, mentioning your interest in guns, or in acquiring one, is a guaranteed conversation-stopper. It can quickly separate a woman from her family, friends, neighbors, and colleagues, marking her as . . .

As *what* exactly? Paranoid? Vengeful? Out of control? Powerful? Independent?

Men and women alike are often deeply ambivalent about a woman who owns a gun and knows how to use it. In a culture where women inject their brows with deadly bacteria to paralyze their facial muscles, relaxing wrinkles that show emotion, an armed, angry female is a deeply unsettling vision.

Especially for women, few decisions are more personal, and perhaps more privately political, than buying a firearm.

It's not the kind of purchase you're likely to discuss casually with your tennis partner or your cubicle mate. In the seventeen states that don't allow citizens to carry concealed weapons, many women have likely only seen guns safely holstered on a policeman's belt or waved about on a television show. Ignorant of firearms, a woman may well find the subject frightening, even repellent. Few women considering buying a gun, especially one for self-protection, would be foolish enough to jeopardize her friendships or professional reputation by talking it over with anyone she doesn't know well; if she lives in one of the nation's concealed-carry states, she can more likely turn to someone whose home contains a firearm and who has some working familiarity with how to buy, own, and store one.

It's a decision, then, women most often make, and live with, in secret. Yet, ironically, this crucial decision is still most often made with no female insights, only with male advice. No matter how uninformed a particular man's opinions may be, they nonetheless often carry great weight. Gun expertise becomes a closed loop, as many women—assuming other women don't know the subject—turn to men, some of whom may be gun-shy or clueless, for advice and guidance.

Once they cross the line into gun ownership, however, some women end up devoted to guns in a way they would once have considered unimaginable. Their homes may contain a veritable arsenal. One forty-five-year-old woman I met at a Springfield, Massachusetts, gun show said she had burst into tears of fear and anxiety the first time a boyfriend showed her his gun. Now, a decade later, when asked how many guns she owns, she lolled her head back onto her current boyfriend's shoulder.

"Honey, how many guns do we have?"

"About a hundred."

Why would any woman want to own a gun, or several? Women, social norms still insist, are primarily nurturers and pacifiers, most interested in compromise, conflict resolution, and cooperation. Pointing the barrel of a .38 or a .357 Magnum or a .380 pistol at another human being—or at a paper target or a deer or moose or pheasant—isn't a dream we're encouraged to share. For many people, the words *women* and *guns* rest uneasily in the same sentence.

Like men, women buy guns for many different reasons: to

hunt, to compete, to shoot socially, to protect themselves or their children. There is no "typical" female gun owner. Female gun owners live in Manhattan, New York, and Manhattan, Kansas. They may own small-caliber pistols like a .22 or .25 or a shotgun, rifle, or large handgun such as a .357 revolver or .45 semiautomatic pistol—or several of each. If a woman's father or male relatives, or (more rarely) her mother and grandmother, lawfully and responsibly owned and used guns, she likely carries no fear of them. They're as unremarkable and familiar a part of the household inventory as a hairdryer or dishwasher.

And women grow up with, and feel daily, the very real fear of assault. According to Department of Justice statistics, *three of four American women over the age of twelve will be victims of crime at least once in their lives.* An educated, urban, middle-class professional, who has always lived in "good" neighborhoods, who once thought crime would always remain safely distant from my own life, I've become a crime victim four times. I never pursued arrest or prosecution, impossible in three of the events, but the sense of violation and impotence it left with me is indelible.

More than a third of women will be violently assaulted, raped, or robbed in their lifetimes.

By the time they think about buying a gun for self-defense, women are simply worn thin by fear, fed up with low-level, life-long anxiety about what to wear, when to travel, what public-transit, pedestrian, or vehicular routes to take. Who wants to spend one's life calculating who is safe to speak to and smile at—and whom we should walk away from briskly? Yet women do. We rarely discuss it, so automatic is the impulse to turn away, to back down, to try to avoid trouble. From puberty onward, women of all ages unconsciously tailor their lives, activities, and work to accommodate the very real threat of violence and crime.

While carrying a gun won't solve the larger and more complex issues of living within a violent society, it *is* one of the few ways a woman can level the field if someone large and adrenaline-charged is determined to do her lethal harm.

Whatever their race, marital status, sexual preference, place of residence, education, or income level, *three-quarters of all women* will become a victim of crime. It's an identity none of us assumes willingly—yet one we have to think about, prepare for, and face head-on if we are to increase our odds of staying safe.

When, in 1993, the National Rifle Association launched "Refuse to Be a Victim," a pilot series of self-protection seminars in Houston, Miami, and Washington/Baltimore, more than twenty thousand women called an 800 number asking for a forty-two-point safety brochure and information on schedules and registration.

A woman considering buying a gun for self-defense, whether as the survivor of an attack, or in preparation for a day she prays will never arrive, must confront several frightening realities:

- Police who might not respond quickly enough to your 911 call to save your life or protect you from serious injury
- Rapists who remain at large or serve short sentences and are soon back on the street
- Vicious, violent, and vengeful spouses or boyfriends
- Ineffectual restraining orders against such men
- Criminals who select as their prey women they perceive as weak—i.e., those emotionally and physically unprepared for attack

It won't happen to me. I live in a good neighborhood. I date nice guys. I avoid rough areas. I choose upscale hotels.
Denial spins a seductive cocoon.

I first became an adult crime statistic as a college sophomore, living alone in a tiny studio apartment in what, in twenty-twenty hindsight, was an affordable but remarkably poor choice—a main-floor apartment at the back of an alley on a busy street in downtown Toronto. Mine was not, per se, a dangerous neighborhood, but there was much pedestrian traffic and loud, drunk passersby heading home from local bars.

One balmy May evening, I lay in the bath reading. Something stirred the heavy, woven cloth of the window curtain, barely three feet above my head. There was no breeze—a man's hands thrust through the cloth, trying to pull my slippery body out the low, narrow window. He failed and, after about five minutes of struggle, rapped the top of my skull with his knuckles and took off.

I never told the police, assuming my assailant would have long since disappeared on foot. I was too shocked even to recall his features. I moved out of that apartment, my first sweet taste of independence, the next day and suffered nightmares for months. Ever since, I've chosen top-floor apartments with no exterior access to my doors or windows.

Despite my experience, I never understood the visceral desire to own a gun for self-defense. Until, twenty-two years later, living in a small, pretty town near Manhattan, another criminal entered my life. A con man who had done jail time in Illinois for widespread fraud placed a personal ad in my local weekly newspaper, posing as a "wealthy Wall Street attorney." Lonely, I answered it. Handsome, well-dressed, witty, attentive, fun, he kept up his manicured appearances for several months, allowing him time to earn my trust and access to my home. After he opened my mail, stole a credit card, forged my signature, and went on a spree, I awoke from my naive coma.

I went to the police to have him arrested and then, in a fit of confused remorse, withdrew my complaint. In their eyes, this made me a hysterical liar whose word was worthless. When I returned a month later with evidence proving his multiple felonies, they dismissed me. So did the district attorney. It was, they said, a simple "he said, she said," my word against his. Whatever I offered in court he would only counter with smooth, practiced deception. His record of fraud convictions elsewhere, which would have strengthened my allegations, was inadmissible evidence. Nor had he gotten much money out of me. There was, legally speaking, little damage. No matter that I was emotionally shredded, far away from my family, terrified, and unable to work.

I was on my own. The man phoned me for weeks, shrieking abuse and threats with impunity; the police, we both knew, would not help me. I changed my locks, bank accounts, and phone number. I refused to move, unwilling to let this criminal force me to sell my home.

But my fear of his venomous rage, his certainty he'd continue to evade arrest and prosecution—and my frustration at the authorities' total lack of interest in my case—made self-defense, and caution, a more compelling issue for me. It still does; I learned, however briefly, what it feels like to be vulnerable to a monster.

When, four years later, my beloved red convertible was stolen in front of my suburban apartment building, I once more felt violated and impotent. I fantasized wildly about confronting the three thieves—seen by a neighbor—with a loaded handgun. I would have shot at the tires, not at them.

Or so I think.

I was twelve when I first held a gun. It felt cold and heavy, something dead and awkward in my hand. My father, who'd been given the Colt .45 by a northern-Alberta fur trapper named Dmitri he'd met while making a film, kept it in an old pine cabinet in his downtown Toronto apartment. I never saw it again. Like most urban Canadian women, guns weren't part of my daily life.

I first touched a gun in the United States, my adopted home of sixteen years, in the elegant Upper East Side apartment of a good friend, then a single woman in her early thirties. She owns a small revolver, a Colt .38. I stared at it in fascination, struggling to reconcile a potentially deadly weapon with the slim, soft-spoken blonde who owns it.

I picked it up. Tiny, compact, with a scored wooden grip that lay cleanly and comfortably in my hand. I felt . . . invincible.

Intrigued by the power and lethality I cradled so easily in my palm, in 1996 I attended a three-day defensive-weapons class at the Smith & Wesson Academy, a school in Springfield, Massachusetts, that normally trains law enforcement officers from around the world. It also teaches civilians of all ages how to aim, shoot, clean, and care for their own weapons.

What I saw and felt there stirred up a potent mixture of emotions. I was terrified to actually fire a gun the first time. Everyone in my class of twelve adults already owned one, or many, and had easily shot their first rounds. In silence, they watched me expectantly. I thought I might faint, but two female instructors, whispering softly beside my ear (muffled by protective headgear) talked me through my fear. I finally squeezed the trigger of the smooth, black Smith & Wesson 9mm. A tiny, loud flame erupted twenty-seven inches away from my face as the bullet flew toward a paper target. The gun recoiled between my palms, the brass casing pinged onto the concrete floor, and a flood of adrenaline coursed through me.

Oh my.

I spent three days there, for hours shooting round after round after round of ammunition. Guns, I soon learned, were loud and smelly. I wore plastic goggles over my glasses to protect my eyes, and long sleeves to cover my arms and wrists from the hot flying bits of brass ejected from each fired cartridge. After a few hours of shooting, my hands hurt from the recoil. But after the initial shock wore off, it was actually great fun.

Like most women who try it, I quickly took to handgun shooting. My shots were clean and accurate, easily puncturing the head and chest area of the man-shaped paper target seven yards ahead of me down the indoor range. Outside, it was July, the sun hot and bright. Indoors, the range was dark and dim, only the paper targets brightly spotlit, powerful fans whisking away the lead dust, smoke, and smell after each shot. Aiming, firing, drilling, loading and reloading the magazine of my borrowed $600 pistol, I glimpsed a new woman inside me, one bristling with an unsettling kind of competence. I could aim, fire, and hit with some measure of accuracy.

I liked the novel feeling of power this gave me—and briefly imagined a life where I kept a sleek, familiar 9mm near me, a life in which I might never fear rape, robbery, mugging. One in which I could walk and drive and travel freely, confident, if necessary, that I could match menace with menace. I don't live in a state of constant alert, nor do I want to. But feeling the chilling nonchalance of my local police and district attorney, and the gloating triumph of a career criminal who knew he'd devastated yet another victim with impunity, *did* change my worldview. I'm a little darker, a little more bruised and wary, certainly, than I once was.

Was owning a gun the answer? Would it protect me—or endanger me even further?

My bullets punched a tidy, tight ring of holes in my targets. With this loud, lethal reply to random viciousness in my hands, I finally felt fearless.

Oh my, indeed.

What was I now to *do* with this knowledge?

But why focus specifically on women and guns? What is it that makes owning or using a gun, or being bereaved by its use, or being around a gun owner, different for women?

For one thing, there are so many of them—an estimated 11 to 17 million American women own a firearm. Forty percent of all American homes contain a pistol, revolver, shotgun, rifle, or combination of these. Even women who hate and fear guns are exposed to them in the hands of their father, brothers, boyfriend, husband, or male friends. Add drugs, alcohol, rage, or depression—each a catalyst for violence, and each of which infects millions of American households—and the odds of an American woman growing up free of contact with guns or gun-related violence are slim.

Women spend their lifetimes in fear of rape. In 1996, 307,000 women were the victims of rape, attempted rape, or sexual assault. (It's estimated three to ten times that number go unreported.) Bureau of Justice statistics show that 44 percent of completed rapes occur in a woman's home (while nearly all the rest take place on sidewalks, or in a park, field, playground, parking lot, or parking garage). As we'll discuss later in more detail in chapter 4, "The Decision to Arm," the most legally defensible shooting incidents in self-defense tend to be in one's own home. Rape usually comes by surprise and at night—and 36 percent of all victims are physically injured in addition to the sexual assault. *Twenty-nine percent of rapists are armed.*

Yet women who choose to own guns receive little media attention, in part because they tend to be law-abiding. Pick up your local newspaper any given week and you'll read of an enraged ex-husband or boyfriend who has gone on a rampage, massacring his former partner, and often her children, before killing himself. When vengeful fired employees return to their place of employment to execute coworkers or managers, the shooters—invariably—are male.

Women who own and use guns tend to keep it quiet: they don't want their guns stolen; neighbors, friends, and family may hesitate to let their children socialize with her children; gun-control advocates may barrage her with their unwanted opinions. It's often a choice best kept secret.

Because of their smaller size and relative physical weakness, women, no matter how strong, angry, or trained in martial arts, remain at a disadvantage when it comes to self-defense; *a gun, police and self-defense experts agree, is the only weapon that truly levels the field in a life-threatening confrontation.*

Whatever their age, race, or income level, women create and nurture a wide web of relationships: to family and friends, to mentors and students, to employers, colleagues, and subordinates, to fellow members of a spiritual community or volunteer group. We are most often defined by, and nourished by, these emotional, spiritual, or intellectual connections.

Yet buying or owning a gun, whether for sport, competition, or self-defense, creates a series of questions especially challenging for women as it challenges our connections:

- Should I tell anyone?
- Whom can I tell?
- When should I talk about it?
- How much information, and when, should I share about this decision with a boyfriend, husband, children, stepchildren, and grandchildren?
- What about non-gun-owning friends and colleagues visiting my home?

For centuries, women have been entrusted with the moral care of their families; keeping a .38 in the night table can complicate matters enormously.

And still, for some women, owning a gun is simply *no big deal.*

My Manhattan friend, like many men, has owned and shot guns all her life. She shops for them with the same fervor and intense pleasure with which she also combs flea markets for old flasks and silver cigarette cases. The three guns in her apartment serve very different functions. Two are for hunting. The third, she explains simply, is her "protection firearm."

Why does she even have three guns? One can logically argue she has no practical need for any of them. This smart, savvy woman, educated in the finest American private schools, now lives with a physically strong and brave husband. But as a young girl, she was beaten routinely and brutally by a family member, until one day, despairing of escape or credibility with her local police, she shot him. He lived and didn't press charges.

She's also American. The U.S. Constitution enshrines her right to bear arms, no matter how shocking the consequences. The Second Amendment protects her rights as effectively as those of a man.

"Guns kill, but guns protect," she says. "They're an enormous equalizer between the weak and vicious."

My friend's guns remain a nonnegotiable part of her sense of self.

There is no "female" attitude toward guns. There are women as passionately attached to the sensuality, utility, and fine design of their Berettas and Glocks as to their well-used copper saucepans or sexy summer sandals. For them, a gun is simply another tool, as useful, personal, and pleasurable an object as a well-designed sports car, timepiece, or computer.

Some women hunt deer, elk, moose, pheasant, quail, rabbits, or squirrels. For some it offers enjoyment, for others the pleasures of being outdoors with friends, testing their skills. It may feed their families or earn them needed income. Some travel on hunting safaris to Africa with their daughters, delighting in the chance to kill big game. Some love to shoot skeet, clays, and trap, mingling easily on country weekends with corporate CEOs and European aristocrats. Some travel the country to hone their skills and test them in regional and national athletic competitions.

Many others, even those whose lives remain personally unscathed by intimate contact with guns, simply find the subject repellent and unpleasant. In their eyes, guns represent only injury, violence, crime, and death.

And some women carry apparently conflicting viewpoints on gun control or advocacy. Several women in this book have lost family members to homicide or suicide, yet remain convinced that gun ownership is a sensible choice, even a necessity.

As a Canadian who grew up in a gun-controlled and pacifist culture, who has lived in England, France, and Mexico, my aim is to examine the intersection of guns and American women's lives, to investigate gun ownership and use, and its portrayal in the media, as both a cultural artifact and historical by-product of a country founded on a distrust of government and institutional authority.

Less dispassionately, the subject endlessly fascinates me, cutting as it does relentlessly and continuously, decade after decade, across lines of gender, age, race, income, or education. None of us is totally immune—physically, emotionally, intellectually, or politically—to the effects of gun violence and its costs to American society. Even in Manhattan, where legally acquiring a pistol remains more difficult than almost anywhere else in the country, gun violence, most often perpetrated by men, is inescapable. As I write this, headlines detail the murder of a talented and ambitious young actress living in downtown Manhattan, shot in the face and killed by her ex-fiancé.

With an estimated 200 million guns in private hands in the United States, regulating their use, defending children from gun accidents, and enforcing current laws often appears a fruitless, if essential, exercise.

In a culture that lionizes individual rights, self-reliance, resourcefulness, and power (not to mention the Second Amendment, allowing the right to bear arms), the gun—whether you love, loathe, or remain indifferent to it—remains an inescapable part of daily American life.

Voices in this book include those of lawmakers and lobbyists, pro-gun and antigun activists, gun manufacturers, female shooters, victims of gun violence, competitors, hunters, teens, women working in law enforcement and the military, women living in fear of gun violence, and those in the media, arts, and entertainment industry whose views help to inform America's gun culture.

You'll hear from women and men, ages thirteen to seventy-two, black, white, Hispanic, and Asian, gay and straight, urban and rural, blue-collar workers and degreed professionals. They are high school students and emergency room physicians, bereaved wives and mothers, elite athletes and law enforcement officials, businesswomen, legislators, lobbyists, and lawyers.

Intrigued by less audible and more nuanced individual voices, I deliberately chose not to seek sources through interest groups such as the National Rifle Association or the Brady Campaign, although I include some of their institutional views and concerns. I found subjects largely through personal contacts, conducting more than one hundred interviews by telephone, email, and in person; when I did not meet someone in person, I have verified their identity. Unless identified and credited to others in the notes, all interviews are the product of my own original, firsthand reporting. I sought the views of girls and women from small towns and major cities, from Maine to Mississippi, Vermont to California, Alaska to Florida. I wanted to hear from women who grew up around guns and those buying their first weapon at midlife and those who would never consider making such a purchase.

Unless otherwise stated, the sources' real names and other identifying details are unchanged.

I chose not to investigate militias, girl gangs, or female crime. I did interview (and quote from the literature on) women who have killed their intimate partners—by far the most common female criminal use of firearms. This is not meant to be an exhaustive catalog of everything women do, or have done to them, with guns, but a look at some of the most important ways that women and guns intersect.

It is not my intent to persuade you that women should own guns, nor that women should eschew them. It is a profoundly personal choice. My goal is to spin a thread across the unbridgeable chasm separating those who enjoy guns and those opposed to them, a persistent cleavage that helps to forestall useful dialogue on thoughtful gun control or regulation.

I do not own a gun, although I've enjoyed target shooting; the social responsibility of keeping a firearm in my home is not one I'm ready to assume.

My aim is to introduce some of the millions of American women—from the earliest beginnings of this country—whose lives are, and have been throughout history, intimately entwined with guns and their effects, overt and covert, subtle and stunning.

Chapter 1
A Moving Target

It's 8:30 A.M. ON A SUNNY SATURDAY, MID-JULY. MANHATTAN streets are silent, parking places plentiful. Twenty-seven women, ranging in age from their early twenties to late sixties, file into the basement of a handsome cast-iron building on the south side of West Twentieth Street. This is Chelsea, a predominantly gay neighborhood of chic bars and shops. The women sign in at the door, each filling out a legally required form testifying, among other prerequisites, that they aren't "habitual drunkards" or the subject of a restraining order. Shyly, curiously, they steal glances at the reason they've come. A shooting range.

Behind the thick wall of glass separating the narrow, cramped lobby from the range, the only such private facility in Manhattan, they can hear a steady, unfamiliar sound, the *slam!slam!slam!* of something large-caliber. The women are the mix you'd see on any subway platform: slim and pretty, two hundred pounds, tattooed and pierced. They include college students, attorneys, a travel agent, City Hall employees, a mutual-funds marketer, an Ivy League MBA, black, white, Hispanic, and Asian. For most, today will mark a communal rite of passage—their first time handling a gun.

They're also making Manhattan history, the first foray by the National Rifle Association's Women on Target campaign, a national hundred-events-a-year effort to win new women shooters, into the heart of gun-control territory. Manhattan is the nation's toughest city in which to obtain a pistol permit.

The day starts with an hour-long classroom lecture on safety, the walls covered in plastic banners for Glock, Winchester, the National Rifle Association, Colt. Mike Bodner, a white, forty-one-year-old electrical engineer and volunteer safety instructor, shows photographs and diagrams of a .22 rifle, the only gun one can legally shoot in New York City without a permit. In his baggy chinos, black lace-up dress shoes, and wire-rimmed glasses, Bodner is a good choice, unthreatening, funny, and friendly. "It's going to be very safe, it's going to be very fun. You'll really enjoy it," he promises.

After demonstrating how to stand, breathe, and fire the rifle, explaining the arcana of caliber and squibloads, it's time to shoot. The women put on "eyes and ears" (heavy plastic protection for both) and file into the range. They're nervous, excited, not quite sure what to expect.

The fourteen narrow wooden booths are lined with white acoustic tile shredded by years of flying brass ejected from thousands of guns. They load the cartridges, no bigger than their smallest fingernail. A paper target is clipped to a metal hook, then wheeled out, clothesline-style, to a distance of twenty-five feet.

Cecelia Fitzgerald, thirty-eight, a soft-spoken New Zealander and a court-appointed attorney in Brooklyn, steps up, cradles the rifle, leans her elbows onto a wooden ledge for extra support, then fires.

She steps out of the booth, her face a kaleidoscope of emotion, her hazel eyes focused on something invisible, unable to speak. After twenty minutes of shooting, she inspects her targets, the small black circle at their exact center frayed with bulletholes. Hers. She's smiling now, relaxed, a little overwhelmed. Her reaction is typical. When women discover they shoot well, and enjoy it, it's unnerving, unexpected. Disarming.

* * *

Americans like to take power into their own hands—and a gun is the simplest and most effective way to do it. After the attacks of September 11, 2001, revealed the nation's intelligence and law enforcement weaknesses, as Tom Ridge and his staff scrambled to create and run the Office of Homeland Security, as Americans learned the new rainbow of risk-status alerts, and as the CIA vainly sought new Arabic-speaking agents, individual self-protection gained sudden urgency.

Wealthy or poor, black, white, Asian, or Hispanic, straight or gay, a new citizen or direct *Mayflower* descendant, every American enjoys the constitutionally protected right to own a firearm, in thirty-three states a weapon you can legally carry concealed under a jacket, on your hip, in your purse or glove compartment.

Ask a foreigner to name a few products quintessentially American: Coca-Cola, MTV, apple pie, baseball, hot dogs.

Guns.

Like those other innocent, ubiquitous icons of Americana, firearms here cross class lines with ease. Only in this country can you find the same object—a gun—tucked into the rhinestone-studded Judith Leiber minaudière of a Dallas socialite or stashed beneath the mattress in a rural Alabama tar-paper shack. At the Fifty-seventh Street Manhattan showrooms of British gunmaker Holland & Holland, a wealthy woman can buy a $50,000 shotgun, while seventy blocks north in Harlem a woman with only $50 to spend can acquire a "Saturday night special," the generic name for a cheap, small handgun.

The essential difference? Only one of those purchases is legal.

The ultimate expression of American values—individual, quick, self-reliant, direct, essential a century ago to frontier survival—the gun today remains as much a symbol of freedom as its guarantor. Owning a gun allows Americans to hew to their frontier need-turned-ideal, protecting oneself and one's family without relying on others.

An estimated 11 to 17 million women now own guns. Forty percent of American homes—many of them headed by divorced women, often with children—contain a firearm. As more women run their households alone, without the protection of a man familiar with firearms, women are increasingly buying guns for themselves. We no longer turn automatically to a man for succor—it's typically a man we are fleeing in fear. When, in the summer of 2002, a serial killer began slaughtering women in Baton Rouge, Louisiana, dozens of women of all ages made the only choice they considered effective: flocking to gun ranges and dealers.

The National Rifle Association, which by 2003 had a record number of female members (170,000), says attendance at Women on Target has increased 300 percent since 2000. In January 2003, the first issue of *Woman's Outlook,* a monthly magazine published by the NRA for women, rolled off the press. Articles included a feature on Annie Oakley, secrets of successful shotgunning, and a first-person account of a midlife transformation from nonhunter to hunter. In the February 2003 issue, writer Katherine Rauch advised women on a wide variety of options for carrying concealed handguns, from handbags to backpacks and briefcases.

More than ten thousand women now belong to Second Amendment Sisters, an Internet-based pro-gun organization for women founded in 1999, when the group organized a rally as a counterpoint to the Million Mom March in Washington. More than five thousand people turned out for the event. A second march is planned for May 2004.

A 1999 survey conducted by *Women & Guns* magazine, a publication with eighteen thousand readers, showed that many of its readers want guns for personal protection. Most surveyed had owned guns for more than ten years. Many were single or headed single-parent households.

And after September 11, 2001, many women are determined to take control of their own safety, just as the women's movement led many to take control of careers and finances.

"There's a sense of danger now, an awareness that there may come a point where I am responsible for myself and other human beings," says *Women & Guns* editor Peggy Tartaro. "So, a lot of women are saying, 'Now is the time to go out to the range and learn how a gun functions.' "[1]

Yet public debate of gun ownership, when it includes female voices, usually focuses only on those opposed to firearms. Conventional wisdom suggests that women, pacific by gender, are uniformly opposed to gun ownership.

A woman's choice to own a firearm, or several, is often private and layered.

It may come from a place of fear, from an abusive childhood or marriage. Or a sense of caution, from a job performed at night, or alone, or alone at night, from driving alone at odd hours through dangerous or isolated areas. It may be motivated by the pleasure of rising at 4 A.M., shrugging into long johns and camouflage, filling a thermos with hot, strong coffee, and heading into snowy woods or misty marshlands with other hunters who share her passion.

Sometimes it's the joy of target-shooting shoulder to shoulder with fellow athletes from across the country, or the world, equally skilled and determined. "I'll be shooting until I'm eighty or ninety," exults Atlanta Olympic gold medalist Kim Rhode, who at seventeen became the youngest woman ever to win a gold medal in trapshooting. "The people are so nice and the outdoors are so beautiful. It's a combination you just can't give up."[2]

Owning and enjoying their antique hunting rifle or former service weapon offers many women gun owners a powerful emotional connection to a beloved brother, husband, father, or grandfather. Sometimes it's the chance to develop skills and confidence while sharing a favorite activity. For Randi Rogers, who became the world champion of cowboy action shooting (rapid-fire precision work using a .22 rifle) two years ago at the age of fifteen, it's a great way to spend time with, be coached by, and get to know her beloved grandfather. "If it wasn't for him, I wouldn't have gotten into shooting," she says.[3]

A gun offers women the same pleasures and privileges it offers men: skill, competence, camaraderie, safety, self-reliance, independence.

When the National Shooting Sports Foundation, which represents the gun industry, held one of its regular media education seminars in Danbury, Connecticut, thirty-six-year-old reporter Karen Ali was quickly hooked. A legal affairs reporter for the *Danbury News-Times,* Ali had never touched a gun before she spent a hot, sunny mid-July day at the range being introduced to a dozen different handguns by some of the country's top shooters. "I got a kick out of shooting and I'm thinking of getting one," she told a fellow writer. "I want to get one. I really do."[4]

A small group had come from *Popular Mechanics,* and as one of their staff stepped back after her first shot, she seemed stunned by pleasure. "This is *fun!"* she whispered.

It *is* fun. Target shooting—which most women do well from their first shot—can be a blast. Like any other sport requiring precision hand-eye coordination and a set of specific athletic skills, shooting can prove alluring.

Once a woman discovers she likes to shoot, her most pressing question becomes "What next?"

The Second Amendment, allowing Americans the right to bear arms (to the letter of the law, as a militia member), remains a source of unresolvable political debate, a thorn deeply embedded in the body politic.

With the majority of Americans living in cities, police a 911 call away, a gun for many of us is now less an object of practical necessity than of desire. And the dogged attachment to firearm ownership continually frays the borders between individual rights and collective safety, creating inherent tension between legal rights and social responsibilities.

What happens when, thanks to my constitutionally mandated

right to own a gun, my son kills yours? My husband blows away his coworkers? Postmortem lawsuits don't address the underlying issues.

Guns legally bought and carefully stored fall, through robbery or carelessness, into criminal hands. Children find guns, show off, and accidentally kill one another. Yet gun deaths, each hideous, each unnecessary and perhaps preventable, do not represent the typical demise of most Americans. In 2001, 17,424 Americans were killed by guns—while 43,501 died in motor vehicle deaths and 16,274 in falls.

Social fault-lines, ignorance, and carelessness help keep the morgues full of bullet-riddled bodies.

Rage-steeped teens open fire on their classmates and teachers. Stray gunfire now demarcates some American neighborhoods as clearly and lethally as coils of razor wire.

Gun safety is an issue we ignore at our peril. Across the country, children play after school in unsupervised homes containing firearms. Which of your children's friends' parents own firearms? Where or how are they stored? Where is *yours*? Are you sure it's unloaded, the ammunition completely inaccessible? As wives and daughters and sisters and mothers and friends of men who may be careless about using, cleaning, or storing their guns, it's an issue we can't simply wish away. Whether you choose to voice your concerns or not, whether you own a gun or could not imagine touching one, as a voter and an American, you're a part of the story. You may not have joined the conversation, nor wish to, but it is one that touches and includes each of us.

There is no way to tidily label responsible gun owners. Any one of us can be or become irresponsible. Rage, depression, drug use, and alcohol abuse infect millions of American homes every day. Each of these additives endangers a household that contains a firearm and ammunition. If someone in your household, no matter how well trained in a gun's safe use, suffers from depression and/or abuses substances, an accessible or loaded gun is your worst nightmare waiting to happen.

Yet millions of gun owners *do* store, shoot, and teach their children to use guns responsibly and enjoyably.

In other countries—Canada, England, Australia, Japan—guns are heavily controlled, if not outlawed. But these are nations with much smaller populations, profoundly different historical roots, and divergent visions of what constitutes polity. Canadians, whose constitution enshrines "peace, order, and good government," focus on cooperation, consensus, and the common good, values that dominate every public policy decision, from government-supplied cradle-to-grave health care to strong labor unions.

Additional forces make Canada less violent, including a wider, deeper social safety net and a social imperative to focus on negotiation and compromise, not confrontation and firepower.

Canada, ironically, carries a much sadder legacy of gun-related mass female murder. On December 16, 1989, thirteen female Montreal engineering students were injured and another fourteen killed by Marc Lepine, a disgruntled twenty-five-year-old who opened fire on them shouting, "I want the women. I hate feminists." Lepine carried a concealed Sturm Ruger Mini-14 semiautomatic rifle into their college, the École Polytechnique, ordered men out of a classroom, lined women up against a wall, and began executing them, shooting himself afterward.

In the United States, a nation focused on each citizen's right to "life, liberty, and the pursuit of happiness," one that relies on the free market to supply affordable health insurance, it's about personal freedom and private choice. The founding fathers broke away from regal authority, creating a new nation—in contrast to other nations that eschew the private ownership of guns—based on the principles of self-reliance and self-determination. Americans fought the Civil War, which pitted citizen against fellow citizen. In the 1800s, thousands moved westward, often far from the protection of a sheriff, confronting wild animals, Indians, outlaws, and bandits. For 140 years after the nation was founded, before the vast majority of Americans moved to policed towns and cities, Americans *needed* guns.

(In some places, the mind-set has changed little. Panhandleshaped magnets sold by Texas souvenir shops, topped with a tiny gun, warn, "In Texas, we don't dial 911." Several towns, including Virgin, Utah, and Kennesaw, Georgia, have made it illegal for a head of household *not* to own a gun.)

Above all, Americans value individual freedom, and anything they think will safeguard it. While we collectively profess horror every time the litany of mass gun violence lengthens—the Luby's massacre, the high school shootings at Columbine, Santana, Santee—we quickly return to business as usual.

Our health insurance premiums, often subsidized by employers, give a falsely reassuring reading. Surely we're not paying for gun violence if a bullet hasn't directly hit us. But we are. Our health care costs, private and public, are inflated by the annual costs of treating gunshot victims, whether they live or die, just as our credit-card interest rates are boosted by the hidden costs of others' theft and fraud.

Hospitals across the country, duty-bound to treat anyone who shows up in the emergency room, are losing a fortune to gun violence. Medicaid only pays about 50 percent of the costs of treating the uninsured, while the hospital eats the rest. Sixty trauma centers around the United States have closed in the past ten years, unable to meet their costs.

"Just putting someone in the intensive care unit costs twenty thousand dollars a day," says Detroit surgeon Scott Dulchavsky. Gunshot victims also require expensive forms of surgery—a laparotomy (opening up the abdomen) costs $41,000, and a thoracotomy (opening the chest) around $26,000. Dr. Robert Wilson, a trauma surgeon who has operated on thousands of Detroit gunshot victims, says, "New high-velocity weapons cause damage inches away from where the bullet was traveling—modern weaponry causes far more devastating injuries. There's no doubt it is harder to save people these days."[5]

It costs more than *$21 billion* a year to treat gunshot victims, according to a 1993 study.[6]

Call it the Second Amendment tax.

This is counterbalanced by income from the sale of firearms;

the 11 percent government excise tax on long guns and ammunition paid by manufacturers in 1998 generated $126,620,000 for the federal treasury. The 10 percent excise tax on handguns in 1998 generated another $35,528,000.[7]

The gun industry represents another significant player in the debate. In 1998, total sales on long guns, handguns, and ammunition amounted to approximately $2.1 billion with rifles and shotguns accounting for $852,819,800, handguns $497,392,000, and ammunition $758,560,000. And hunting adds yet another boost to the U.S. economy. According to its most recent five-year study, the U.S. Fish & Wildlife Service reports that hunters and shooters spent $20.6 billion on their activities in 1995. Annually, hunters spend approximately $2.5 billion on food and lodging with another $1.7 billion spent on transportation. Aside from their expenditures on firearms and ammunition, hunters annually spend over $7.4 billion on equipment, clothing, camping gear, decoys and game calls, telescopic sights and binoculars, boats and campers, and related items. Approximately $652 million is spent on hunting licenses, special stamps, and game tags each year.[8]

The manufacture, sale, and use of firearms not only affects thousands of American-owned businesses but fills government coffers. In a closed loop, much of this money is recycled to state hunting programs.

It's somehow easier to dismiss a woman's desire to own a gun, certainly for self-protection. The very idea leaves many squeamish. Shooting and killing is a man's job, they argue, a dirty business best left to police, security guards, the military, a husband or father skilled with a weapon. Yet, if a large, angry man is trying to rape you or beat you or kill you, the odds of someone armed and efficient arriving quickly enough to stop the crime are slim.

It's easier to dismiss a woman's desire to own a gun for self-defense if you've never been a crime victim, haven't felt the cool disinterest of police or the judicial system, have never heard the peculiar whiz of a bullet splitting the air over your head, or attended the funeral of a friend or relative shot in anger or by accident. Gun control remains an academic debate, often moderated by those who enjoy the security of a gated community, a well-policed suburb, or a neighborhood with private armed patrols—like those employed by middle-class whites and blacks alike in New Orleans.

"My children are my life," wrote novelist Susan Straight, discussing her ex-husband's growing, and initially hidden, fascination with guns that ended their marriage. "I don't want scars on their bodies or in their brains and hearts. The way parents were afraid of polio in the 1950s, scared of public pools and free-floating germs, I am afraid of guns."

Yet, she admitted, "when I think about a wild stranger touching my children, I wish, even briefly, for a handgun. On our strolls to 7-Eleven for Slurpees, I watch everyone passing us on the busy street, on the eucalyptus-lined sidewalks. I plan what I will do to an attacker. I admit it—I visualize 'the great equalizer,' the peacemaker, the one thing that would make me, five-four and 105 pounds, able to repel anyone who tried to hurt my girls."[9]

However ambivalent, women must still decide for themselves. And the issue is hardly color-blind.

Black women accounted for 41 percent of the female homicide victims in 1992. "They have it the toughest," says police sergeant Malissa Sims, of Waco, Texas. "Being black and being a woman—it's a double negative."[10]

Most vulnerable to violent crime, poor women of color often live in dangerous neighborhoods or buildings with no security, rely exclusively on infrequent public transit, and walk through dark, unmonitored hallways to reach their front door. Drive-by shootings and stray gunfire from drug-related turf battles are common. Young children in inner-city neighborhoods learn to hide in the bathtub, where bullets cannot penetrate. Police may arrive late, or not at all. For these women, the debate is hardly academic.

Even when a young black man struggles to leave a life of crime, he's not safe. Ask Paula Reynolds, whose seventeen-year-old son, Omain Gullette, had, after four arrests, become so determined a student-athlete he was offered a football scholarship to Syracuse University. Gullette was shot and killed one July afternoon on a Philadelphia street by three men. "It wasn't meant for him," said a friend wounded in the attack. "He was trying to be a negotiator."[11]

Only after a woman has suffered an attack with or a bereavement from use of a firearm does the debate hit home. Yet indignant, emotional attacks on gun owners, often made by other women, are relentless.

"This is what I want to know," wrote Sallie Tisdale. "Why do we need to balance the 'needs and desires of gun enthusiasts' with anything at all? It is exactly this hedged liberal urge to satisfy everyone that has gotten us into the dreadful mess we find ourselves in today—a mess that the writers of the Constitution would have deplored. . . . Why must we listen to the claims of gun lovers, or make any effort at all to satisfy their irrational appetite for weapons? Why should we bow to the rage and hunger of a single-issue lobby? . . . I am no longer an advocate of gun control. I am an advocate of gun elimination."[12]

Depending upon where they live, women considering a gun purchase—certainly for hunting or self-defense, which by definition involve the readiness to kill—can face powerful social disapproval from other women. A white forty-year-old fund-raiser working in Manhattan was "creeped out" by her coworker's enthusiasm when she discovered her colleague had bought a rifle and was simply training for the summer biathlon, an athletic event that combines running and shooting. "Guns *kill*. Men *kill*. Women don't kill!" she said. She has since softened her position, but initially found the very idea of a gun used for sports "bizarre."

No wonder so many women stay quiet.

Despite the feminist movement—and sometimes because of it—arming oneself remains a highly divisive choice. Mainstream feminists, typically, are eager to distance themselves from guns, arguing that women should choose, and focus on, nonviolent alternatives. Some women opposed to firearms bolster their argument by quoting poet Audre Lorde: "One cannot dismantle the Master's house using the Master's tools." Only by abandoning the symbols of patriarchal oppression, they argue, can women create and strengthen kinder, gentler new paradigms—theoretical constructs of no practical use in the middle of a rape, robbery, or assault.

Real feminists remain unarmed.

Or do they?

What kind of guns do women buy? A survey of six hundred U.S. firearms dealers found that the number of female gun buyers had increased "a lot" (17 percent) or "significantly" (19 percent), with 87 percent of women buyers arming themselves to protect themselves and their homes. Fifty-eight percent of these women were between thirty-one and forty, and 46 percent of them had "some" university education. Barely 4 percent of gun buyers had Ph.D.'s or the equivalent, the survey reported.

Fifty-three percent chose a .38 special (a gun whose smaller size and lighter weight is often easier on smaller female hands). More than three-quarters of women, 76 percent, said they prefer handguns for self-defense. Typically, though, women in this survey prefer to leave their guns at home.

Handguns represent one-third of the total number of guns in the country, and *probably 90 percent of them are kept loaded. Yet handguns are involved in only 20 percent of the accidental firearm fatalities; its victims have a 90 percent survival rate, while those wounded with a rifle or shotgun face wounds four times more lethal.*[13]

Depending on her social class, political persuasion, and neighborhood, an American woman faces wildly differing peer pressure to accept or reject gun ownership. In Southern states and rural areas with a long tradition of hunting or shooting skeet, trap, or clays, guns are ubiquitous, admired, and enjoyed, no more remarkable a domestic possession than a toaster or microwave oven. Several upper- and middle-class white women I interviewed in Texas and Louisiana said they felt significant peer pressure to get a handgun and know how to use it. "I'd feel like a wimp if I didn't have a gun," said one. "All my friends have one."

Every instructor and police officer I interviewed is adamant on this point: *a woman who buys a gun for self-protection* must *know how to use it.* A Glock in your handbag is worthless if you don't practice enough to use it with total confidence.

In addition to the basic differences among handguns—larger frame, tighter trigger, heavier weight, and larger caliber—there are many subtler distinctions between a semiautomatic pistol and a revolver, a rifle, and a shotgun.

While researching this book, I shot a .22 rifle, a 12-gauge shotgun and AR15 rifle, a .38, a .45 ACP, .357 Magnum and 9mm, both pistols and revolvers. I wanted to feel, and hear, the differences, and there were many. I have large, muscular hands, and the .38 and .22 felt too light and too small. When you fire a gun, the power discharged causes it to recoil. When the gun is smaller, there is less room for the power to dissipate, which hurt my hand after just a few shots. The .45, with its larger bullet, felt loud and sludgy, slow and awkward, and the powerful recoil made the whole experience unpleasant.

Like Goldilocks searching for her bowl of porridge, I finally found a good fit, the 9mm. It just feels right in my hand—and the tight circle of bulletholes in my targets when I shoot one confirms it.

The difference, for me, between shooting a pistol (in which the grip, which you hold, contains the receiver, which contains the magazine, which contains the cartridges, which contain the bullets) and a revolver, where the cylinder literally revolves before your eyes, was significant. With a pistol, after loading the magazine and slapping it upward into position into the gun with the heel of your hand, you don't see the bullets again. With a revolver, every time you shoot, the chamber revolves to move the next cartridge into place. Smoke curls out of the barrel after each shot is fired. As you slowly squeeze the trigger, the chamber revolves before your eyes, a visual reminder you're about to shoot.

A rifle or shotgun further dehumanizes your target. With a .22, the recoil and noise are minimal. No matter how lethal, it feels like a toy. At a hunting lodge in central Texas, I shot an AR15 (a modification of the M16, standard U.S. military issue) loaned to me by a businessman from California.

It was night, the air cool and studded with stars. The gun felt trim and compact, easy to lift, aim, and fire. It was a totally different experience from shooting a handgun or even a rifle—much quicker to fire and less emotionally engaging.

Fun. Powerful. A potent combination.

Some women grow up with guns and take their presence in a home for granted. Others, especially those who have never even touched one, often fear or hate them, convinced that bullets can somehow explode on their own. Ignorant of how firearms function, they can't begin to imagine any attraction to gun ownership.

I began to feel like the Pied Piper as friends and acquaintances, none of whom had ever shot, began to want to join me whenever I went to a range. First my eighteen-year-old research assistant, Rachel, then my thirty-three-year-old neighbor, then a thirty-four-year-old interior designer. I was their entrée into a mysterious, unknown, and alluring world, someone not a "gun nut," yet someone they trust who also enjoys shooting.

A sunny Saturday in Manhattan, when the NRA's Women on Target program made its first foray into the city, offered proof of guns' allure. No matter that the event received little publicity, or that even saying the word *gun* in many parts of downstate New York is a guaranteed conversation-stopper—organizer Amy Heath, a thirty-four-year-old freelancer who works in film production, and who had advertised the event very little, was turning women away. That day, more than fifty women showed up, this in a city that makes acquiring personal protection extremely difficult.

One woman, a petite, blonde, forty-eight-year-old former actress who shares my name, said she'd first encountered guns in November 2001 after dinner with friends in a West Village restaurant. She was led downstairs to a private, members-only range. "I liked it a lot!" she said, laughing at the memory. "My girlfriends were horrified. They all asked, 'Why don't you just take a yoga class?' "

Sonia Vargas, thirty, a slim, Hispanic woman in a tank top and jeans, was delighted to hit nothing but bull's-eyes right from the start. "This is awesome!" she said, grinning. Every woman that day, many initially apprehensive about shooting, was soon giggling and laughing, stunned by her competence, her exhilaration infectious.

For Raquel Angelos, a twenty-two-year-old forensic-science student with a thick black ponytail, white T-shirt, and baggy jeans, shooting a .22 was simply the latest step in her growing familiarity with firearms. She had already shot a Glock and a derringer, a tiny gun that holds only two cartridges. "I want to start a collection," she said unapologetically. Her friends don't like her fascination. Fellow bus passengers give her dirty looks when she carries a copy of *Guns & Ammo:* "You see *Vogue,* you see *Maxim,* you don't see a gun magazine." Shooting is something she's proud of, a skill that tells the world she's capable. "I think there's a stereotypical view that women are careless, not in control of their own situations. This is good. This shows women *can* do it. It's female empowerment."

Jennifa Willis, forty-two, a travel agent originally from Trinidad, came with her two daughters, Kizzy and Keshalle. Keshalle, who shoots at a range in New Jersey, encouraged her mother to come that day. Jennifa was positively giddy with pleasure at her rapid progress. "I didn't want to have anything to do with a gun. But it's nice. I'm going to tell everybody I did it. I'm going to brag!"

Most of the women produced extremely tight groupings of shots, many of them bull's-eyes. All were eager to take their paper targets to work, joking they'd flaunt them the next time they asked for a raise.

While women shooters have their own magazine, *Women & Guns,* it's not easily found on your local newsstand. The image of a traditionally nurturing female bearing arms still scares many people—although Paxton Quigley's unapologetically pro-gun book, *Armed and Female,* has remained in print since 1989.

Don't rely on the mass media to discuss the issues in any depth. Many urban reporters and editors, certainly, have never shot, would consider the idea distasteful, and know better than to pitch a piece that might paint gun owners in anything but a negative light. New York City, home to the country's largest and most powerful television, newspaper, and magazine companies, also has the country's toughest gun laws, significantly reducing the odds that media decision-makers, if they have ever shot, currently enjoy shooting or know much about guns. Most women's magazines are run by women editors, many of them ignorant of, or squeamish about, this issue. Add to this, at the time of this writing, a recession in the publishing industry and a desperate scramble to woo, win, and keep readers and risk-averse, deep-pocketed advertisers—and the odds of coverage favorable to gun owners drop further.

The public, visible, and vocal world of guns remains overwhelmingly male.

As Carol Oyster, a professor of psychology at the University of Wisconsin, La Crosse, and fellow hunting enthusiast Mary Zeiss Stange, a professor of women's studies at Skidmore College, quickly discovered when coauthoring their book on this subject, women remain largely absent from the national conversation on guns. While lobby groups on both sides of the debate fling statistics at one another, women's voices are almost inaudible.

"We were intending to document the experiences of invisible women. Not only is it impossible to ascertain the precise number of women who own or have access to or regularly use firearms, the extensive social-science literature on guns and their use almost invariably fails to take gender into account."[14]

You'll also search in vain for women's voices in academic journals on law, violence, and criminology—a landmark 1995 edition from the Northwestern University School of Law, *Guns and Gun Violence,* contained only five women of twenty-one contributors. The annual Shot Show, the largest and most important gun-industry trade show, attended by as many as thirteen thousand vendors and buyers, typically welcomes about three thousand women. Although women work as instructors and salespeople for such major gun manufacturers as Colt, Glock, and Beretta, only two women have recently run gun-manufacturing companies in the United States—Elizabeth Saunders, CEO of American Derringer, in Waco, Texas (founded by her late husband and now closed), and Kay Clark, CEO of Clark Custom Guns of Princeton, Louisiana (founded by her late father).

Guns whose names are household words, such as Remington, Glock, Browning, Ruger, Colt, and Smith & Wesson, are named for the men who invented them.

At a gun show with about a thousand people a day packing the aisles in Springfield, Massachusetts, I gathered skeptical glances, so rare were women buyers or vendors at that event. Once people realized I was not "antigun" and had shot and enjoyed it, they were happy to share their knowledge and experiences.

While the NRA officially represents gun owners, it takes a strong-armed stance, and some members tell me privately they long for more moderate language and a less macho approach. Some female politicians are propelled to the forefront of the gun debate by personal tragedy—Suzanna Hupp, a pro-gun Texan whose parents were shot and killed, or gun-control advocate Representative Carolyn McCarthy of Long Island, whose husband was killed and son wounded by a gunman on a commuter train.

Most often, though, regardless of gender, politicians simply toe the party line: Republicans favor gun ownership, Democrats gun control. How and where do they get their information? Often from aides and consultants, who, in turn, rely on gun-control groups or the NRA. Rarely is fresh data uncovered that is not immediately repackaged and spun in whatever direction seems most useful. Gun-control advocates aren't shy about telling gun owners what to do, while gun owners bristle at the temerity of those bossing them around who have little or no personal familiarity with guns.

When it comes to gun legislation, individual gun owners and gun-control advocates alike watch from the sidelines, both feeling frustrated and impotent.

When, if ever, should a woman consider buying a gun for self-protection?

Rape

Rape is the most underreported crime in America; the government estimates that 17.7 million women are survivors of rape or attempted rape. That's about 20 percent of American women— *one in five*.

Rape survivors face a host of medical, psychological, emotional, and professional problems, both immediately after their ordeal and many years later. A study published in the *Annals of Emergency Medicine* found that half of all women who are sexually assaulted are not given recommended treatments to prevent pregnancy or sexually transmitted diseases.[15]

Effects linger for decades. In a study of 558 female military veterans, comparing a group who were victimized (physically assaulted, raped, or both) with those who were not, those who were raped and physically assaulted did worst of all. Their general and mental health, pain, vitality, and physical and social functioning were on a par with those of people suffering from major chronic illnesses such as Parkinson's disease or diabetes. "More than a decade after rape or physical assault, women reported severely decreased health-related quality of life, with limitations of physical and emotional health," says Anne G. Sadler, R.N., Ph.D., the study's principal investigator.[16]

"Rape is not just a psychological problem; it's a social and public-health problem," says Kathleen Basile, Ph.D., a behavioral scientist in the Centers for Disease Control and Prevention's violence-prevention division. "It affects the physical and psychological health and well-being of half the population, and it's preventable."[17]

"The rapist took more than my confidence, self-esteem, and sense of the world as a safe place," says writer Melissa Chessher, who was raped and stabbed near Fort Worth, Texas. "He stole the Technicolor out of my life."[18]

After many years of depression and post-traumatic stress disorder, Chessher finally hired a personal trainer, learned to box, and reclaimed her "power and strength."

What if she had never gotten raped at all?

But will owning a gun prevent a rape?

Women hoping to forestall rape—often a crime of opportunity—need to prepare physically and psychologically to fight back. "Attackers are not looking for partners to fight with when they pick a woman to attack," writes Gail Groves.[19] "Men do not begin an attack on a woman thinking, 'I'm going to attack her and then she's going to hurt me.' Rather, they see women and girls as easy targets, weak and helpless."

Studies of rapists and other criminals have shown that they are most likely to choose women as victims on the assumption they are unarmed and/or unable or unwilling to fight back effectively.

"I don't advocate weapons under any circumstances," writes Frederic Storaska, former executive director of the National Organization for the Prevention of Rape and Assault.[20] Yet, he concedes, "The only weapon worth talking about is a handgun. . . . Most important, do not become dependent on any weapon." If a woman feels she must have a gun, Storaska suggests keeping it in only two places, her home or her car. Those who decide to buy a gun, he cautions, must (1) check with police to ensure they are legally able to own one; (2) train often and consistently in its use; (3) be absolutely ready to use it.

What about other self-defense methods? Some options, in addition to the *absolute last resort* of using a gun, include:

- Self-defense courses such as Model Mugging
- Tasers, which operate (only within a range of twenty feet) by delivering a shot of low-dosage electricity
- Pepper spray
- Tear gas
- Mace
- Manual self-defense
- Awareness of your surroundings, reading situations quickly, and trusting your instincts
- A large, powerful dog

Older Women

Visibly vulnerable, many older women lack the necessary physical strength to respond effectively to attack. When, in the early 1980s, twenty-six-year-old writer Pat Moore disguised herself to experience life as an eighty-year-old woman in New York City, her most indelible emotion was fear, especially after she was mugged. "A frail woman bent over by osteoporosis—it's hard for her not to look weak and vulnerable. It's hard not to look frightened because you *are* frightened in that situation."[21]

For frail older women and those with disabilities, one-on-one, hand-to-hand self-defense methods are simply impractical.

Elderly women are more likely to have their purses stolen; for elderly people of both sexes, burglary, household larceny, and motor vehicle theft are most common.

When the elderly do become crime victims, it's most often in or near their home. Single elderly people are most vulnerable; in later life as earlier, members of racial minorities are more often victimized than whites.

One reason for stopping an attack before it starts: older victims are more likely to suffer serious injury that requires medical attention.

The good news? Statistically, older women—despite their high level of *fear* of crime—remain at relatively low risk. Those over the age of sixty-five make up only *2 percent of crime victims,* with that rate dropping after the age of seventy-five.[22] And elderly women are even less likely than elderly men to become crime victims, especially violent crimes perpetrated by strangers.

Black Women

Black women, in particular, feel the brunt of gun use and gun violence. With crime highest among young black men, low-income and even middle-class black women—whether in big cities like Chicago, Detroit, New York, Philadelphia, Los Angeles, Houston, or smaller but equally deadly centers like New Orleans—live in daily intimacy with guns, drive-by shootings, gang and turf wars. Even if they live safely distant from a ghetto or public housing project, friends, schoolmates, and relatives may not.

Dale Atkins, a black woman running for district attorney in New Orleans, had barely kicked off her 2002 campaign when a random bullet from a drive-by gang shooting killed her sister—sitting on the family's front porch after the funeral of another relative who had been shot. From earliest childhood, black women are disproportionately hurt by gun violence, losing a progression of fathers and friends, husbands, sons, and boyfriends.

Emergency room nurses and physicians across the United States witness the carnage firsthand, racing to patch, stitch, or declare dead body after shattered body, almost all of them black, male, and young.

According to the Congress of Racial Equality, the small, cheap guns known as Saturday night specials are most often bought for self-defense by poor people—especially poor black women. With the high percentage of households headed by single black women in public housing, arguably one of the most dangerous places in which to live and raise children, you might expect to find women residents buying handguns for their own protection. Yet, under HUD regulations, residents of public housing are forbidden to own firearms.

Not only are black women more likely to live and work in dangerous neighborhoods, they're prey to violence through their relationships to men who use guns. A three-month investigation by *Cleveland Plain Dealer* reporter Elizabeth Marchak, conducted in 1997, found that the single most dangerous place to live in America for a black woman was Youngstown, Ohio, a working-class town of ninety thousand, which saw seventy murders of black women in one year. "A lot of these people weren't the intended victims. They're just the victims of circumstance," said Youngstown police captain Robert Kane. (Other areas with the widest racial disparities in murder rates after Youngstown were Fresno County, California; Lake County, Indiana (home to Gary); and Washington, D.C.)[23]

Yet much gun-control advocacy still comes from women, and men, whose income, race, marital status, or neighborhood protect them from any threat of real violence. Such high-profile and vociferous advocates of gun control as actresses Rosie O'Donnell and Meryl Streep live in wealthy enclaves and, when traveling, can well afford to hire private bodyguards, relieving them of the politically messy consequences of arming themselves.

Carol Oyster and Mary Zeiss Stange note in their book *Gun*

Women, "The generally antigun tenor of mainstream feminism reflects, and is to a large degree insulated by, a comfortably middle-class, white perspective. It is surely easier to forswear violent resistance if one belongs to a group less likely to fall prey to violent attack. According to Bureau of Justice statistics . . . certain women are far more vulnerable than others, [including] women aged twenty to twenty-four, African-American women, divorced, separated, or single women, urban dwellers, women who never graduated from high school, and women who earn less than $10,000 a year. Women of color and poor women, many of whom share several of these risk factors, seldom have the luxury of debating about whether the Master's house can be dismantled using the Master's tools.[24]

There's another issue. You won't find it discussed in journals or on talk shows, but it came up in private conversations with women of all ages, and often from those who publicly profess liberal views.

Rage.

Some women offer politically correct gun-control positions on the record, laugh nervously, then guiltily admit how personally seductive a gun might be. Their true trepidation is *not* their distaste for, or potential incompetence with, a deadly weapon, but the opposite—that owning a powerful method of potential redress might somehow tap into or unleash years of fury and frustration.

No matter their income level or education, women spend decades ignoring or minimizing male aggression and hostility: lip-smacking noises from strangers in the street, the "accidental" hand brushing against your breast, thigh, or buttocks in a crowded bus or bar, the manager who always leans in just a little too close.

If we haven't already become crime victims ourselves—and I experienced four crimes by the age of forty-five—we know a woman who has. We smile, swallow our retorts, or fail to alert police, often to avoid the public humiliation or frustration of a trial, and try to pretend we don't care.

Oh, but we do.

Most women realize that shifting a manual transmission on a steep hill, or changing the diaper on a wriggling infant, is physically more difficult than pulling a trigger. Not buying a gun simply ensures they can warily circle that pent-up rage, avoiding the allure of a dangerously definitive way to express it. Several women I interviewed told me point-blank—they don't want to own a gun because they *know* how angry they are.

Remember Lorena Bobbitt, the wife who sliced off her husband's penis with a kitchen knife and tossed it into a field?

"The widespread understanding among women of Lorena Bobbitt's act, even as one feminist spokesman after another publicly condemned it, reveals a certain off-the-record vein of vengefulness, a mother lode of anger, a vast buildup of unrequited insults and injuries," wrote Ann Jones in *Ms.* "Mostly we pretend it's not there. We're ladylike and polite. But there it is, welling up from time to time when you least expect it. Women exchange high fives in the street when Lorena Bobbitt is acquitted. Women cheer in the movie theater when Louise pulls the trigger on that scumbag wanna-be rapist [in the 1991 film *Thelma & Louise*]. It's a lot like living on an emotional fault line; we go along calmly and then, one day, boom, some little incident sets us quaking with laughter that smacks of sweet revenge."[25]

Says Michelle Dubos, a white, upper-class New Orleans accountant, "I don't want to find out about myself, so I don't want to buy a gun." Dubos sees a double standard—after thirty years of feminism, some men no longer feel much compunction to protect women, yet neither are they comfortable knowing a woman can protect herself without male help. "The white man keeps looking over his shoulder for the black man, but he should look for the white woman—because they're pissed."

A liberal New York writer in her early thirties, encountering her boyfriend's gun, found herself entangled in a welter of powerful feelings:

> As someone who has always been very antigun, I had a rather startling response to weapons a few years back when I started to date a police detective. The first few times that I caught a glimpse of his gun in his holster under his jacket, I was startled. I found it rather sexy.
>
> And, once I admitted that thought to myself, I was enraged. "How could I find a weapon sexy?" This was a question I asked myself over and over again.
>
> As I continued to date him, I found myself secretly intrigued by the gun. Whenever he got home after work, he would lock his gun away. I found myself wanting to be around just to see him do that. Once, I told him that the gun was interesting to me and I asked him if I could hold it. He made sure it was locked and then put it in my hand. I was overwhelmingly surprised at the weight of the piece and the idea that such a simple tool could cause such horrible damage when fired.
>
> I handed it back to him and never touched the gun again. The sensation of holding the weapon—even momentarily—is one I will never forget. It was cold, yet hot. Heavy and powerful. My hand did not feel large enough to grasp it, but I did not want to clutch it too tightly. I thought about a hundred things in the brief moment the gun was in my hand. Wars, drive-by shootings, police officers defending citizens, crazy men who terrorize their wives. I did not hold it for too long. I really don't want to touch one again. I think they belong in the hands of police officers and members of the military, not in the possession of ordinary citizens.

Even if they never own or touch a gun, many women admit to powerful, mixed emotions regarding guns. Dubos, the New Orleans accountant, is fascinated by women who kill: "For a woman to commit an act like that is even more violent [than a man] because you're going against what society has taught you." As someone who knows women who have lost friends or siblings to gun violence, hers is no idle fantasy.

Dubos was so outraged when a local gallery presented a show of artworks using guns that in reply she staged her own show, "Feminine Protection," using items such as tampons and vibrators; fifty artists from around the world contributed.

Yet it was less the gun itself than the macho assumption that the gun, and its power, remain a male preserve that riled her. She easily concedes their appeal: "So many of the women I talk to are getting a gun for self-protection. This has been going on for years. Women are often afraid of guns, afraid of the fact that, deep down inside, they may use it. That's a real thing with the women I've talked to over the years. Women joke about it, but there's a real fear that they'd use it."

Dubos says she knows a dozen college-educated professional women who feel this way. She also says that black women face a far different reality.

"It's a different issue for them. In the African-American community there *are* more guns. There's more access to guns. It's more of a reality for them.

"For a white woman, it's more of a big deal. It's something we're not supposed to do. My dad had a rifle, but it was never considered that a girl would have a gun. Guns were in the male world, not the female world." Dubos only knew that her father's rifle was kept in the closet, "an object of fascination."

Language complicates the conversation. For those who oppose guns, the preferred term is *weapon*, implying aggression, violence, and destruction. For those who enjoy guns or use them professionally, the term is *firearm,* a technical word implying an end use that remains neutral.

It's reminiscent of the irresolvable debate over abortion, whether one aborts a fetus or kills an unborn child. The fundamental issues for women, especially—choice, self-determination, valuing one's life over that of another—are not dissimilar. Terminating a pregnancy and firing a gun in self-defense are final, zero-sum acts of desperation, the last links in chains of accident, poor choices, or bad luck.

Both solutions are choices no woman wants to face, both forcing personal, political, and life-changing decisions.

Ending a pregnancy, a private decision, affects the woman, the erstwhile father, and the unborn child. Buying a gun tosses a boulder into the pond of community, the ripples of consequence growing ever larger as they potentially extend far beyond your nightstand or gun safe. They touch your husband, boyfriend, or lover. Their friends. Your roommate. Their friends. Your friends. Your children, stepchildren, grandchildren, and their friends. Their schoolmates and teachers.

Women are still largely valued, and value themselves, for their ability to create and nurture close relationships. It is they who are most often expected to set an example, to inculcate and uphold moral values, to teach their children well. The greatest gift a woman can make is still one of self-sacrifice—ferrying the kids to soccer/ballet/Boy Scouts; working a split shift to be able to put them to bed; skipping sleep to efficiently handle the "second shift," which is what writer Arlie Hochschild calls the household duties many full-time working mothers also assume at day's end; struggling to care for aging parents as part of the "sandwich" generation caught between the competing needs of children and elders.

Owning a gun and storing it safely—while keeping it accessible and useful in time of need—always presents a significant social responsibility.

How, then, can a woman remain responsible to herself, to her own perceived need to feel safe and protected (or to simply enjoy a gun for hunting or sport), *and* to the competing needs of her intimates? Perhaps this is why so many women, still, enter gun ownership *not* through the advice, wisdom, and experience of other women but, most often, through that of men.

Do we really, still, need their permission?

Chapter 2
Annie, Get Your Gun

IN THEIR HANDS, AND OTHERS', GUNS HAVE ALWAYS TOUCHED American women. They have buried loved ones shot on the battlefield and the street corner. They have lost friends, colleagues, neighbors, and relatives to suicide. They have stalked deer and game to feed their families. In earlier times, disguising themselves as men, they enlisted as soldiers, fighting bravely, their gender irrelevant until wounded and discovered—or they gave birth, stunning their unsuspecting comrades-in-arms.

In civilian life, American women have taken up arms to defend their lives and their families against intruders, bandits, rapists, and thieves. Until the early 1900s, in a country both thinly populated and poorly policed, it was dangerous to be unarmed alone at home. Learning to shoot, to load and reload under heavy fire, to find the loopholes in your cabin walls quickly enough to fire accurately through them when Indians arrived in the night, were domestic skills as essential to colonial and frontier women's survival as cooking, sewing, or midwifery.

"As soon as we came to the door and appeared, the Indians shot so thick that the bullets rattled against the house, as if one had taken a handful of stones and threw them. . . . The bullets were flying thick, one went through my side and the same through the bowels of my dear child in my arms." So wrote Mary Rowlandson in 1678, of an attack on February 10, 1675, that killed her eldest sister. Her son died eight days later, at the age of six years and five months.[1]

The first female soldier in the U.S. army was Deborah Samson, born in Plympton, Massachusetts, in 1760. At the age of twenty-two, Samson, a schoolteacher, disguised herself in men's clothing and hiked to Boston, where she enlisted in the Continental Army under the name Robert Shurtleff. She served for over a year in the Fourth Massachusetts Regiment and was commended as an outstanding officer. Near Yorktown, New York, she engaged and killed a British soldier. She hid her first serious wound, a saber slash to the neck, from physicians for fear of being discovered. Wounded again in a skirmish near West Point, New York, she removed a musket ball from her own thigh with a pocketknife rather than risk discovery by allowing a doctor to do it.

After the wound later flared up, she received an honorable discharge—given the money to travel home by General George Washington himself—and settled in Sharon, Massachusetts, where she married a farmer, Benjamin Gannett, and had three children. As Gannett's business failed, Samson took her skills on the road to raise money for her family. Dressed in her old army uniform, she would give a short lecture about her military adventures, then dazzle the audience with a precision rifle drill. Finally, in 1792, at the urging of her friend and neighbor Paul Revere, she applied for and received veterans' benefits.[2]

Mary Ludwig Hays McCauley, known as Molly Pitcher, carried water in hundred-degree heat and humidity to soldiers fighting the battle of Monmouth on June 28, 1778; she also loaded cannons and fired them. She became a sergeant, received a military pension, and is buried at West Point. Her name became the generic term for women who carried water to artillery in battle and occasionally substituted for fallen men in the critical job of cleaning the insides of hot cannon barrels.

Away from battle, women enjoyed little respite from violence or its daily threat. "The life of the pioneer woman, from the earliest times, was . . . to a large extent, a military one. She was forced to learn a soldier's habits . . . on guard-duty, [acting] as the sentinels of their home fortresses."[3]

Disguised as men, some four hundred women, three of them African-American, volunteered for and served in the American Civil War. Their reasons for joining ranged from boredom to patriotism. Some followed a fiancé or husband into the service. Honeymooners Martin and Elizabeth Niles enlisted together on September 2, 1862, in the Fourteenth Vermont Infantry and served together for ten months. Some women soldiered with their brothers, and at least two went to war with their fathers.[4]

Military life offered a secure, substantial income in an age with few jobs open to women, most of them domestic drudgery. "In New York City in 1860 maids earned between $4 and $7 a month, 'good' cooks $7 or $8 a month, and laundresses up to $10 a month. On the other hand, three months' service as a private in the Union Army yielded a hefty sum of $39 in an age when most monthly salaries for men ranged from $10 to $20."[5]

"Women soldiers were present as combatants in numerous battles, skirmishes, and campaigns from the beginning of the Civil War to the end. Women fought for their country from the first engagement at Blackburn's Ford, Virginia, on July 18, 1861, to the surrender of the last Confederate army. They served in both the eastern and western theaters throughout four years of bloody conflict. Women soldiers were wounded, maimed, and killed in action, and just like men with whom they served, they inflicted their share of pain and death. Despite the fact that they were not required to perform military service and in fact were barred from enlisting as soldiers, women nevertheless served the Union and Confederacy as armed combatants. Testimonials of their comrades leave no doubt about their effectiveness on the field of battle or their bravery under fire."[6]

Although their gender was most often discovered during medical treatment, a few female soldiers fought the entire war undetected; nineteen-year-old Jennie Hodgers joined the ranks of the Ninety-fifth Illinois Infantry on August 3, 1862, and served three full years as Private Albert Cashier before mustering out on August 17, 1865.[7] The idea of a woman soldier was so unlikely that many men likely shrugged off some of their high-voiced, slight-shouldered comrades beside them as male teenagers.

"Soldiering was the very antithesis of idealized Victorian womanhood. That romantic ideal of the weak and timorous female made many individuals, both civilian and soldier, incapable of recognizing the women hidden away in the ranks, for surely no woman could perform the hard, sometimes horrifying, and indisputably masculine duties of a soldier."[8] So deep in denial were some men that they only realized a woman lived among them when she went into labor. In April 1864, at Rock Island Prison in Illinois, "a portly young fellow in Confederate gray was . . . delivered of a fine boy."[9] Six soldiers were known to have performed their military duties while pregnant, and none of their comrades noticed until the moment of birth.

While facing the rigors and terrors of combat, women soldiers also enjoyed a new sense of power and independence, unheard-of luxuries for women of that era. Once the press learned of their presence, women soldiers such as Frances Clayton, Rebecca Clark, and Georgianna Peterson became celebrities, with much adoring coverage in newspapers and magazines. Then as now, journalists hungry for a great story chased those who confirmed a comforting stereotype, such as joining up for love of man or country.[10]

Based on her own experiences as Private Franklin Thompson, in 1864 Sarah Emma Edmonds wrote the best-selling *Nurse and Spy in the Union Army*, which was reprinted twice and sold 175,000 copies. Accounts of the deeds of women soldiers were standard fare in books and newspapers from the beginning of the Civil War until the beginning of World War I; only in the 1930s did women soldiers finally disappear from the media.[11]

Belle Boyde, also known as Ma Belle Rebel, was arrested and released six times in her work as a spy. When, in April 1862, she braved army pickets to hand-deliver a letter to Stonewall Jackson that helped him maintain control of a key bridge during the battle of Front Royal, he wrote, "I thank you for myself and for the army for the immense service you have rendered your country today."[12]

Women were also essential to the Civil War effort making munitions. On March 15, 1863, "Richmond [Virginia] was greatly shocked by the blowing up of the laboratory, in which women, girls, and boys were employed making cartridges; ten women and girls were killed on the spot."[13]

In the West, the greater part of the U.S. army that in peacetime had been stationed from the Red River in the north to the Rio Grande in the south was withdrawn during the Civil War, leaving many settlements so poorly garrisoned that women and children were left almost entirely unprotected from Indians, Mexican bandits, and American outlaws and desperadoes.

As Americans pushed westward to settle the country, guns were indispensable to men and women alike. On the frontier, every home contained a gun, and most women knew how to use it; until the Bureau of Land Management declared the end of the frontier in 1890, women inhabited a world whose normal population density was two people per square mile.

> *The westward crossing was an extraordinary undertaking—one that took its toll on the minds and health of women in a variety of ways. . . . Living on the frontier— alone or with family—required a special brand of courage. Women wrote repeatedly of the fear they felt when alone at night. They were fearful of Indians, fearful of animals, fearful of anything that rustled or stirred outside. Much of their fear—and that of the men, too—came from their inability to read their environment with any accuracy. They repeatedly misinterpreted Indian behavior, reacting in terror to the sudden appearance of any curious Indian. . . . Equally frightening were the swarms of vagrant men, either displaced by the Civil War or turned out of work in the mines and fields. Footloose soldiers, out-of-luck miners, ex-slavers,*

ruffians, and outlaws roamed freely throughout the countryside, and women had no way of knowing if the customary "Halloo!" that rang out from the forest belonged to an honest man or not.[14]

Only a gun, and her readiness to use it, could protect the woman who guessed wrong.

A California woman remembers, "In the early part of 1853, strict laws and the vigilantes sent an ever-moving stream of human microbes from the cities—gun men, gamblers, blacklegs, and all the new class of the sporting elements (men and women) to this county. They considered our hard-working miners lawful prey. . . . Every succeeding year brought thousands to California."[15]

"The wild world into which emigrant wagon trains ventured would physically transform women into robust, hardy creatures and give them tough, crucial duties." Contemporary guidebooks warned women readers to develop male characteristics of "strength, resilience, and resourcefulness to survive the trip."[16]

No matter where they went, American women could count on facing danger head-on, often alone. Men were often absent, whether hunting, attending to matters in town or the county seat, working in the fields, fighting Indians, or off in military service or training.

The great Sioux uprising in Minnesota, the bloody border wars in Texas, Cheyenne and Arapaho raids in Colorado, all involved settlers more directly than the later military campaigns that are such a familiar part of American history. Most women's diaries for these places and periods at least mention the Indian problem, and many relate from firsthand experience the terrors and horrors surrounding these events. During the Washington Indian wars of 1854-55, Caroline Sexton fled from her home on horseback "squaw fashion" to Fort Levens where she "took her gun and stood at a port-hole and fired upon the indians [sic] all night. . . ."

Although men were certainly more aggressive in their response to and dealings with Indians, women could be provoked to direct action. Threats to their safety or that of their children usually elicited an immediate and violent response. Women armed themselves with rifles, revolvers, and knives and stood ready to defend themselves and their families when they felt it was necessary.[17]

A group of little-known American women-with-guns are the "girl homesteaders," thousands of whom settled in the Great Plains. Records in Lamar, Colorado, and Douglas, Wyoming, for example, indicate that in the years 1887, 1891, 1907, and 1908 an average of 11.9 percent of the homestead entrants were women. Although homesteading was considered a male occupation, these women were readily accepted, spurred on by the Homestead Act of 1862, offering homesteaders 160 acres, and the Kincaid Act of 1904, doubling it to 320 acres. Whether facing Indians or animals alone, these women relied on their guns.

Bess Corey of South Dakota called her claim a "regular rattlesnake den . . . it's nothing to kill half a dozen just crossing it."[18] During the Oklahoma land runs of the 1890s and early 1900s, hundreds of women added their names to the list of claimants— and more women than men (43 percent of women versus 37 percent of men) toughed it out long enough to keep the property.

Yet some women of the Wild West were as notorious as the men, among them stagecoach robber Pearl Hart, Martha Jane Canary (better known as Calamity Jane), and Belle Starr. Calamity Jane acquired her nickname for several reasons, partly "because she carried guns ostentatiously" and "because her lovers, sometimes miscalled husbands, developed habits of dying violently."[19]

Like many American women who gained notoriety for their gun use, Calamity Jane was less interested in breaking the rules of polite American society than in writing her own. "Ladies who would not have recognized Miss Canary socially were enduring ostracism, scorn, and ridicule less than two thousand miles away by preaching that women had the same inalienable rights as men.

Miss Canary had never heard of them and would have been amused if she had. She was a man among men and what was the use of talking about what was simply a matter of meeting the boys on their own ground and doing as you damn pleased?"[20]

Belle Starr, who from 1875 to her death in 1889 sheltered fellow outlaws in the Indian lands, was born Myra Belle Shirley on February 5, 1848. She had eight common-law husbands, beginning with outlaw Jim Reed, losing every one of them to murder. By 1878, left on her own with two children to support, she rode the ranges of northwest Texas and the Oklahoma and Texas panhandles "with as thoroughgoing a group of desperadoes and cutthroats as ever missed a deserved national celebrity."[21] They rustled cattle, held up banks, and stole horses. One day, with a gun in each hand, she strolled into a gambling house and raided the pot of $7,000. She noted, "There's a little change due one of my friends, gentlemen. If you want it back, come down to the territory and get it."[22]

Starr almost always dressed in a long, dark velvet gown, carried six-shooters at her side, and rode sidesaddle with a high collar, chiffon waist, and black leather boots, often crowning the effect with a cream-colored Stetson with an ostrich plume.[23] When one day her hat blew off and her accomplice, a Cherokee named Blue Duck, failed to retrieve it, he found himself staring down the barrel of her revolver. "Damn your greasy hide. You pick up that hat and let this be a lesson to you in how to treat a lady!"[24] Convicted of stealing a single colt, she served six months in 1883 in the Detroit House of Correction.

She settled down with Sam Starr in a log cabin on the Canadian River and sheltered outlaw Jesse James there for several weeks. "The best people in the country are my friends," she told the *Dallas News* on June 7, 1886. "I have considerable ignorance to cope with . . . surrounded by a low-down class of shoddy whites who have made the Indian country their home to avoid paying tax on their dogs. . . . I am the constant theme of their slanderous tongues. In all the world there is no woman more peaceably inclined than I."

She was killed with a shot to the back from a double-barreled shotgun near her home on February 3, 1889.

Rose Dunn, known as the Rose of Cimarron, rode with the Doolin gang of Oklahoma, known for cattle rustling. She was involved in several shoot-outs with law officers, keeping her lover's guns loaded as he shot.

Ironically, it was a young Canadian woman, Pearl Hart of Lindsay, Ontario, who became a legend in the American West. On May 30, 1899, a stagecoach rumbling up through the Cane Springs Canyon of Arizona was halted by a man and what appeared to be a twelve-year-old boy—Hart in disguise. One traveling salesman yielded $380, the driver $10. But Hart and her accomplice hadn't even planned their escape and were captured a few days later barely twenty miles away. "It was, from the standpoint of resourcefulness and organization, one of the worst stage robberies ever pulled."[25]

Yet, thanks to a contemporary hunger for outlaw heroes, Hart became a celebrity. "Stage robberies, good or bad, were getting so rare now as to be romantic. . . . Old-time road agents . . . had never used women in their field operations," and "while Calamity Jane was drinking whiskey and passing into an ancient folklore, and Belle Starr [was] dead and forgotten, Pearl was exalted into a sort of archetype of contemporary wild western womanhood. This was the land where men were men, every dime novel reader and cheap melodrama patron repeated to himself, and now it had suddenly transpired that women were likewise. If Mrs. Hart had not been shackled with various binding engagements with sundry Arizona jailers and penitentiary wardens, she might have made a modest 1899 fortune in vaudeville."[26]

Instead, after being jailed, she kept her name alive, happy to pose for newspaper photographs cuddling her pet wildcat or with two guns or a rifle drawn.

Prostitutes, who followed soldiers, miners, and others across the country, often carried tiny pistols, two-shot derringers, small enough to tuck into a corset or boot. One, Etta Place, made her name as the lover of the Sundance Kid, helping him and Butch

Cassidy rob trains in the 1890s, then fleeing with them to South America, dropping out of sight around 1907.

Certainly the most famous female shooter in American history was Annie Oakley—the name chosen by Phoebe Ann Moses of Greenville, Ohio. Born August 13, 1860, she grew up poor, her mother widowed at thirty-three with seven children under the age of fifteen. She started shooting as a youngster to catch birds and rabbits for her hungry family, selling them for cash or ammunition to a local shopkeeper, who resold them to hotels as far away as Cincinnati. According to legend, she was one of the few hunters who shot game through the head, thus supplying meat free of bits of lead shot.[27]

Five feet tall, one hundred pounds, a woman who eschewed makeup and jewelry, she met her future husband, Frank Butler, in 1881 when she scored 25/25 in a shooting match against him, winning $50. (He scored 24/25.) Their childless marriage proved a happy, companionable partnership that lasted fifty years.

She came to national attention beginning in 1885—and held it for forty years. So badly did Oakley want to work for Buffalo Bill Cody and his Wild West show that she did three shows free to persuade him of her potential value. He hired the couple. In their first season on the road, they traveled to more than forty cities in the United States and Canada. Oakley's skills stunned audiences everywhere. She could shoot four clay birds at a time. With rifles and pistols, she shot glass ball after glass ball, sometimes even shattering marbles. To finish her act, she would lay down her gun, throw balls into the air, retrieve the rifle and break the balls before they fell. On July 31, 1888, before an audience of twelve thousand, she broke a record by downing 49/50 live pigeons.

In 1893, the Wild West show cleared $1 million in profit; Annie was earning $100 a week, the highest salary in the troupe. By 1900, she was making $150 a week—more each month than the average American earned *per year*.

On August 11, 1903, the Hearst newspapers *The Chicago American* and the *Chicago Examiner*, with no proof, proclaimed her a cocaine addict and a thief. It took her six grueling years,

1904 to 1910, and much cross-country travel to testify in court, to settle her fifty-five libel suits; she won or settled fifty-four. Hearst paid her the most in damages, $27,500.

Oakley was evangelical about the joys, and value, of women shooting and taught hundreds. "I think sport and healthful exercise make women better, healthier, and happier."[28] Moreover, women shooters would gain confidence and self-possession; most women, she said, were "greatly handicapped when danger comes."[29]

In her ability and her determination to earn a handsome living, her relentless work ethic, her insistence on extraordinarily high domestic standards, her international fame, and her ability to combine competence with femininity, Oakley presaged another American icon, a woman who, a few decades later, even lived in the same New Jersey town of Nutley.

Martha Stewart and Annie might have found much to discuss: both fought hard for years to ensure their financial independence, a holdover for both from chaotic, unhappy, and straitened childhoods. They worked for many years, traveling constantly, holding themselves and their colleagues to punishingly high standards.

"Annie maintained her costumes, tent, and homes with such meticulousness that she frequently annoyed those around her. Even family members lamented Annie's tendency to act 'particular,' and her husband, Frank, deplored her ability to drive away cooks and other domestic helpers. . . . Annie sometimes responded in an irritable fashion to complaints regarding her near-obsessive behavior. That Annie was not above sharpness is revealed in her autobiography, which gives evidence of how her quick wit could turn into a caustic tongue. . . . She saw family members only intermittently, and . . . seemed to make little effort to . . . develop truly intimate relationships."[30]

Her appeal to turn-of-the-century America, like that of Martha Stewart today, also lay in her ability to reconcile conflicting notions of womanhood—highly competitive businesswoman and smiling, gracious domestic goddess. "During an age of accelerating industrialization, war, divorce, and fear of moral decline, people evidently appreciated a shooting star who covered her ankles and calves with pearl-buttoned leggings, set riding and shooting records from a sidesaddle, and did fancy embroidery between shows. Oakley's [fans'] . . . growing nostalgia for open spaces and simpler times, and their fear that the values Annie embodied were declining, encouraged them to see her as a model western woman."[31]

Just as the name Martha now connotes for many Americans a standard of domestic perfection, for a while Oakley's was synonymous with a free pass to an entertainment event—a punched ticket showing admission looked like one of her targets punctured by bulletholes.

As more Americans moved into cities, women were still widely accepted as sport shooters and hunters, long before they won the right to vote. Smith & Wesson produced the first LadySmith, their first gun designed for, and sold to, women, from 1902 to 1921.

The 1920s and 1930s added several female names to the roster of gun-toting legends: Arizona Donny Clark (Ma Barker) and Bonnie Parker. Ma Barker was best known for her four sons' exploits—three kidnappings, ten murders, and robberies nabbing $10 million. She was killed after a four-hour gun battle, the longest in FBI history, on January 16, 1935, in Lake Weir, Florida.

In a 1933 photo, Bonnie Parker appears as cool and elegant as a *Vogue* model in a dark knit suit, stogie clenched in her lips, revolver dangling from her right hand. With her broad cheekbones, hair slicked back into a beret, and left leg cocked atop a car bumper, she exudes cool. Parker killed thirteen people with her partner, Clyde Barrow. "She has been described as both beautiful and homely; as a Robin Hood and selfishly greedy; as diabolical and simpleminded; and as in love with Clyde Barrow and infamy. Few other criminal women have inspired such public fascination."[32]

Parker married Roy Thornton at sixteen, but was left behind when he went to prison; she met Clyde Barrow the following year after losing her café job. Within a few months of meeting him, she was a well-known criminal. She first gained notoriety when she slipped a gun to Barrow so that he could escape his prison cell. In the next two years they crisscrossed the South and Midwest— deliberately creating media "buzz" as they went by sending dramatic photos to newspapers. Between 1932 and 1934, they killed nine law enforcement officers; when she was simply robbing banks—in an era of popular support for those who victimized the wealthy and powerful—Parker stayed a sympathetic figure. As a cop killer, though, she quickly lost favor.

Parker wrote and published poems about her life. One, "The Story of Bonnie and Clyde," written in 1933, predicted her death the following year: "Some day they'll go down together; And they'll bury them side by side; To few it'll be grief—To the law a relief—But it's death for Bonnie and Clyde."[33]

She and Clyde were gunned down in a hail of two hundred bullets in Louisiana on May 23, 1934.

The years after the Depression saw the rise of another legendary female shooter, Elizabeth "Plinky" Topperwein, of San Antonio, Texas. She was a member of the trick-shot team for manufacturers such as Winchester, once breaking 485 of 500 clay pigeons at a Texas gun club.

Congress created the Women's Army Auxiliary Corps (WAAC) in May 1942; in July that year the navy created the Women Accepted for Volunteer Emergency Service (WAVES), with the same status as male reservists. By November, the U.S. Coast Guard had created SPAR, from its motto, *Semper Paratus* (Always Ready), and the Marines followed in February 1943. In all, 350,000 American women served in uniform in World War II, with a peak strength of 271,000. In June 1943, Congress upgraded the WAAC into the permanent Women's Army Corps (WAC), with full military status. The WASPs (Women's Airforce Service Pilots), all volunteers, flew planes, ferried bombers, tested fighters, and tested targets.

Catherine McBride D'Arezzo, interviewed in 1996, recalled her days training in the Texas Women's Defense Corps during

World War II. "We'd go to the pistol range and we learned how to take apart a Colt .45 and clean it and put it back together. Then we had to learn to fire it. They were preparing us for duty that might be necessary. You never knew."[34]

In civilian life of the 1940s, riflery was a popular choice for young coeds, as much a part of genteel campus athletic life as tennis, field hockey, golf, and riding. At Texas Woman's University (now coed, then named the Texas School for Christian Women), the 1941 rifle team defeated a much larger rival school, Texas A&M, for the second time in two years. In a shoulder-to-shoulder shooting match on the rifle range, the Tessies scored a two-point victory, and by May 1943, photos of the shooters appeared throughout the world in newspapers from India to Iceland.[35]

By the fall of 1943, with war production at its peak, 17 million women represented a third of the total U.S. workforce, 5 million in the war industries. "They were working harder then they had ever worked, at home and elsewhere. They did heavier and more dangerous work than they had ever done before."[36] While women's labor was essential to the war effort, it also dislocated and isolated them, placing women in unfamiliar cities and towns, far from family and friends, newly vulnerable to crime. Not only were women working long hours, and sometimes odd hours or overnight shifts, they were moving constantly, following jobs or their men.

When women studies professor Martha McCaughey compared self-defense pamphlets from the 1940s and the "feminist" 1970s, she found the language of the 1940s guides much tougher and more direct, those from the "liberated" 1970s more polite and circumspect. While manuals of the 1940s advised women to throw a punch into a man's face or light a book of matches and do the same if necessary, a Bureau of Justice pamphlet from 1977, for example, warned women not to "invite" a forced sexual encounter.

Did American women arm themselves with guns during World War II, this uncertain era? No historian I asked could answer the question. It's likely that many homes already contained a firearm belonging to an absent husband, father, or brother, making that choice easier—and obviating the need for women to obtain one of their own.

The 1950s offered women shooters a "feminine" gun; from 1955 to 1956, a company called High Standard targeted women buyers with its Sentinel model, a nine-shot .22 revolver that came in pink, baby blue, nickel, or gold finishes.

"Times have changed and so has the woman's role on the shooting range," noted *The American Rifleman* in June 1956. "Particularly since 1945 have women competed in sizable numbers in pistol, small-bore rifle, and high-power rifle matches. This year, 1955, will truly go down as a milestone in the history of shooting, and because of a woman." Viola E. Pollum, at the National Matches at Camp Perry, Ohio, beat 488 men and women to capture the national small-bore rifle championship, becoming the first woman to win an overall national shooting match in the NRA Annual Matches, held every year since 1873.[37]

One group of women in the 1950s and 1960s deeply affected by gun violence were those active in the civil rights movement, such as Fannie Lou Hamer, Rosa Parks, and Daisy Bates. "By the time I was six, I was old enough to realize we were actually not free," writes Parks in her 1992 autobiography. "The Ku Klux Klan was riding through the black community, burning churches, beating up people, killing people. . . . At one point the violence was so bad that my grandfather kept his gun—a double-barreled shotgun—close by at all times. . . . I remember thinking that whatever happened, I wanted to see it. I wanted to see him shoot that gun."[38]

After Parks married, and her husband began organizing activists' meetings, they held one in their home. "This was the first time I'd seen so few men with so many guns." She had hoped to serve them refreshments, but "with the table so covered with guns, I don't know where I would have put [them]."[39] Parks never carried a gun, although other women in the movement did.

Some of the most violent reprisals by those opposed to civil rights were made against women, and the homes of women activists were regularly fired upon.[40] When Fannie Lou Hamer ran unsuccessfully for Congress in 1964, she had already been jailed and beaten and the subject of death threats. "My house is so full of holes it wouldn't hold water," she told a meeting of the Mississippi Freedom Democratic Party.[41] On September 10, 1962, she took refuge at a friend's home. "They shot in that house sixteen times tryin' to kill me." As the nighttime terrorism continued, she moved again. "We would have to have our lights out before dark. It was cars passing that house all times of the night, driving real slow with guns and pickups with white mens in it, and they'd pass that house just as slow as they could pass it . . . three guns lined up in the back."[42]

Ruby Hurley, director of the NAACP youth program from 1943 to 1951, and the first NAACP staff person in the South, never wanted to carry a gun herself. But she grew accustomed to riding beside a man who did, Mississippi's NAACP field secretary Medgar Evers. "Many times when Medgar and I would be driving together, Medgar would tell us about carrying his gun. I said, 'Medgar, it's not gon' do any good to carry a gun.' He used to sit on it, under his pillow." Hurley was convinced that carrying a gun would be of little practical use should Evers really need it. "They're cowards. They're not gonna come and tell you, 'I'm gonna shoot you.' And sure enough, that's the way he died. A sniper got him."[43]

After Evers was shot in the back by a rifle on June 13, 1963, it was Hurley who cleaned up the mess. "Everybody was in such a state of shock that nobody had done anything about getting the blood cleaned off the driveway or off his car or anything. So that was the first thing I did—get that blood up—before his wife sees it and before the children come back home."

Hurley's job was typical. From earliest colonial days, American women, when not victims themselves, have been cleaning up the bloody aftermath of gun violence, digging bullets from the bodies of their loved ones, burying them, and mourning them.

Robert Williams, an early civil rights activist later discredited by the NAACP for his call to violent action, says some black women joining the movement wanted to learn to shoot, but male activists dissuaded them from doing so. "They had volunteered and they wanted to fight. But we kept them out of most of it."[44]

Daisy Bates, who had been instrumental in the desegregation of Little Rock's Central High School in 1957—and who had been fired at in her home and on the street by segregationists—spoke frequently across the country telling audiences she carried a pistol and that she knew how to use it.[45] Yet Bates's calls for armed self-defense did not make her a pariah as it did Williams. "In a world where manhood and violence were so intertwined, the fact that she was a woman muted the perceived threat," writes historian Timothy B. Tyson.[46] Black women occasionally drew their weapons; when black physician Dr. A. E. Perry was arrested for performing an abortion on a white woman in October 1957, a furious crowd of armed black women, whom Perry had treated for many years, "housewives with hatchets and shotguns and pistols," flocked to the jail in Monroe, North Carolina, to protest.

White Detroit housewife Viola Liuzzo joined the list of civil rights martyrs on March 25, 1965, when she was shot twice in the head by three Ku Klux Klansmen who ran her down on an Alabama road after the Selma march. The thirty-nine-year-old white woman who had driven to the South to help register black voters left behind five children.

By the end of the 1950s, no single moment had yet galvanized gun-control activism. The most recent presidential assassination had been that of President McKinley in 1901. (Abraham Lincoln was shot in 1865, and James Garfield in 1881.) The 1960s changed that forever. Four young, charismatic leaders—John F. Kennedy, Robert Kennedy, Malcolm X, and Martin Luther King—were assassinated within five years. Jacqueline Kennedy, her chic suit spattered with her husband's blood, burned into our collective memory. Certainly, no woman who saw it could expunge that horror.

Over the next forty years, private gun ownership became a matter of heated public debate even as crime rates rose and, in the 1970s with the rise of feminism, women began to gain and test new political, social, and economic freedom. No longer were many American women relying on a man at home to defend them. As the number of divorced women rose dramatically, some of those who wanted to feel safe in their homes alone, with or without children, began to acquire guns for self-protection.

Today, 17 million women own guns. Yet widespread and persistent discomfort with this choice still begs the question: Should they?

Chapter 3
Thelma, Velma, and the Fembots

$\longleftarrow\bullet\!\!\blacktriangleright\!\!\blacklozenge\!\!\blacktriangleleft\!\!\bullet\longrightarrow$

From gangster molls of the 1930s to *Thelma & Louise,* 1940s comic book heroines to Lara Croft Tomb Raider, pop culture images of women with guns have horrified, amused, and intrigued us for decades. While sharpshooter Annie Oakley made headlines in the 1880s, her legend has yet to die, thanks to comic books, films, a television series, and a perennially popular musical, *Annie Get Your Gun,* based on her story.

A woman killer offers durable dramatic material. Serial killer Aileen Wuornos, who murdered thirteen men between 1989 and 1990, quickly became the subject of a television movie, a feature documentary, two feature films, an opera, and a play. In 1926, the first iteration of the phenomenon *Chicago,* whose female characters shoot their lovers, and which became a Broadway show and an Oscar-winning film, was a play written by Maurine Dallas Watkins. When Ann Woodward killed her husband, millionaire sportsman William Woodward, on Long Island in 1955, the case inspired a miniseries starring Ann-Margret and the late Claudette Colbert and a 1985 novel, *The Two Mrs. Grenvilles.*

While guns remain iconic within American culture, from

gangsta rap to white-walled art galleries, the women who use them are usually de facto Bad Girls transgressing social boundaries. If they actually *enjoy* shooting, they had better feel guilty. A woman able to kill challenges preconceptions of female vulnerability and attractiveness. With the power to blow you away whenever and wherever she feels like it, she's scary as hell.

A woman shooter remains most sympathetic when—like Ellen Ripley in the *Alien* films or Clarice Starling as a young FBI trainee in *Silence of the Lambs*—she's carrying lethal force on behalf of others, especially when protecting the lives of children. Things get messier when a woman decides to stand up for herself. Women who possess lethal power, women wreaking violence, *women who fight back,* make many viewers, and would-be directors and producers, deeply uncomfortable. Most often, when women tell the stories, they offer *not* a passive victim awaiting rescue, but a female willing and able to do it herself.

Film

Hollywood has never comfortably reconciled women characters both attractive and dangerous, armed and lethal. "According to society's accepted role definitions, which films have always reflected in microcosm . . . a man is supposedly most himself when he is driving to achieve, to create, to conquer . . . a woman is least 'womanly' in the pursuit of knowledge or success," wrote film critic Molly Haskell twenty-seven years ago.[1]

Little has since changed. In the 1996 film *Set It Off,* four black women use guns to redress their wrongs, yet only the butch lesbian character, Cleo, played by Queen Latifah, can safely express the deepest wish for serious weaponry: "We ain't robbing stagecoaches. I need something I can set it off with." She dies for her hubris in a shoot-out with the Los Angeles Police Department.

Women's studies professor Martha McCaughey thinks such violent images are just fine: "We need to stop asserting that nothing is what it seems, that all of women's attempts at resistance in movies lead to failure. . . . We find most of our university students cheer when we screen such images. Male students say it teaches them not to 'mess with the wrong female,' and women students say it makes them realize they can fight back if attacked."[2]

Seeing tough women in the movies altered McCaughey's worldview. "My usual anger at the violence [in films] changed dramatically when I watched *Terminator 2* in 1991. Sarah Connor's competence with weapons and hand-to-hand combat exhilarated me. I remember driving my car home differently from the theater that day, flexing my arms as I clutched the steering wheel. That's when I realized that men must feel this way after seeing movies—all the time."

She dismisses dismay at the ugliness and brutality of violent women in film. And some of the images are indeed horrific: the opening scene of the 1992 film *Naked Killer* shows a woman shooting off a man's penis. When a man moves too quickly from foreplay to intercourse, Mallory in the 1994 film *Natural Born Killers* whips out a handgun from her purse and blows his brains out, shouting, "Next time don't be so fucking eager!"

McCaughey, an associate professor and director of the women's studies program at Appalachian State University, calls these killers "mean women," playfully mocking the horror they evoke. "Depictions of women's violence seem more horrific to many people, perhaps because we find far fewer of them than we find scenes of male violence. Moreover, cultural standards still equate womanhood with kindness and nonviolence, manhood with strength and aggression."[3]

Many cultural changes created a hunger for "mean women" in film in the early 1990s: the health and fitness movement that redefined women's bodies; the student antirape movement that sparked nationwide conversation about gender, violence, and power; and the movement of middle-class white women back into the paid labor force.[4] A banner year for violent women in film was 1991; films that year included *Silence of the Lambs, Terminator 2* with Linda Hamilton, and *La Femme Nikita.* Foster won her second Oscar for her role as Clarice Starling (in addition to the

Golden Globe, British Academy Award, New York Film Critics Award, and Chicago Film Critics Award).

Hamilton in *The Terminator* and Sigourney Weaver as Ellen Ripley in the *Alien* series offered viewers fearless Amazons cradling enormous weapons, their chiseled arms gleaming with sweat. They were powerful—but they weren't real. When Louise, a housewife in the 1991 film *Thelma & Louise,* killed a would-be rapist in a parking lot with a .38, public and critical reaction was rough, not like the adulation offered Jodie Foster in *Silence of the Lambs.* A woman trying to professionally outwit a psychopathic, serial-killing cannibal was sympathetic—a hausfrau-turned-vigilante was not.

Thelma & Louise, written by a woman, Callie Khouri, ushered in a whole crop of gals-with-guns movies in the early 1990s. In *Blue Steel,* Jamie Lee Curtis played rookie police officer Megan Turner, who kills two men while on the job, followed by *Guncrazy, Point of No Return,* and *My New Gun. Copycat,* a 1995 film, starred Holly Hunter as detective M. J. Monahan, a skilled shooter. In the 1998 film *Out of Sight,* Jennifer Lopez played gun-toting federal marshal Karen Sisco, a character who reappeared in the fall of 2003 in the ABC television drama series *Karen Sisco.*

But critics often dismiss female firepower. In *The Long Kiss Goodnight,* a 1996 film, Charlie is a CIA operative who kills "efficiently and often."[5] Geena Davis played the role, so blood-soaked it disgusted *San Francisco Examiner* film critic Barbara Shulgasser: "Why would an actress with [her] obvious ability want to keep making movies designed to demonstrate that women can be just as insensitive, bloodthirsty, and repulsive as men have been for years?"[6]

"When, if ever, is too much?" asked film critic Andrew Sarris. For him, the violent women of 1990s film were deeply disturbing, lacking the clear boundaries marking earlier cinematic Bad Girls, making clear their choices were unacceptable. While film noir portrayed enormous violence, "those morally marginal characters . . . were not the people who won Oscars or who became box-office champions. The tough guys and their dames had a following, but they were the exception rather than the rule."[7]

Images of women who simply enjoy shooting for its own plea-sure—*not* the retaliatory, morally defensible pursuit of criminals, aliens, or abusive men—are rare. Who can forget the manic joy on Annette Bening's face in the Oscar-deluged 1999 film *American Beauty*? A suburban mother and wife smothering in a stalled career and dead marriage, Bening's character picks up a gun at her local range and fires with fierce pleasure, exulting, "I love this!"

Instead, male-dominated action films are where the big money lies. "The assumption that only men can make action films is built into the Hollywood culture," says Anne Thompson, west coast editor of *Premiere* magazine. "There's so much money at stake; the studios go with what's proven."

Even when women end up in action films, they "either get killed or screwed, and I think *screwed* is the polite word," says Denise Di Novi, who produced the 1994 film *Little Women* and 2002's *A Walk to Remember.*[8] One recent notable exception was the 2000 film *Charlie's Angels,* produced by veteran actress Drew Barrymore and distributed by Columbia Pictures, one of the few studios with a woman president, Amy Pascal. The film grossed $122.8 million, the twelfth most successful film of the year, just behind *Erin Brockovich* ($125.5 million) and ahead of *The Patriot* ($113.3 million).

Barrymore starred in the 1992 film *Guncrazy,* playing a sexu-ally abused young woman who shoots and kills her stepfather. Yet, as a producer of *Charlie's Angels,* she insisted that the three Angels, Barrymore, Lucy Liu, and Cameron Diaz, use no guns in their many death-defying adventures. "We wanted to try and cre-ate something different, set a new tone, create a new genre," said Barrymore. The challenge was to make them strong *and* likable. Said the director, McG, "They have to make the men say, 'I want to be with her,' and the women to say, 'I want to *be* her.' "

The decade's most sympathetic woman-with-a-gun? Perhaps heavily pregnant, unfailingly polite Marge Gunderson, the police officer in *Fargo,* the 1996 film starring Frances McDormand as Marge—who won an Oscar for her role.

Women with guns occasionally surface in documentaries.

Canadian filmmaker Wendy Rowland made *Packing Heat: Does Safety Come from the Barrel of a Gun?* about gun owners, in 1996. In 1994, Cambridge, Massachusetts–based filmmaker Margaret Lazarus won the Academy Award for Best Documentary Short for *Defending Our Lives,* a $135,000, forty-two-minute film about eight battered women who killed their husbands. It has since been seen by millions, she says, most often screened in college classes and as an educational tool for domestic-violence agencies.

"I think it's extraordinarily important to get it out there. People don't realize how bad it can get," she says. In the film, women describe in chilling detail, with still photos of their injuries, what their husbands did to them—and their losing battle with the legal system. *Guns and Mothers,* a fifty-four-minute, 2003 documentary written, directed, and produced by Thom Powers, looked at both sides of the issue of gun ownership, focusing on Brooklyn-based activist Frances Davis, who lost her three sons to gun violence, and on Maria Heil, spokesman for the pro-gun group Second Amendment Sisters. The film aired May 13, 2003, on more than a hundred PBS stations. *Bowling for Columbine,* of course, won the Oscar for Best Documentary for 2002 for filmmaker Michael Moore—who, interestingly, said not a word about women and guns in his wildly popular two-hour antigun diatribe.

Women in the cinema were bubbly flappers and socialites in the 1920s and dizzy dames or dimpled baby-girls in the 1930s, although that decade also produced a crop of films with molls, detectives, con artists, and spies. The 1940s produced the "treacherous woman," "one of the most striking phenomena of [that decade], [where] actresses like Rita Hayworth, Jean Peters, Eve Arden, Ann Sothern, Lana Turner, and Dorothy Malone . . . played women of dubious ethics or unconventional femininity who were as likely to be found on the wrong side of the law as not."[9] In the 1949 film *Beyond the Forest,* Bette Davis is a crack shot and hunter. By the end of the 1940s, though, as women were abruptly shoved out of the workforce with the end of World War II, brave female characters comfortable wielding physical power rapidly disappeared from the silver screen. They would not return to prominence for more than forty years, in the early 1990s.

In contrast to male action films, where firepower equals strength, the more violent they become, the less credibility female characters enjoy. In the 2000 French film *Baise-Moi* ("screw me" is one translation), a woman sodomizes a man with a handgun and fires it inside him, killing him. Writer Richard Brooks described the film as "a more explicit mélange of *Thelma & Louise* and *Pulp Fiction* in which two young, disillusioned women embark on an extraordinarily violent journey across France after one is raped and the other sees her best friend shot dead."

"It's not real violence after all," said filmmaker Coralie Trinh Thi, bemused by the uproar and a censorship battle over its ratings in England and France. "It's comic-strip violence." The film is based on a book by cowriter and codirector Virginie Despentes, who was raped as a teenager.[10]

In the spring of 2002, as America moved toward war with Iraq and women soldiers across the country prepared to head overseas, *Time* magazine critic Richard Corliss tried to make sense of the latest crop of women-with-guns films:

"The recipe is simple: put a woman in a room with a psycho, and let us watch. If the woman has an ailing daughter for the baddies to terrorize, good. If the man she loves has a dark past and maybe a homicidal kink, better. If she must confront two mad-genius kids, best. Just put our heroine in dire peril before she emerges victorious. It's a lesson in female resiliency. Also, these days, big box office."[11]

Corliss described April 2002 as "a beam of hope to those desperate for gender equality on-screen. The two top films for the April 5–7 weekend were thrillers starring women: David Fincher's *Panic Room,* with Jodie Foster besieged by three burglars, and Carl Franklin's *High Crimes,* in which lawyer Ashley Judd defends her enigmatic husband in a high-stakes court-martial. In *Murder by Numbers,* Sandra Bullock plays a cop on a homicide investigation that points to two brilliant teenagers. And Jennifer Lopez [stars in] the spousal revenge drama *Enough.*

"These films do let audiences see top actresses playing strong characters. 'People want to root for their favorite female stars,' Foster says. 'Audiences don't want a woman just to be the sister-of, daughter-of, wife-of. This proves they're not only open to, but absolutely behind, the idea of a woman going through some terrible danger and finding the gumption and the brawn to fight against it. . . . It's just that it's been happening to men for centuries, and now it's happening to women.'

"Women are always in danger in modern movies," Corliss adds, "in danger of being left out of them. In teen-boy farces, women are usually just a priapic prop. In adult action pictures they may be no more than a trophy, a pawn, or a poignant memory. So the very notion that women are not on the margins but at the center of medium-budget, mass-appeal films is refreshing."

"Some female leads are really male leads," says *Murder by Numbers* producer Susan Hoffman. "For a while in action scripts, it was as if they just changed the name from Robert to Roberta. The question is, can there be scripts that have all the dynamics, the strengths and insecurities, of a woman? . . . There's still a ways to go in the writing of these characters. What we're really missing is more female writers."

Or are we missing a more complex idea of what women, and movies, can be? "Years ago, in the fifties and film noir," says Irwin Winkler, a producer of *Enough*, "women were tough and often very bad. Nowadays, the women are very good and have to become tough to defend themselves." Their goodness is usually defined by the bad things done to them.

"In the thirties and forties," writes Corliss, "movie women had little need for revenge; they weren't imperiled; they were liberated. They and their men talked, fought, and loved as equals, and audiences flocked to see these battles of wits and wills. Often women dominated the most popular movies. Until 1965, Hollywood's top-grossing film was *Gone With the Wind*, which was succeeded by *The Sound of Music*—two films of women in peril (Yankees! Nazis!). Among today's heroines in jeopardy, there's no room for Vivien Leigh's classy spoiledness or Julie Andrews's sassy sweetness.

"The fact is, the women-in-peril films are like most other recent U.S. movies, from *Pearl Harbor* to *In the Bedroom:* they are revenge fantasies, playing on the understandable but infantile belief that every atrocity can be overcome by a righteously violent response. But life doesn't work that way, and neither did most of the best old movies. *Casablanca* and *Gone With the Wind* did not end happily for their heroines; the frustrations of duty and destiny intervened. In the end, the new women-in-peril films betray a simultaneous naïveté (that the heroine will triumph) and cynicism (that moviegoers won't believe justice is done unless they see the bad guy blown away)." (© 2002 TIME Inc. Reprinted by permission.)

By the time *Chicago* had been filmed again in 2002, starring Catherine Zeta-Jones as killer Velma Kelly and Renee Zellweger as Roxie Hart (Zeta-Jones won the Oscar for Best Actress and the film the Oscar for Best Picture), a vengeful woman with a gun had lost its ability to shock. Woman-as-killer had almost become a cultural cliché, commented male critic Terry Teachout. A real-life parade of female shooters had made front-page headlines for several decades: Valerie Solanas, Amy Fisher, Jean Harris, serial killer Aileen Wuornos . . .

In the film, when small-time chorine Roxie Hart shoots and kills her lover, a slick defense lawyer uses her crime and a scandal-addicted press to make her name a household word. "Those who fondly recall the colossal dramatic punch that *Chicago* packed in 1975 may not realize that while the show remains more or less the same in 2002, the world around it has changed utterly," Teachout wrote. "Twenty-seven years ago, it was still startling to be told that an uneducated, untalented slut could become a full-fledged star simply by virtue of having killed someone. Now it's old news."[12]

It was interesting to see the contrast between two of the 2002 Christmas season's most heavily promoted films—both of which featured women-with-guns. In a print ad for the James Bond film *Die Another Day,* Pierce Brosnan thrusts out his handgun while a leather-clad Halle Berry shies backward at his side, her arms and hands invisible, a passive, pretty victim. (Other ads for the film showed her with her arm, and gun, extended as aggressively as his.) In the full-page ad for *Chicago*, Zellweger and Zeta-Jones stood with their backs to the camera, each holding a tiny, snub-nosed .38 revolver. Gun as accessory, if not to murder, to their beaded, fringed, short dresses.

Sometimes film's most compelling armed women aren't even women. Discussing her admiration of the "fembots" in the 1997 film *Austin Powers: International Man of Mystery*, sex writer Susie Bright talked about how, when she's sitting in bumper-to-bumper traffic or dealing with a slow, rude salesperson, she wishes she had the robots' unique skill—firing bullets from their nipples. "It's just so . . . inspiring!"[13]

Television

Women on such popular contemporary television shows as *N.Y.P.D. Blue, The Sopranos, CSI, Alias, Law & Order: Criminal Intent, Law & Order: Special Victims Unit,* and *Fastlane* carry guns and use them proficiently. By the late 1990s, chic, pistol-packing women starred in *La Femme Nikita* and the wildly popular Fox television show *The X-Files*. In that show, FBI agent Dana Scully was a complex amalgam of demure and daring. Always clad in modest pantsuits, her red hair immaculately coiffed, a tiny crucifix dangling in the hollow of her throat, she was as adept with her pistol as her male partner, Fox Mulder. Gillian Anderson played Scully, a role for which she was nominated many times for Screen Actors Guild, Golden Globe, and Emmy Awards; she won the Emmy and the Golden Globe in 1997.

Many remember the 1950s for television shows offering saccharine images of domestic bliss: *Ozzie and Harriet, Leave It to Beaver,* and *I Love Lucy*. Women were generally portrayed as pristine housewives or ditsy housewives. Yet that decade also offered viewers a woman starring in her own long-running adventure show, who carried a rifle and shot it proficiently. *Annie Oakley,* a syndicated show that ran from 1952 to 1956, was a children's western set in the town of Diablo and starred Gail Davis as a gun-toting rancher whose horse was named Target. Davis did her own riding and shooting; the series made television history—the first ever to star a woman in a western. (It was produced, perhaps not surprisingly, by Gene Autry's Flying A Productions.)

Throughout the century, images of guns work best in context: on the range, on the ranch, or on the job.

Perhaps reflective of the 1960s and 1970s cultural ambivalence toward women's increasing economic and political power, many television shows portraying women with guns flickered briefly before their inevitable cancellation. There was Honey West, owner of a private detective agency; *The Girl from U.N.C.L.E.;* and an undercover LAPD cop in *Get Christie Love.* The most popular girl-with-a-gun show of that decade, a sixty-minute show on ABC running from 1968 to 1973, was *The Mod Squad,* starring long-limbed, blond Peggy Lipton as Julie Barnes, an LAPD undercover agent.

Perhaps the most infamous show using women and guns was *Charlie's Angels.* The series, which ran on ABC from September 1976 to August 1981, was the most popular show of the 1976–77 season. The one-hour program featured three young female police academy grads who had signed up with Charles Townsend Associates, a private detective agency. In the first season, more than *3 million* posters were sold of lean, blond actress and "Angel" Farrah Fawcett.

As shows portraying women as police officers slowly gained popularity, so did the image of a woman handling a pistol or a revolver with competence.

Cagney & Lacey was the turning point in television's treatment of women and guns in its groundbreaking willingness to show tough, risk-taking female cops. It was the first television crime show in which the two central characters were women. The series, starring Tyne Daly and Sharon Gless, first aired on CBS on March 25, 1982, and ran until August 25, 1988. It was the first show allowing women to play credible police officers, struggling with some of the real emotional and physical risks in being on the job. Daly made history by winning four consecutive Emmy Awards for Outstanding Lead Actress in a Drama Series.

The most prolific television writer in America, David E. Kelley (who in 2002 had four prime-time network shows in production), wrote women's gun use into several episodes of his Emmy Award–winning hour-long crime drama *The Practice,* about a Boston criminal-defense firm. Guns in women's hands showed up elsewhere, from two episodes of *The Simpsons,* an animated series on Fox, to a remake for TNT of the Shakespearean drama *King Lear.*

Theater

Female violence prompted Carson Kreitzer, a thirty-four-year-old American contemporary female playwright, to create what she calls her "women-with-guns triptych," three plays whose main character was a woman who shot and killed.

"I'm very interested in issues of women's anger and violence because I'm a very nonviolent person myself. Women are trained to *avoid* conflict and to make things nice for everyone else. When I started writing about women who shot and killed, I wondered why it didn't happen more often. This fascinated me."

The first play, *Valerie Shot Andy,* was about Valerie Solanas's shooting of Andy Warhol, written when Kreitzer was a senior at Yale in 1991. The second, *Heroin/e (Keep Us Quiet),* was a dialogue between the sister of a patient of Sigmund Freud's and Ellie Nesler, who on April 2, 1993, in a Jamestown, California, courtroom, shot and killed Daniel Driver, the man she said had been molesting her son.

In her third work, *Self-Defense, or the Death of Some Salesmen,* Kreitzer used the life of serial killer Aileen Wuornos—and her shooting of seven clients in what she said was self-defense—to show how glamorized Wuornos became as "serial-killer woman."

A *New York Times* reviewer gave the play a lengthy and favorable review, calling it "a sympathetic, even affectionate portrait."[14]

Gun violence inspired another recent American play, one deliberately didactic. In 1999, disturbed by an incident at his son's school, William Mastrosimone, an award-winning playwright, wrote a one-act play called *Bang, Bang, You're Dead,* about a youth who shoots his parents and five classmates. The play, whose message is the futility of violence, is available free at www.bang bangyouredead.com; it has been produced more than fifteen thousand times. (It was also made into a television film for Showtime, broadcast October 13, 2002; the *New York Times* called it "an eloquent and moving plea for understanding.")

The play has clearly found a niche; when I checked the website in January 2003, there were performances scheduled almost every day of the week across the country: a middle school in Houston, Texas, and high schools in Charlotte, North Carolina; Stanford, Kentucky; and Tomales, California.

The play, says Mastrosimone on his website, is "a free gift for students to perform in schools, garages, street corners, parks, houses of worship—anyplace there can be communication and discovery about how we've made the world's violence our own. And how we can change it."

It was performed in April 1999 at Thurston High School in Springfield, Oregon—a case of art imitating life. It was there, on May 21, 1998, that a student opened fire in the cafeteria, killing two students and wounding twenty-three. "I don't want any other school to go through the hell that Thurston went through," said Nichole Buckholtz, an eighteen-year-old who played a role in the drama and who was shot in the leg that day in 1988. The students performed at the Hult Center for the Performing Arts in Eugene; said drama instructor Mike Fisher, "If it's on campus, the wounds are too fresh and too deep."[15]

In *Gun Club,* peformed in Manhattan in 2003, thirty-five-year-old New York playwright Holman Hunt used a gun to make a larger point about parental neglect and teenage angst; in the second act of his two-act play, Klaus, a teenage boy, shoots Heidi, a teenager he met at a local gun club. Hunt wanted audiences to exit the theater less outraged about guns than by teens ignored by their parents and teachers; Heidi dies because she rejects Klaus, a young man trying desperately and ineffectually to connect with his parents.

The most popular, longest-running, and best-known shows whose women characters wield guns, *Annie Get Your Gun* and *Chicago*, are stylized escapist fun, safely distant voices from the past.

Video Games and Toys

Even the youngest Americans get little respite from a culture saturated with violence. For Christmas 2002, Forward Command Post—a bombed-out dollhouse with smashed furniture, broken railings, and bullet-pocked walls (and accessories including a machine gun, rocket launcher, magazine belt, and explosives)—was being marketed for children ages five and up.

Female action figures, from an LAPD officer to an F-15 pilot, are increasingly popular, although most buyers aren't children but adult men. Blue Box, a private Hong Kong–based company, manufactures a line of combat-ready women who come accessorized with the appropriate weapons made to scale. The figures sell for $39.99, obsessively accurate in every detail. Twenty-First Century produces a line of female soldiers, and the Rescue Heroes, targeted to preschoolers and made by Fisher-Price, was the second-best-selling action figure brand in 2002. The best-selling female action figure of all time was Princess Leia from *Star Wars*, which sold largely to girls.

Christopher Byrne, a consultant for twenty years to toy companies who has interviewed families across the country, says many women just don't like guns. "What we've observed is that women don't generally approach conflict resolution by picking up weapons. Women are more sensitive to introducing guns into their children's play than men. Many men grow up playing with toy guns and figure, 'Well, I turned out okay.' Women don't have that same experience. Just as collectible dolls don't resonate with men, neither do action figures resonate with women. People buy toys that reflect themselves and their culture."

Byrne has found significant regional differences in attitude. "I've talked with families in the Midwest and the Southwest where the family gun is as much a part of the household as the family cat. At the same time, on the coasts, the gun is seen as dangerous."

The country's best-selling video game is a PlayStation 2 game called Grand Theft Auto 3, sold in Wal-Mart, Best Buy, Toys "R" Us, and other retail chains. It's a game, writes *New York Times* columnist Bob Herbert, "in which all boundaries of civilization have vanished. You get to shoot whomever you want, including cops. You get to beat women to death with baseball bats. You get to have sex with prostitutes and then kill them. (And get your money back.)"[16]

Grand Theft Auto: Vice City was released in October 2002, selling for $49—Grand Theft Auto 3, released in October 2001, sells for $50—and is the country's second-most-popular video game. (The third and fourth best-sellers, as of January 2003, were Madden NFL 2003 and Super Mario Advance 2.)[17] Shooting prostitutes in the head is part of the fun—and it's wildly profitable. The Manhattan-based public company that produces the GTA series, Take-Two Interactive Software Inc., reported $794 million in sales for 2002—a 76 percent jump from 2001. The company's net growth for 2002, in one year, was 1,136 percent.[18] The company won't disclose whether more men than women are buying or playing the games.

Most black women portrayed in many of the nation's most popular video games are violence victims, according to a study by Children Now, an Oakland, California–based nonpartisan advocacy group. The study—called "Fair Play?"—documented that 86 percent of the African-American women in the games are physically assaulted in some way. The researchers looked at best-selling games played on Nintendo 64, Sony PlayStation and PlayStation 2, Game Boy Advance, and Game Boy Color. The games also showed no Latina characters. Nearly all the heroes were white.[19]

Female video-game characters are starting to hold their own, fighting back with a variety of weapons, including serious fire-power, prompting queasy distaste from some observers, fist-pumping cheers from others. "I love having images in popular culture and these games that include women as fighters," says feminist author Jennifer Baumgardner. "You should see the letters we've gotten from mothers and daughters and sisters thanking us for Lara, the first real action figure they identified with," says Paul Baldwin, vice president for marketing at Eidos, the video-game publisher with the biggest franchise starring a female character, Lara Croft Tomb Raider.

Feminist theorist bell hooks is less impressed; in video games, as in the cinema, women with guns are often also portrayed as hypersexual, pneumatic fantasies, all breasts and no conscience. "The women kill as ruthlessly as and brutally as any men, but when it comes to sex, that drops out and they are little girls. It's a tremendous burden."[20]

The fighting women in video games put up a respectable fight against an array of male and female opponents in Tao Feng: Fist of the Lotus, created for the Xbox console. In games like Cy Girls, Brute Force, WarCraft III: Reign of Chaos, and Enter the Matrix, female characters have as much chance of winning as the men do; video-game makers say their tough new women reflect the grow-ing number of aggressive women on film and television screens and in the military.

Comic Books and Cartoons

Ninety-five percent of American comic-book buyers are male, so it's no surprise that American comics show a dearth of gun-toting females. They pop up occasionally, but there's nothing like the array of female superheroes who dominated newsstands 60 years ago.

Only when guys are gone can girls get strong.

In 1942, nearly ten strips were drawn by women in daily newspapers; most of the men drawing cartoons were of draft age, and as in every other industry, women took their places. In 1942 the number of women working for comic books tripled, and their numbers stayed high until the end of the 1940s. As a result of the influx of women into the consistently most male-dominated of media industries, typical wartime heroine titles included *Yankee Girl, Blond Bomber,* and *Girl Commandos.* In 1946 and 1947, there was *Toni Gayle,* a fashion-model/detective.

"For four glorious years, young girls could open a comic book and read that it was possible for women, too, to defeat Fascism."[21]

One comic book company, Fiction House, started in 1936 by two men, hired more women than any other. Their six titles, *Jumbo, Jungle, Fight, Wings, Rangers,* and *Planet* specialized in stories with strong and beautiful female protagonists. "These women were in charge," writes cartoonist Trina Robbins in her history of female cartoonists. "They could be jungle girls, pilots, 'girl detectives,' or outer space heroines. Dressed in two-piece leopard skin bathing suits or ripped Army nurse uniforms, they leaped across the page in graphic role reversal, guns blazing or knife in hand. And they were likely to be drawn by women."[22]

In 1948, Timely Comics brought out a comic book featuring a version of Annie Oakley as a contemporary career girl. In the first issue, foreman Tex Collins tells his boss, ranch owner Bruce Barr, he's just found a terrific new cowpuncher. Says ranchhand Slim, "What a shot! What a roper!"

"He's a her," says Tex.

From 1940, when she was twenty, to 1961, Ruth Roche (also working for Fiction House) made history by being the company's major writer and, later, editor. After the war ended and men came home to reclaim their jobs, men took back their action comics. By 1952, *Brenda Starr* (an ongoing newspaper strip about a female reporter) was the only adventure strip drawn and written by a woman.

"There aren't many female characters in comics who use firearms," says Calum Johnston, an owner of two comic-book stores who has been in the comics business for twenty years. Forty percent of his customers are female. "Most of the superheroes in comics eschew guns and use special powers or devices instead. Witchblade has a magic gauntlet that transforms into a sword; Wonder Woman has her bracelets, which deflect bullets, and she also has a magic lasso, which compels people to tell the truth. Catwoman usually uses a whip if she has to fight." Black Canary uses a knife, and the Huntress a crossbow.

A few do use guns, well and often. They include Ghost, a female version of the Shadow, who hoists a pair of .45s. In western comics, *Gunsmith Cats, Dirty Pair, Ghost in the Shell,* and *Appleseed* all have female lead characters, says Johnston, "who are no stranger to firearms." Barb Wire is a female Mad Max figure while Tara Chase is a British espionage agent. Tank Girl, says Johnston, is "totally cool and living in a postapocalyptic world and determined to make the best of it"—toting guns. *Matador* tells the story of a Latina cop pursuing a contract killer, while the characters of *Grrrl Scouts* use firepower in their battles against drug dealers.

Women comic buyers enjoy images of women who are able and willing to fight effectively, "female characters [who] are not just 'screamers' or 'hostages,' Johnston says. "Female characters' appeal is strongest when they are fleshed out, having more depth than 'Superman's girlfriend' or 'Batman's date.' "

But Johnston thinks the majority of female characters winning by their wits, not their 9mms, is no accident.

"I think there is an effort, going back to the 1950s, where comic creators have tried, perhaps subconsciously, to get away from using guns, and in fact, tend to showcase their use as being 'bad' or 'evil.' Only the villains use them."

Popular Music

Guns have long appeared in American music of all kinds. In one nineteenth-century ballad, a young woman unhappily betrothed to a nobleman puts on men's clothing, adding a hunting rifle to her male disguise, to find the farmer she loves. In "The Death of Polly van Luther," a man shoots and kills his fiancée in a hunting accident. In "Poor Ellen Smith," a traditional song told by the man who killed Ellen Smith as he sits in prison, she was found "shot through the heart lying cold on the ground."

The classic folk song "Frankie & Johnny" tells the story of Frankie, who shoots her faithless lover three times with a .44. "Hey, Joe," sung by Jimi Hendrix, the Byrds, and the Surfaris in 1965, tells the tale of Joe, a betrayed lover who shoots his female sweetheart. In Lead Belly's "Bill Martin and Ella Speed," Martin, a bartender "long an' slender," shoots two-timing Ella in her side, breast, and head with a Colt .41: "All you young girls better take heed, Don' you do like po' Ella Speed."

Perhaps the best-known and most-recorded lyric starring a female shooter is "Pistol Packing Mama," written in 1943 by Al Dexter. Her cheating lover, whom she finds in a cabaret dancing with a blonde, pleads for his life after she shoots out the lights— and kills the blonde: "I'll be your reg'lar Daddy if you'll put that gun away."

San Diego teenager Brenda Spencer, who opened fire on an elementary school across the street from her home in 1979, inspired a hit that year from the punk-rock group Boomtown Rats. The chorus echoed her excuse: "I don't like Mondays."

Rock music critic Gillian Gaar says few contemporary songs celebrate women's use of guns. One is "Dark Lady" by Cher, in which a woman kills her lover and the woman he's cheating with. "Men see their use of guns as asserting their masculinity," she says. "Where women have guns, they're more often seeking revenge on a cheating lover, almost as if it's one of the few acceptable realms in which women can be violent. If it's a crime of passion, [the women] never seem to be sorry about doing it, either!"

"Miss Otis Regrets," written by Cole Porter, sung by Kirsty MacColl on the compilation Red Hot + Blue, "is more of a revenge thing, too. I can't think of any examples of women being empowered by guns," Gaar says.

Men reference guns more than women, she adds. "And even then, it's probably a lot more common in rap and country than in rock. "When men talk about guns, they talk about the *violence* of the gun," says Gaar. "They use it against women or men, and it's about the violence. Women [using guns] are playing a character. It's not necessarily reflecting their own experiences."

In "If I Had a Gun," by the Dead Milkmen, a father facing financial hardship considers killing his wife and children. In Aerosmith's "Janie's Got a Gun," a sexually abused stepdaughter kills her stepfather with a handgun, while Tori Amos in "Me and a Gun" describes how she was raped at gunpoint. In "Gun," rocker Mick Jagger begs his female lover to end his heartbreak by shooting him.

In Willie Nelson's "Seven Spanish Angels," a woman caught in a desperate shoot-out picks up her dead lover's gun, knowing it's empty, knowing "she couldn't win. But her final prayer was answered / When the rifles fired again."

A woman kills in "The Thunder Rolls," a song cowritten by contemporary country singer Garth Brooks. It describes her "pacin' by the telephone in her faded flannel nightgown askin' for a miracle," hoping her often absent husband is not cheating. After he arrives home at three-thirty in the morning, she hugs him in relief—but, sniffing his lover's perfume, finally takes her revenge by shooting him.

While rap and hip-hop music lyrics are rife with guns and ammunition, firefights and revenge, few lyrics offer women shooters; most are bitches or 'ho's, often the victims of violence. While some female singers despair at the brutality surrounding them, few espouse picking up a weapon and fighting back.

"These rappers, when they step into the [recording] booth, they rap about what they feel and see . . . the things that happened in their own homes," says Mia X, a New Orleans–based rapper who spoke at an *Essence* music festival panel in July 2003 on rap music. Fellow panelist Mona Scott of Violator Management, who represents some of the biggest names in rap, including 50 Cent, Busta Rhymes, and Missy Elliott, said she has generally "functioned in a vacuum" when considering the effects, on men or women, of the graphic, violent, and misogynist images her artists put forward.[23]

"The rap industry has made street violence and street culture integral to the music," argues Bakari Kitwana, author of *The Hip-Hop Generation: Young Blacks in African-American Culture*. "I don't think the industry has attempted to control it, because it helps to push the sales. The more 'ghetto' the better."[24]

A 2002 survey of two thousand African-Americans between sixteen and twenty found striking disparities between the music young men and women prefer: 54 percent of black sixteen- and seventeen-year-olds chose hip-hop/rap as their favorite musical genre, while the percentage drops to 40 percent of 19- and twenty-year-olds. Twice as many young black men prefer hip-hop/rap—65 percent—than young women, 32 percent of whom chose it as their favorite genre.[25]

Buffalo-based folksinger Ani DiFranco channeled her rage at the shooting deaths at Columbine High School in the title cut of her 1999 album, "To the Teeth":

> *School kids keep trying to teach us what guns are all about*
> *confused liberty with weaponry*

Art

A show featuring guns and ammunition backfired in 1999 for Mary Boone, one of America's best-known and most-respected art dealers. She was led from her eponymous Fifth Avenue gallery on September 29, 1999, in connection with a show by sculptor Tom Sachs that included a vase full of live 9mm cartridges for visitors to take home. Boone, forty-eight, was charged with unlawful distribution of ammunition and with resisting arrest. She faced up to a year in jail and $2,000 in fines if convicted; she received a year's probation.

In 1996, New Orleans artist Brian Borrello gave seventy-five sculptors, painters, and photographers a quarter ton of guns either seized or bought by the New Orleans police, to use as they saw fit. Madeline Faust's sculpture, molded from the soft lead of bullets, re-created the face of a man who had recently held her up at gunpoint, forcing his way into her car. She had managed to escape unharmed. "I thought maybe this would purge me," she said.[26]

The same year, the University of California at Riverside's Museum of Photography held *In Our Sights: Artists Look at Guns,* a show by twenty male and female artists, "as a catalyst for larger community dialogue."

Stephanie Cress, shot in her Oakland driveway beside her husband, who was killed, showed photos of her entry and exit wounds. Joan Barker offered portraits of women gun owners, while Bradley McCallum's *Shroud: Mothers' Voices* included the voices of mothers whose children were gunshot victims. Cynthia Stahl and Cynthia Rettig Pancher, both of whom grew up with guns in the home, explored that intimacy with firearms. Nancy Floyd's photos focused on women who armed themselves.

After the attacks on New York City of September 11, 2001, several Manhattan artists went to Santa Fe to recover. One was Margaret Evangeline, who works on aluminum plates, whose surfaces she grinds to create shimmering 3-D effects, then usually paints in abstract patterns. In the silence and fresh air and sunshine, she tried a new technique unavailable to her at home—firing at the plates with a variety of guns. "I hate to admit it, but I felt much better after I did it. It cleared something for me."[27]

Advertising

You'll find few contemporary images of women and guns in advertisements outside the gun industry and the gun press. I found two—both for Texas companies in Texas-area editions of national shelter magazines. One was for gravy, of a woman with a dead bobcat slung over her shoulder, Mrs. Smith from Glenrock, Wyoming; so few are historical photos of women with guns, I later recognized her in a History Channel video. (Formal portraits were preferred during that period.)

Green Pharmaceuticals, a company in Wilsonville, Oregon, ran an advertisement in the February 2003 issue of *Vogue* and other national consumer magazines for their only product, SnoreStop Extinguisher, a homeopathic antisnoring oral spray. "Wife Shoots Husband and Rests in Peace," read the headline, with a sleeping young white couple above it. Would the ad have reached its target audience, or even been accepted, if the genders or race were different? Only twelve consumers contacted the company to comment—three-quarters of whom liked it.

There *was* a time when many images of women-with-guns appeared, at least within early American firearms advertising. Annie Oakley was then still a nationally recognized and respected name, and women were emerging from Victorian corsets and petticoats into a wider world of athletic pursuit. A 1909 poster for the Winchester .22 automatic rifle shows a lone woman, her red hair piled into a loose bun, at an overgrown lakeshore, staring down into her canoe, her duffel, paddles, and rucksack on the ground beside her, gripping her rifle in her left hand. A perenially popular 1917 poster, distributed in all Spanish-speaking countries and in South and Central America, shows a woman in a middy blouse and fringed leather gauntlets, sitting astride a western saddle with a hazy Western landscape behind her, holding aloft a Winchester rifle. Both images convey a sense of solo adventure and excitement, while a poster featuring a fashionably dressed woman on the shotgun field suggested the pleasures of trapshooting.

"More American women joined the ranks as hunters and shooters . . . national advertising for armsmakers or ammunition companies regularly featured women wielding six-gun or shotgun, with the new growth in sporting arms fostered by the development in 1886 of smokeless powder. Gun catalog covers frequently incorporated distaff shooters armed with the latest lightweight repeaters. . . . Advertising aimed at new shooters took the form of calendars, envelopes, and posters, [and] ammunition containers and gunboxes were also embellished with advertising motifs aimed at the women taking up the shooting sports."[28]

Editorial Coverage

Realistic or positive images of women and guns, whether enjoying the shooting sports, competing athletically, or using a gun professionally, remain extremely rare in the mass media. For all the images of women *subjected* to cinematic (or real) gun-related violence, very few show a woman ready and able to fight back and reclaim (fire)power. Rarity amplifies its shock value. A girl-with-a-gun, like the sexy, skimpily clad seductresses of B movies and Agent 007's "Bond girls," has instead become a fashion-layout cliché, her slim hand with long red nails languorously caressing the cool, polished steel of a firearm and its phallic shape. The most likely place you'll see a woman with a gun is in a men's magazine like *Maxim* or *Playboy.*

Putting a gun near a woman whose appearance is elegant, aloof, upper-class, and polished sends a powerful, coded message, at least to male viewers. She's hot, dangerous, probably out of your league. Don't mess with this one. Because skill and comfort with guns remains, at least in mass-media images, so male a prerogative, a gal-with-a-gun has already crossed the line. What else is she willing to try?

Check out the slim, elegant white model in a fashion layout in the October 2002 issue of the upscale men's magazine *Esquire,* one whose story line mimics a film noir. Wearing a beaded Ralph Lauren gown, the model aims and shoots a .38 revolver. There's no blood, no explosion of tissue and bone, but rather the fantasy woman classy enough to be comfortable wearing a gown produced by the *haut*est of WASP designers—who can also fire off a few rounds if needed.

In 2002, I found only one positive contemporary reference to gun ownership in a mass-market national women's consumer magazine. The December 2002 issue of *Vogue* asked wealthy young socialites for their holiday gift suggestions. More predictable choices included T. Anthony luggage, Frye boots, and Paul Smith cuff links, all safely stylish status names. Sculptor Hope Atherton offered a $1,625 Hermès dog carrier, a vintage dress, a diamond ring—and a $5,830 leather Holland & Holland gun sleeve.

Occasionally, guns become fashion accessories. Designer Rudy Gernreich showed a military look in 1970 after the shootings at Kent State University, equipping his models with rifles in response. Ralph Lauren, whose fashion empire relies on iconic American images, recycled the Wild West—à la Annie Oakley—for a November 2002, nine-page, color *Vogue* retrospective of his work featuring supermodel Carmen Kass, her hair in a pompadour, clutching a handsomely chased rifle.

Only stylized faux violence makes the final cut.

Chapter 4
The Decision to Arm

———❖❖❖———

No matter where you live, read your local paper carefully for a few weeks. Look for men killing women.

"Man Held in Nurse's Death" *(Dallas News);* "Two Dead in Bronx Slay & Suicide" *(New York Post);* "Handling Sinners and Victims of Domestic Hell" *(New York Times);* "Here, Queer and Armed" *(New York Post);* "Man Shoots Fiancée" *(New York Post).*

And that's just a small two-month sample.

Psychologist David Barash, in an essay on evolution, males, and violence, writes, "Uncountable private episodes of violence receive little national attention, but are the stuff of many a personal tragedy. Admittedly, an occasional Lizzie Borden surfaces, but for every Bonnie, there are about a hundred Clydes. Male brutalizers and killers are so common, they barely make the local news, whereas their female counterparts achieve a kind of fame. A man who kills—even his own children—gets comparatively little notice. . . . When it comes to violence, the two sexes are not in the same league."[1]

"Men assault their former, estranged, or current wives,

fiancées, and girlfriends with near impunity. *Women are more likely to be killed by an intimate partner than by a total of all other categories of assailants"* (emphasis mine).[2]

Should guns be marketed to women?

Opponents argue that when gun advertisers target women, they manipulate them through an exaggerated fear of crime into purchasing handguns more likely to be used against them. The decision remains deeply personal. Anyone who is well-trained and psychologically prepared to aim and shoot *to kill* is arguably less endangered as a woman crime victim passively awaiting the arrival of police or a sympathetic neighbor or passerby. In the terrifying, paralyzing moments when a woman feels her life at risk, a lack of mental and physical preparation creates hesitation, and it is hesitating while armed most likely to endanger her.

Many women won't buy a gun, no matter what the pitch. A 1995 study of 396 men and women found that "women's attitudes toward guns and the ownership of them do not seem to be influenced by marketing campaigns directed at them, but instead seem to be complex reflections of societal and personal influences." In other words, women choose guns for more complicated reasons than simply seeing an advertisement or hearing a fear-mongering slogan.[3] None of the women I interviewed said that reading a gun advertisement had prompted her to consider buying one. Having been a crime victim, or a fear of becoming one, was far more compelling.

But a gun is not, as some women fantasize, an easy equalizer, a tough-looking retort to wave about under duress.

You must only point a loaded gun at someone or something you are fully prepared to destroy, and once you have pointed the barrel, you must be ready and able to squeeze the trigger as many times as necessary. If you truly feel yourself incapable of ever doing so, even to prevent your own death or severe injury, *do not buy a gun primarily for self-defense.* You are far more likely to be injured or killed with your own weapon *if you hesitate,* misfire, or fire a few rounds wildly in the hope of merely wounding.

"If you have a gun for defense, you must give serious consideration to the legal and moral responsibility of having that gun," writes Boston-based lawyer Karen L. MacNutt, legal affairs editor for *Women & Guns* magazine.

Gun owners are held to a higher standard of behavior than nonowners as the repercussions of a short fuse and a handy weapon can be, and often are, fatal. When actress Joan Rivers, then sixty-nine, flew off the handle at a Manhattan car rental office in December 2002, allegedly tossing a pen at an employee's eye, her tantrum filled tabloid gossip columns. But the potential consequences of her tirade were more serious—the loss of her two handguns, registered under her married name, Joan Rosenberg. If she had been arrested and charged with assault, her handgun license could have been suspended. If convicted of assault in the third degree, she would lose her license, although she could reapply in a year.[4]

Many non–gun owners fear that those who own a firearm, certainly a portable handgun, will automatically escalate any argument to its lethal conclusion. Yet those who own guns face an even greater legal responsibility *not* to draw their firearm for precisely this reason. Contrary to popular belief, owning a gun does not confer an unlimited or reflexive legal right to use it, even for show.

"Your use of the gun could not only result in your being charged with a crime, but you may·also find your would-be attacker suing you for everything you own. Even if you win, your legal fees may result in financial disaster," writes MacNutt. "Owning a gun for self-defense is always your last line of defense, not your first. *Caution is always your first line of defense* [italics mine]. Be alert to what is going on around you. Avoid compromising situations."[5]

The decision to buy a firearm for self-defense often pushes an already fearful woman into a new, unfamiliar, and intimidating world, one dominated by men. However overwhelming the new jargon of the gun world, she must decipher the subtleties of ballistics and ammunition, choice of caliber and holstering, of responsible firearm storage. She needs to learn the law and look deep into her own psyche, determining when she might actually aim and fire her gun at someone. If—as is common—she relies on a male friend or relative for advice, she is likely to stumble into a confusing, macho world of half-formed opinions, bluff, and bluster.

Because women who already own firearms tend to stay quiet about it, those considering the purchase of a gun for self-defense or recreation most often turn to the men they know—and to the males' presumed expertise. They turn to local gun dealers, those at gun shows, to books and to instructors, a few of whom teach women-only classes, such as writer and instructor Paxton Quigley.

There are two main groups of firearms: long guns and handguns. Long guns, designed to be fired from the shoulder, include rifles and shotguns. A familiar midpriced manufacturer is Remington; high-end sporting guns from J. Purdey & Son, Holland & Holland, and Perazzi can run to more than $100,000. They are sorted by gauge, the size of the cartridge; a 12-gauge is larger than a 20-gauge. The larger the gauge, the more recoil or kick the shooter experiences when the gun is fired.

Handguns are designed to be fired with a single hand and are usually defined as having an overall length of less than eighteen inches. A "pump" or slide-action shotgun, some argue, is a great choice for a woman alone at home because racking the action (i.e., readying to shoot)—which produces a distinctive *shuck-shuck* sound—may be enough to deter a would-be intruder who hears it through the door. But a shotgun is larger, longer, and in a hurry or in a small space, unwieldy. A handgun, easily concealed and carried in a purse or backpack or hidden in a drawer, is easily accessed and, if a pistol using magazines, easily (re)loaded in a hurry. But it's also less accurate; a shotgun sprays the target with "shot," loose pellets whose trajectory is much wider and more likely to hit something than a single bullet fired from a pistol or revolver.

Should you choose a pistol or a revolver? It depends upon which feels more comfortable. Many women prefer revolvers because they don't malfunction as often—but they usually hold a maximum of six bullets. A pistol, whose magazine can legally hold up to ten cartridges, is more prone to malfunction, but carries more ammunition and, in a worst-case scenario, is more easily and quickly loaded and reloaded by slapping in a new magazine. Handguns are made by firms such as Taurus, Glock, Smith & Wesson, Colt, Ruger, and Sig Sauer; some of them, such as the S&W Ladysmith, specifically manufactured for a female market, are designed to be lighter and smaller and therefore easier for female hands.

The caliber is, again, a matter of personal preference. Some women like smaller-caliber guns such as the .22, .25, or .38 because they are light, small, and more easily carried and concealed than larger-caliber guns such as a .45, 9mm, or .357. But smaller guns also produce much more recoil, which can be uncomfortable and can affect your aim if you shoot quickly and repeatedly. Whatever you buy for protection, you must practice with it regularly; shooting a larger and more comfortable gun only at the range is of little practical use if you switch, terrified and shaking, to something smaller yet unfamiliar at the last minute.

Whatever gun you think you want, try it out before you buy and practice with it consistently. Practice dry-firing it (without ammunition) and work on your stance. You must know how to load and unload, how to safely clear the barrel in case of a malfunction, how to clean it and maintain it. Like a car or computer, a gun is a sophisticated piece of machinery that requires upkeep, cleaning, and an understanding of how it works—and what to do when it doesn't. Your life may depend on your weapon, and its safety, reliability, and ease of use. A gunsmith can customize your gun in many ways—reduce the pressure needed to squeeze the trigger or install a smaller grip, for instance.

All gun buyers purchasing from a licensed dealer must first fill out a two-page form from the Bureau of Alcohol, Tobacco and Firearms, with thirty-four sections to complete. It asks, among other questions, if the buyer has been judged mentally incompetent or committed to a mental institution; if s/he has been convicted of a felony or is subject to a restraining order; and whether s/he has been convicted of a misdemeanor crime of domestic violence. This is used before an additional phoned-in background check, performed by the FBI.

Like men, women learning defensive shooting are taught to aim for the chest, for two reasons. Bullets shot into the heart and/or lungs are most likely to create massive, quick blood loss that will quickly weaken or kill your attacker. Large areas are also easier to hit. Aiming to cripple an assailant by shooting at their arms, hands, or kneecaps, for example, significantly ups your odds of missing small, rapidly moving body parts.

When should a woman buy a gun for self-defense? For some, never. For others, when they can't take one more minute of living in fear for their life. The decision is deeply personal.

Some battered women are encouraged by friends or family to arm themselves, although many are so traumatized that they crave comfort, silence, and kindness, not cold steel and ammunition. "They want teddy bears, not guns," says Larry Preston-Williams, a private detective in New Orleans who has trained abused women in firearms use.

Many abused women also fear the presence of a gun will further provoke their partner, that the gun will be taken away from them and used against them or their children, that it will escalate already unpredictable violence to a lethal level. Some, more practically, just can't get one. They don't have the money, live in a region with tight gun-control laws, or don't have access to the criminal networks that can supply one illegally.

"Your typical domestic-violence victim is isolated, cut off. You're cut off by being a victim. They're probably out of the loop. Who are you going to call?" asks Elisa Koenderman, a lawyer who has for eighteen years worked with the domestic-violence/sex-crimes unit of the Bronx district attorney's office, and who now supervises the work of forty-four assistant district attorneys. Stabbings are more likely, she says, as women "grab what's handy" to defend themselves.

"I just don't think they kill very often," says Koenderman, who has seen maybe a dozen cases of women who killed their abusive partner. "They continue to take the abuse or they finally leave."

Many women come to New Orleans shooting instructor Wade Schindler emotionally and physically scared, uncomfortable in the predominantly male gun culture. "Most women have never held guns before. Most of them aren't sure they can even fire the gun, and all of a sudden their fingers kick in, they coordinate it with their mind and they're fine. At least now they're confident enough to know what to do with it." Most of the seven hundred women he has trained, in the thirty years he has run his New Orleans–based Orleans Regional Security Institute, choose to buy a 9mm, "because they don't have the strength to keep firing the revolver."

While celebrities can afford to, and often do, hire bodyguards, those who own guns are reluctant to discuss it. Every year, producer John Laughlin organizes the Hollywood Celebrity Shoot, an event that draws national press attention and many male actors. Women, however, don't want to be publicly identified as gun owners.

Occasionally, a wealthy and well-connected woman gun owner appears in the media, usually by accident. In January 2003, Debi Dobbs, the forty-nine-year-old wife of CNN *Moneyline* host Lou Dobbs, was stopped at Newark airport with a fully loaded semiautomatic .25-caliber pistol in her handbag. Her husband said she needed it for security at their sprawling horse farm in rural Sussex, New Jersey. "It's very isolated up here," said a neighbor. "There are no streetlights, and the homes are very far apart."[6]

Cassandra Sefelt, a fifty-seven-year-old widow, lives alone in a bungalow in a wooded suburb north of New Orleans, on the north side of Lake Pontchartrain. Sefelt keeps a loaded .38 Smith & Wesson revolver, her husband's old gun, in a leather holster in her dresser. "I didn't believe in having guns in the house originally." But, involved in a real estate dispute in which, she says, she received telephone death threats, she decided that having a loaded handgun was a smart choice after all.

"If someone's in your house, you better shoot and you better shoot to kill. I could do it," she says. Yet, she admits, she knows she needs to practice and does not. "I should. I used to practice all the time." Cleaning and maintaining her gun is "on my to-do list," she says sheepishly.

Doris McClellan, seventy-four, armed herself for the first time on March 23, 1995—and saved her own life. McClellan lives on 9,600 acres of land, across the road from another 128,000 acres, one of the largest ranches in central Texas, where her husband, Bill, works as a cowboy. Their road is a bone-straight slash of asphalt, running fifty miles between the two nearest towns, Sterling City and Colorado City. The land is empty and silent, except for the rattle of a windmill and the gobbling of wild turkeys. McClellan loves the peace and quiet, savoring it as she walks out under the cottonwoods every morning. One morning, for a reason she still can't explain, she felt the unprecedented need to wear a .38 revolver on her walk. She'd never done so before, although she knew how to use it.

She headed out of their large bungalow into the early morning silence to pick mint growing along the creek bank about thirty feet from her screened veranda. She heard a weird, wild yowling and no sooner realized its source—a rabid bobcat running toward her—when it sprang for her throat. McClellan flung up her right arm in reflex and the thirty-pound animal latched on and hung from her forearm, screeching and slashing her legs with its razor-sharp claws. She had managed to get her revolver out and into her right hand. She had fired twice as it leaped toward her, then, with the cat's claws dug deep into her forearm, she transferred the gun to her left hand, firing another shot point-blank into the cat's belly. It let go and ran away.

"I could feel the blood squishing in my shoes," she recalls calmly. She walked back into the house—Bill was far away, working the cattle. Ever poised, the former schoolteacher put on fresh lipstick and dialed 911. The gun, without question, saved her life. She needed fifty stitches in her arm.

McClellan started shooting after she married her husband, a former marine. "My dad had a gun. My brother had one. Bill insisted I learn to protect myself from snakes, rabid raccoons. I thought my predator would be two-legged, a person I'd have to defend myself against. I was reluctant at first to learn, but I was proud of myself. You just have to learn independence when you're out in the country like this."

"I really do not wish to shoot anyone," says Kari Baldwin, a twenty-three-year-old from Verbena, Alabama. "I have had a self-defense class. But I really want to carry a handgun so that if I ever get stranded out in the middle of someplace, I will have something a little more powerful. I travel a lot, sometimes by myself. I go to places like Texas, which in some places has nothing. If I ever got stranded out in the woods and needed a gun, I would have one."

Toy Long, a forty-nine-year-old who lives near Lovington, New Mexico, a town of 9,471, has spent her adult life on ranches so remote that a call to police or 911 might more practically be a call for a hearse, she jokes. It's not that police don't care to help—there just aren't enough of them to cover the enormous distances fast enough. "We lived in remote places because that's where the cattle were. I moved many times to many ranches because I was married to cowboys who moved like tumbleweeds."

To reach her nearest town, Long often travels alone over rough roads, often leaving predawn and returning late at night. Sometimes the roads flood and she has to sleep the night alone in her truck. In most places, a cell phone doesn't work.

"I can't rely on a cell phone for safety. I have to take care of myself. When people in town go out for the day, they take their credit cards. When I go out, I take supplies: water, peanut-butter crackers, and a gun."

One ranch she lived on was thirty miles from the nearest town, another was eighty miles away; her children spent three hours a day on the school bus.

Long bought her first gun when she was twenty-six and moved to Counselors, New Mexico, with her first husband and two infants. She bought a Smith & Wesson .38 special and now owns two of them. She would drive her son to the county line to meet his school bus, waiting alone with her two-year-old daughter. Residents of two local Indian reservations, often intoxicated, had a habit of lying in the road, forcing drivers to stop, then demanding the car's battery or some other part they wanted.

"There were many times I needed my gun to show them they

weren't going to take a piece of my vehicle. They wouldn't move away from my car. I couldn't show fear. I've never had to use my gun, but I've had to show it, to make a show of force. Once I did that, they got out of the way."

While Long has shot rattlesnakes threatening her children on the ranch, she faced her worst and most persistent threat when she lived for a while in the town of Lovington, where a man stalked her. Two judges backed her wish for a restraining order, but the district attorney denied her request. She quickly moved far out into the countryside again, where she has always felt safest. "Now I live so far out, if you're following me, I know it, and you better have a darned good reason. The only sounds I hear out here are calves bawling, horses whinnying, the wind whistling across the prairie. My sister lives in Houston—in a house with burglar bars."

Ana Rodriguez, a twenty-six-year-old health-care lobbyist in Tallahassee, Florida, has owned a gun since 2002. "My father bought me a gun for Christmas 2002 as a gift. I never owned my own prior to that. Since I spend so much time traveling on Florida's highways, I thought it would be wise to protect myself in case my car breaks down on the side of the road and someone tries to assault me." Rodriguez credits her father with introducing her to gun ownership, "one hundred percent."

She has never drawn her .38 special, titanium, five-round revolver and hopes she never will, although she nows feels "empowered, safe, and in control." In 1994, Rodriguez was followed home one night around midnight and held up at gunpoint in front of her home. "Fortunately, I was not hurt, but the trauma has never left me. I was scared to even go outside for a few weeks." Today, she says, "I'm simply more aware of my surroundings."

For Claudette Gadsden, a forty-two-year-old residential consultant for Verizon who lives in Baltimore (America's most dangerous city in 2002), buying a handgun is as much a gesture of self-determination as protection. Gadsden is black, and a proud member of a particularly low-profile group—women of color who own guns. "People don't want us owning guns," she says. "Laws were enacted to make sure people of color couldn't gain access to guns." She grew up in a household with guns her father used for hunting. In June 1999, she was visiting relatives in New Jersey when an uncle took her to "minority day" at a local gun range. "We worked on aim, stance, breathing. I thought, 'This is cool!' "

She hadn't shot in many years, but quickly rediscovered how much she enjoyed it. She now practices several times a month, less than she should, she admits. But her guns are not for pleasure: "My thing is being able to protect myself." Gadsden lives with her brother, who also shoots, and has a security system in her home. She says her Baltimore neighborhood is safe enough, but she still wants her handguns; she won't say how many, what brand, or which caliber. "I don't want to take anyone out," she hastens to add. "But I don't want to be taken out."

Her sister shoots and so does her college-age daughter. For these women—as for many others—their shooting competence confers a heady feeling of power. And letting men around them know they possess these skills sends a clear, larger message: "Don't f--k with me!"

Women keep their gun ownership private, and women of color feel even greater pressure to do so, says Gadsden. Like many white women, even those black women who have shot for years may hide their interest; only after Gadsden began shooting did a friend of twenty years reveal that she, too, is a gun owner.

Gadsden herself now holds "minority days" for the fourteen-member gun club she started in Baltimore. "I want to teach women to be safe and responsible, not just from an intruder but from the gun itself. This is something we need to share! I know some women like to keep this knowledge a secret, but it's something we need to know." To attract potential new members of color, Gadsden hands each of her members two hundred to five hundred flyers, instructing each of them to get rid of them all. They do, posting them at church, at work, in local businesses.

Sheara Cox, Gadsden's fifty-year-old sister, acquired a gun when she lived from 1993 to 1998, alone with her two young children, in a tiny town near Wilmington, North Carolina, at the end of a dirt road surrounded by woods. Her husband, then in the military, was often gone for six months at a time—and the town was so small everyone knew when he was absent. "He thought I should have something to protect me and my children. It was just kind of scary. I didn't like the idea of getting a gun. I *really* didn't like it, certainly with children in the house." Acquiring a gun in North Carolina, a concealed-carry state, was quick and easy—and a popular choice, Cox learned. "Everybody did it! *Everybody.* They had just put in 911.

"I really didn't want to learn it, but thought I'd better be able to do whatever I needed to protect my kids." Reluctantly, she learned how to use a .38 pistol. "I wanted something that was light."

But twice now, grabbing the gun has pushed her or her husband to the brink of disaster. One night at 1 A.M. a neighbor started banging on her door. She couldn't see out her peephole, couldn't hear his entreaties for help with his ill child. All she knew was it was very late, she was alone, and she had to do *something*. Holding the gun in her shaking hand, Cox pointed it at the door until she realized it was someone she knew, not a would-be assailant. "I was more scared of using it than whatever might have happened," she admits.

Cox now also lives in Baltimore, and is usually alone at night while her husband works the 11 P.M. to 7 A.M. shift. Again, he insisted on buying a handgun. "I really didn't want him to get another one." Whose protection does it guarantee? Cox asks, laughing bitterly. "All of us, I guess."

Yet, once more, the presence of the gun in their home at a moment of anxiety pushed them to the edge of using it, a high precipice too easy to fall from. One night her husband learned that a neighborhood tough was beating up one of their sons. Reflexively, he grabbed his gun and ran to find the perpetrator. By the time he arrived, the fight was over and his son was unharmed. But the Coxes were deeply shaken.

"I couldn't believe he did it," Sheara says quietly, dismayed by how quickly their fear escalated into the potential for murder. "*He* couldn't believe he did it." Cox said they were both seriously reconsidering their decision to keep a gun in their home. "We could have gone to jail. People react before they think."

For Cloe Cabrera-Gutierrez, a thirty-eight-year-old newspaper reporter at the *Tampa Tribune,* who is both black and Hispanic, racism she encountered after winning a major beauty pageant pushed her into gun ownership.

"Back in 1987, I won the Miss Florida–USA pageant. I was the first black and/or Hispanic woman to win the pageant in its forty-year history. Needless to say, a lot of people did not share in my excitement. One of my first appearances as Miss Florida was at a Kmart in Panama City, Florida."

"An older man, in his late sixties or seventies, approached me for an autograph, and while we were speaking, he informed me of his disgust that a black woman was representing his state. He told me that he hoped I would come to the backwoods and allow him and his friends to show me the kind of welcome niggers like me really deserved, and to watch my back. I was infuriated and I told him so. We exchanged some heated words. My father thought it was in my best interest to own a gun.

"It was more for his peace of mind than mine. He bought me a small-caliber handgun. I went to a few shooting ranges and learned how to use it. I became comfortable with it. I rarely carried it on me, usually it was in my car glove compartment or under the seat. But just knowing it was there gave me some sense of security.

"Shortly after my reign ended, I put the gun in a closet and it has remained there ever since. I do occasionally take it out, clean it, and put it back in its case. I hope I never have the opportunity to use it. That is the only gun I have ever owned," she hastens to add. "My husband and I are not gun lovers. We have a great deal of respect for guns because we are very aware of the power they have. In the wrong hands they can be deadly."

Named by *Newsweek* as one of the "Top 50 People Who Matter Most on the Internet," Aliza Sherman is an on-line marketing expert, published author, international speaker, and regular contributor to national magazines and websites.

She's also a handgun owner, and former crime victim. Sherman, now forty, single, and living alone in Cheyenne, Wyoming, with her three Chihuahuas, decided to learn to shoot in 1994. She was living in New York City, where few women own handguns. For her own protection, at her father's urging, she had always carried Mace and/or pepper spray. "Before I decided to learn to shoot a gun, I knew nothing at all about guns. I had never even seen one in person, up close, much less touched one."

She began taking shooting classes in Manhattan.

"Eleven days later, I was held up at gunpoint and kidnapped with a friend of mine—three guys, three guns. I had lived in New York City for seven years at that time and nothing bad had ever happened to me."

It was an August night, at 1 A.M. after a late-night dinner. "My ex-boyfriend and I were in front of his apartment building, on Ninety-fifth between Amsterdam and Columbus [not a high-crime neighborhood, on the Upper West Side], and three guys came down the steps toward us with guns in their hands and told us to give them our money. Throughout the fifteen-to-twenty-minute ordeal we were not physically hurt. One guy had a nine-millimeter in his hand, one had a small pistol, one had a nine-millimeter tucked in the back of his pants that he showed."

They forced Sherman and her boyfriend to walk to the nearest bank and remove cash from the ATM. She stayed calm and maneuvered their escape into the street without injury. "The self-defense classes I took probably saved my life. In them, we learned to breathe, to not look directly at our assailant but to look at them surreptitiously to note identifying clothing and features, and most of all, to negotiate for our lives.

"We learned later that the nineteen-year-old was out of jail for only three months before our holdup. He was in for assault, talked down from attempted murder. He had held up another couple, and when the woman got hysterical, he beat her with a baseball bat, knocked out eight teeth, and nearly killed her. We escaped but found out later they had shot a guy a few blocks away a little while before they held us up.

"After the incident, we videotaped each other talking about the whole thing. It was intensely traumatic for me, and until they were put in jail, I suffered from extreme post-traumatic stress disorder. The minute they were in jail, all my symptoms disappeared."

Traumatized, Sherman nonetheless continued her shooting lessons. "Deciding to continue was also a way to face my fears. I decided I could not give these idiots power over me and my decisions. Getting back to the range with a gun in my hand became therapy."

Initially, she refused to move out of the city. "Leaving Manhattan was not an option. I couldn't give them power over my choices, my life. I had a tiny apartment, so a big guard dog wasn't an option, but also I didn't feel unsafe in my neighborhood or my apartment."

Three months after the incident, Sherman got her target license and a $700 Sig Sauer 228, 9mm pistol. "I went to the gun shop and held guns in my hand, going for the sleekness, all-black, and the feel of it. I wanted it to feel good in my hand.

"When I went to the shooting range with my gun, all the men wanted to touch it. Turns out it is most guys' dream gun—something they cannot afford, unless they are in law enforcement, so they all wanted to hold it and clean it for me.

"Revolvers to me seemed so old-fashioned and clunky. In a way, there was a mystique about guns in my mind, sort of like in other people's minds the way that smoking cigarettes was cool. In my mind, carrying an all-black nine-millimeter gun was cool in some totally forbidden way. This has to be because of the movies I enjoyed watching—there were no other influences in my life to give me this impression."

Yet when Sherman told her New York girlfriends—college-educated professionals—that she shot guns, some were uncomfortable. "Many were antigun in general, for no other reason than it was all they knew." Many women in her self-defense class were also deeply ambivalent about defending themselves competently. "I do believe women are brought up to be nurturing and trusting, which is wonderful until faced with any form of evil. They will definitely protect others before themselves—not because they are so totally selfless but because there is a strange disconnect in many women between their own self-worth and safety.

"So many women had emotional breakdowns during class, and breakthroughs, because they had never felt worthy of self-protection until the class. Many could not shout or scream for help; many could not bring themselves to hit an assailant; many had not been faced with a man calling them names and they really freaked out when the padded assailants did this."

In 2000, Sherman left New York for good. In Wyoming, "guns are no big deal. I live in a renovated barn on eighty acres and my landlord has built a small shooting range on the land so I can shoot whenever I want." She's now taking tae kwon do, "mostly for the exercise and discipline. Bottom line, if I'm attacked, chances are I will not be able to overpower my assailant.

"If someone tried to break in right now, into my barn, which is pretty secluded out in the open plains with only a handful of houses in view in the distance—closest a little over a mile away— then I know I can reach for my gun and shoot them the moment they step across the threshold. Without hesitation."

Sherman is proud of her choice. "Knowing I overcame my superstitions and fears about guns, and that I gained a skill and have a hobby, target shooting, that I'm good at, is all part of being true to myself, finding ways to gain wisdom and strength, and not letting fear dictate my life."

For Erin Rose, formerly a male army officer, now a forty-five-year-old female transsexual law student in Tucson, getting a handgun carry permit is a priority, "so that I do not accidentally end up with a weapon too close to me in a traffic stop that is not legally covered; so that I can carry in other states without as much difficulty. If I need to work security to supplement my income, armed guards make more money, and a carry permit is a little more of a certification than showing up with a holstered .44 on your hip.

"Safety *is* also a part of the equation, a growing part that I had not considered originally, but one that is more of a concern now that I am living as a woman," she says. "This is a twofold issue, because there are times when I am not 'read'—recognized as a transsexual—and am hit on by questionable men. Then there are times when I *am* read and am either pursued by men who think I am an easy score—one almost got out of his car and came after me—or am insulted and threatened for being who I am. This is relatively rare, but is a high-stress situation because usually the people involved are young males—race and ethnicity are immaterial—with more than one in the car out to demonstrate to the world that they are macho men."

Vulnerability to attack is a new and unwelcome sensation. "This is becoming more of a key consideration. I have noticed an increasing feeling of vulnerability since I began living part of the time as a woman, and now full-time. A big part of this is a number of my friends have been attacked by men with sexual intentions. Also important is that I have never been very strong in the upper body, and the adjustment of my hormonal makeup has decreased that even more.

"The weak are always seen as targets. Women are *seen* as weak by men and easier prey. Therefore they are more prevalent targets. Rapists, too, usually look for someone they are sure they can brutalize with little or no chance of retribution. Tall women draw attention. Tall transsexuals may draw attention, then, if read, become the focus of attack because the man or men involved have to 'save face or regain their manhood' after being taken in by a queer, faggot, or trannie."

Rose is six feet four inches and weighs 240—"on my way towards 200 or—hopefully—180 or 185. But the size is deceptive," she explains. "As TS women continue taking estrogen, their muscle mass decreases and the slow-twitch fibers turn to fast-twitch fibers, good for endurance, but lousy for strength. Endurance is decreased somewhat by changes in blood oxygen levels, and other factors. And as I continue to lose weight, I will be seen as even more vulnerable."

A 1999 *Los Angeles Times* survey found that one of three California adults owns firearms; 75 percent of them are white, 40 percent are female. One of three polled said they'd bought a gun for self-protection; gun sales spiked in the wake of the 1992 Los Angeles riots, the Y2K hysteria in late 1999, and after the September 11 terrorist attacks. A cover story in the *Los Angeles Times Magazine* with the "armed and anonymous" included:

- Deborah Fuller, a white school-bus and truck driver in Madera, who reluctantly bought a gun, a .357-caliber pistol, in 1998 to help protect their home while her husband, Butch, a trucker, is away on the road.

- Cori Harris, a white, twenty-five-year-old single parent in San Diego, bought a 9mm Glock handgun in 2001. "It's just everybody is so violent. You're always hearing about campers or hikers getting raped and beaten. And you have all the school shootings and you start thinking, 'I need to learn about [self-protection]. I have a daughter and we live alone together. With all the drugs and crime, it's scary. I just feel better [having] something to defend myself [with] if someone comes into the house."

- For thirty-two-year-old Mexican immigrant Aracelia Parra, who runs a gift shop in Compton [a particularly dangerous area], a daytime break-in while she was at home destroyed her sense of personal security. When she bought her first house, in Long Beach, she also bought a .22-caliber pistol. Parra has three children and cares for her brother's three children as well. "I know they probably could take it away from me," she says of her weapon. "But it might scare them away."[7]

Some women who travel alone—over great distances, at night, and through unfamiliar neighborhoods—carry a gun. In the 1930s, a young black woman, Zora Neale Hurston, later best-known as the author of the novel *Their Eyes Were Watching God*, traveled throughout rural Florida doing field research while studying anthropology at Barnard College. "Evidently she cut an unusual figure—a single black woman, driving her own car, toting a gun, sometimes passing for a bootlegger."[8]

For Shelley Kane, a white, well-dressed professor in her sixties who often drives the twelve-hour, six-hundred-mile trip from her home in Dallas to her weekend home in Santa Fe, New Mexico, a gun is as crucial as a cell phone. "I travel late at night. I'm alone. I drive a nice late-model car. I'm a target."[9]

Maurer Culpeper, a white New Orleans housewife, is an avid hunter, but also has guns in her home for self-defense, so many she couldn't enumerate them. "I try to watch what I do and where I go." She stopped carrying a gun when she had children and instead got a large dog. Now that her children are grown, she keeps unloaded guns handy. "If you need to, you can easily put in a clip quickly."

For Peggy Landry, seventy-two, the first woman in Louisiana to win a concealed-carry permit, a gun is and always has been a necessity. She started carrying, illegally, in her fifties when she lived in New Orleans. "There were killings all the time. My worst fear, always, is being raped." Now she lives alone, a widow in Natalbany, about forty-six miles west of Baton Rouge. But Landry isn't your typical small-town widow; as thanks for helping him pass concealed-carry legislation by publicizing the night her gun saved her friends, Governor Mike Foster appointed her vice chairman of the Louisiana State Board of Parole, a paid position she has held since 1996.

"I'm very independent. I want to live alone. But a lot of families don't like the decisions I make and they may come looking for me. I carry my gun from room to room. My house has a lot of windows.

"I'm not afraid. I've been trained and I go every month to the range to practice. A man tried to break into my house the other day," Landry recalled calmly. "It was about three P.M. If he'd broken in, I would have shot him. I hope and pray I never have to use my gun, but if my life or the life of anyone with me depends on it, I'm going to use it."

"I've simply never been a 'gun person' and I suppose that's something as innate as my being vegetarian for thirty-four years. It is something having to do with the soul you've been dealt; something you never second-guess." Yet Cathy Mong, a fifty-two-year-old reporter in Dayton, Ohio, is someone who might have bought a handgun after being raped in her home in Richmond, Indiana, in 1980.

She had returned from a reporting workshop where she'd turned her ankle, leaving her on crutches. She caught up on a week's worth of unread papers and fell asleep, clothed, in bed. At 1:10 A.M. she was awakened by the sound of a man on the stairs; his face was grotesquely flattened by a panty-hose mask. He forced her downstairs from her bedroom to the kitchen, where she saw that he had kicked in her locked door so hard the frame was destroyed. "Anyone who would break into someone's home to hurt you would be dangerous. I just wanted to survive."

After she reported the incident, Mong discovered that three other women on her street had also recently been raped. Why had the police not mentioned this in their daily crime reports? she asked. They didn't want to scare anyone. She moved into a duplex apartment, with "a big teddy bear of a guy at work. I didn't want to be alone."

Of course, the majority of American women, even those who live and work in dangerous neighborhoods, *don't* arm themselves. Some choose one or several alternatives: a dog, carrying pepper spray or Mace, learning self-defense methods, installing an alarm system in their home. Some live with friends or relatives, while others get to know their community and avoid trouble spots. Shannon Frattaroli is a researcher at the nine-year-old Johns Hopkins Center for Gun Policy Research, located in East Baltimore, a neighborhood where the sounds of gunshots are common.

Frattaroli, who is white, says the black women she knows facing gun violence are not rushing to arm themselves.

"They're *not* afraid. They see the downsides of a culture saturated with guns, and they're suffering terribly for it." Frattaroli points out that women who have the least to fear—suburban whites in safe neighborhoods—often choose to arm themselves. "While we're immersed in this culture of fear, the women we'd suspect who would feel the most vulnerable are the toughest and the least fearful. The women you'd think would be the most interested in this form of protection are the *least* interested."

Kit Senter, seventy-nine, is a lean, petite white woman who has lived since 1978 in a huge, three-story home in New Orleans, a city famous for a high crime rate, and the resulting middle-class white flight to the suburbs. She knew when she bought the house how dangerous the city could be and usually has tenants living with her. An ardent activist on behalf of many causes, Senter feels passionately that keeping a gun in her home is simply not an option. "I'm completely opposed to guns, to the NRA and the gun lobby."

Her principles were tested one January night in 1983. Fast asleep in her second-floor bedroom, she was awakened by the cold steel of a knife blade pressed against her throat, a man sitting astride her. Her daughter was away, as were her tenants, male college students. The man had broken into the basement apartment then crept up the wide staircase to her bedroom.

"Give me your gun!" he demanded.

"I don't have one," she told him truthfully.

The burglar was incredulous. "Why not?"

"I don't believe in them."

The man stole her jewelry and threatened to rape her, but Senter talked him out of it and, even after being bound, escaped—by leaping out her window onto the first-floor roof of her sunroom, then onto the sidewalk. She broke her back, but suffered no permanent injury.

Today, Senter says proudly, she relies "not only on a burglar alarm, but on better locks, other weapons, and on my own wits."

Chloe Polemis, a twenty-three-year-old senior at New York University, owns a Beretta shotgun she uses exclusively for clay- and trapshooting. She sees buying a handgun for self-defense as unacceptable. "Maybe that makes me a hypocrite, but I am perfectly willing to be one. I don't think anyone needs to own a handgun. I think that where I grew up, Manhattan, had a huge impact on me. In New York City, people tend to have very negative images of people who shoot or hunt, and of the gun culture in general."

A woman's decision to arm may bear little relationship to her true, statistical vulnerability. The violent crime rate in the United States *has decreased by almost 50 percent* since 1993. Violent crime fell by 9 percent in 2001, according to the National Crime Victimization Survey; experts said the drop was a result primarily of the strong economy of the 1990s and tougher sentencing laws.

From 2000 to 2001, assault was down by 10 percent—although injuries increased by 13 percent. The share of violent crimes involving guns held steady at about 26 percent. Rape fell 8 percent and sexual assaults (which include verbal threats and groping) fell 20 percent.[10]

The Decision to Shoot

A woman buying a gun for self-defense needs to know local laws and a local criminal-defense lawyer, preferably one with expertise in this area, and to keep her cell-phone number handy. Should she ever fire in self-defense, she will face the judgments and persistent questions of police. She may face tough interrogation by prosecutors and a judge. The jury may include twelve men and women who know nothing about guns or ballistics, have never seen or touched a gun in real life. The gun will be taken away as evidence, possibly for years.

Waving a gun, let alone using it, subjects a woman to high standards of legal behavior, warns *Women & Guns* legal affairs editor and Boston lawyer Karen L. MacNutt. "If you use, or even threaten to use, deadly force to defend yourself, your actions may end up being judged by a jury sitting in a quiet court room far removed from the place you felt endangered."[11] If you use the gun at the wrong time, "you are going to be in big trouble *even if you do not fire the gun*" (italics mine).[12]

Several factors are crucial in fashioning a sustainable legal defense after a shooting. Danger must have been "imminent"—a word so subjective lawyers admit they often turn midtrial to the dictionary for help. Bronx ADA Elisa Koenderman has done this herself, finding the definition as "immediately or soon," terms frustratingly vague. Is "soon" within the next five minutes or the next month?

"What a struggle it is between the prosecutor, the judge, and the jury," agrees Manhattan criminal defense attorney Michael Dowd, who since 1979 has defended twenty-four women who have killed their abusive partner. Dowd, who has faced Elisa Koenderman in court, has also consulted Webster's himself to make sense of the word, equally stymied by the same unclear definition.

(The one point lawyers agree on? Made-for-TV scenarios—such as the 2002 Jennifer Lopez film *Enough* and the 1984 film *The Burning Bed* with Farrah Fawcett, in which vengeful abused wives kill their husbands—are pure fantasy. You can't legally shoot an abusive partner while s/he is asleep, after s/he has walked out of the room, or after s/he has disengaged from an argument.)

You *can* use deadly force to protect yourself if you have a reasonable belief that your life, or the life of another, is in serious danger. In some states, you are required to retreat from your attacker, if you can do so in safety, before the law considers your life to be in danger. If you cannot retreat safely, you do not have to. Even in those states that require you to, there is usually an exception if you are within your own home or place of business.

Some states have adopted "home castle" laws, which reaffirm old English law that your home—however humble—is your "castle"; if someone invades it, you can use whatever force is needed to evict them. But *these states are in the minority,* and in most jurisdictions, your use of force has to be reasonable.

The woman who shoots an aggressor must argue she was using "proportionate force"—not difficult if she is 100 pounds and five-three and he is six-four and weighs 250. But what if your attacker is another woman or a slightly built man? What if they weren't threatening you with a gun, but with a knife, baseball bat, or other weapon—or no weapon at all?

A woman who uses her gun in self-defense, even if she didn't fire it or kill with it, may still face the full weight of the judicial system—arrest, arraignment, a grand jury, indictment, and possibly a jury trial.

Pro-gun women's groups such as the Liberty Belles, Armed Females of America, KeepAndBearArms, and Second Amendment Sisters exhort women to consider using a gun in self-defense. But if a woman does, she's alone, far from her erstwhile cheerleaders, facing the suspicions and scrutiny of family, friends, colleagues, neighbors, and the media, whose insatiable appetite for titillation is often only matched by their ignorance of the law and of firearms. A woman accused of shooting frequently enters a courtroom at a disadvantage; if she can't afford a seasoned criminal defense lawyer, she may find herself at the mercy of an uninterested, incompetent, and likely poorly compensated court-appointed attorney. Manhattan criminal defense attorney Michael Dowd usually works pro bono; few women can afford his normal fee—between $100,000 to $450,000 depending on the complexity of the case.

In one study, of forty-two women convicted in California for killing their abusive partner, 55 percent used a public defender and only 33.3 percent a private attorney. An additional 12 percent began with a public defender but later switched to private counsel.

As many as forty-five hundred women are currently in prison for the death of their violent male partner.[13] Criminologist Elizabeth Dermody Leonard recently conducted the largest-ever study of women who have been convicted for killing their abuser—forty-two women in the California prison system. California has the highest number of incarcerated women and is home to the world's largest women's prisons, two of which, the Central California Women's Facility and the Valley State Prison for Women, alone house nearly seven thousand women.

Comparing battered women who kill with 294 women in the general female prison population, Leonard found that:

- Killers are older, with a median age of forty-seven, fourteen years older than the average for other prisoners.

- Most—67 percent—are white; while African-Americans represent close to half of all female inmates, they are only 17 percent of this group. Latinas, 14 percent of California prisoners, make up only 7 percent of battered women who kill.

- They're well-educated. Sixty-four percent have had some college education versus only 13.5 percent of other prisoners.

- Seventy-three percent of women who killed had been married versus 55 percent of other prisoners.

- Most of the women who killed had supported themselves through paid employment (52 percent) with only 4.8 percent on public assistance and another 4.8 percent selling drugs. Corresponding numbers for the general prison population were 21.8 percent on public assistance and 15.6 percent selling drugs.

- Their sentences were severe. Twenty-six percent received fifteen years to life; 34 percent, twenty to thirty years to life; and 15 percent, life without parole.

- Fewer than 20 percent *(half the rate* of the general prison population), had been previously arrested—and the most common reason was for motor vehicle violations.

Leonard offers much evidence of America's judicial ambivalence toward abusers. Thirty-three states currently uphold exemptions that protect husbands from rape prosecution, for example.[14] "American law has been slow to label as criminal the actions of men who assault their wives. As a result, abusive men tend to face little punishment for their violence against women, and female victims receive little protection from them."[15]

Leonard cites four studies showing the futility of relying on law enforcement: "One study of domestic homicides found that in 85 percent of the cases, the police had been summoned at least one time before the final incident, and in half the cases, police were called five or more times before the woman killed. Exacerbating the problem, Department of Justice data reveal that the police are likely to respond more quickly if the attacker is a stranger than if he is known to the victim."[16]

Most intimate-partner victimizations are not reported to police at all, according to the Department of Justice. Women (1) consider it a private or personal matter; (2) fear reprisal; (3) view the crime as minor or are not sure it was a crime; (4) believe police will not bother, are biased, or are ineffective; and (5) want to protect the offender.[17]

For any woman who chooses to arm herself, lawyer Karen MacNutt's slim, simple volume, *Ladies Legal Companion,* makes sobering reading.

"If someday you have to use a gun or some other object to defend yourself, you will suddenly find yourself under a magnifying glass. You may also find yourself charged with 'assault with a deadly weapon' or murder, no matter how justified you believed your actions were. If you go to court, you can expect the prosecution will do everything in its power to make you look bad. Look at yourself, your home, and your car as others might." MacNutt cautions female gun owners to eschew T-shirts or bumper stickers with pro-gun slogans. "Things like that are hard to explain to twelve fellow citizens when the only thing they know about you is that you have been charged with murder."[18]

Cross-examination may prove far more frustrating than cathartic.

"When I tried saying my husband mentally abused me and I was afraid of him, all that was thrown out [of court] because *he* wasn't on trial and he wasn't there to defend the allegations I was making—*I* was on trial for murder, not his abuse," one woman told criminologist Leonard. Said another, "We couldn't [talk] about the threats. Every time we tried to get anything in, it was dismissed because [my husband] was the victim. And he was dead. . . . Nobody testified about the abuse."[19]

The concept of "initial aggressor" is also key to a woman's defense strategy, says Michael Dowd.

- Who started the attack?
- Was he or she provoked?
- Did anyone try to walk away and defuse the situation?
- Does the woman, or the man, bear defensive wounds?

Police working in jurisdictions where they can choose not to arrest a domestic abuser often feel stymied by what the law demands and what women need most, Dowd says. "They fear being [physically] attacked at a minimum, and sued at a maximum. Generally, they'll arrest the person who strikes the first blow, but with important exceptions: Who's injured? To what degree? Educating police officers and prosecutors to appreciate these distinctions presents an ongoing challenge."

Says Dowd, "You have to understand the context." Until women are truly viewed as equals, police, courts, and others may not offer battered women all the help they expect, and need, he argues.

"Our society comes to the place where there is a domestic dispute with a predisposition that the woman is not equal to the man. I rest my case on the issue of equal pay—women still earn seventy-three cents on the dollar to what men earn." Until police and prosecutors, most often male, truly perceive women as equal, in work, in the home, and under the law, domestic abuse victims face tough structural obstacles, Dowd says. "We have to understand the imbalance that still exists between men and women. There's a residue of prejudice and ignorance that will linger. You can pass all the laws you want, but these things die slow. You have to change people's minds."

Like many others who track domestic violence and deal with its bloody outcomes, Dowd says it must be stopped before it can start and escalate. "The way to attack the problem is to deal with it in a way to prevent it. By the time you're dealing with a homicide, it's too late."

Chapter 5
The Dark Side

SHE HAD NEVER TOUCHED A GUN AND NEVER WANTED TO. WHEN Anita Rodger killed her husband with three shots, she used her father's gun in a last-minute, split-second, lifesaving decision.

Living in a small town in Indiana, in 1986 she finally left her abusive common-law husband of nine years. In one of many assaults, he had shattered her eardrum, yet she was loath to leave him, wooed back repeatedly by his apologies, "the Romeo part that comes after the beatings. But it got worse. I couldn't take it anymore."

She had never seriously considered arming herself. "I was sure I could never shoot him, that I'd chicken out. I was scared he would take it away and shoot me."

Leaving him precipitated even more violence and threats, an escalating cycle of stalking and intimidation that kept her moving locally every few months. "The time I spent with him was frightening, but the time I spent apart from him was even more frightening. I was being hunted. I didn't know at the time it was more dangerous to leave, but I learned fast."

He shot at her car, stole her animals, and as she worked cleaning houses, would suddenly appear at the window pointing a gun at her. "When the police arrived, he'd be gone." In desperation she started to hide her vehicle in friends' garages—still, he always found her. After five months, one October night at 9 P.M., Rodger and her father went out to the man's farmhouse to confront him. As the two men argued, fighting for control of a baseball bat, Rodger stepped back in fear. She stepped on something hard and metallic; her father's .38 revolver had slipped out of his pocket.

As her ex-husband lunged toward her in rage, she picked it up, about to toss it into the bushes. Convinced he would kill her, she fired three times.

"One in the head, one in the heart, and I don't know where the third one went. I didn't have time to aim. I didn't even have time to think. I just know that if I hadn't shot, I wouldn't be speaking with you today." He was six feet tall and 185 pounds; she was five feet seven inches and 135 pounds. She had never shot a gun before, never been charged with any crime.

She threw the gun in a nearby river and turned herself in to police an hour later. "I knew I'd better get it over with." Like many lower-income women, Rodger couldn't afford a lawyer and had no idea how to choose one, so a public defender was appointed. She initially faced a sentence of fifteen to twenty-five years: "I couldn't even comprehend it." A jury voted eleven to one in her favor, forcing another trial, but she was able to plea-bargain and received only a six-month sentence, of which she served four and a half months.

She wasn't ordered to do so, but later worked as a volunteer both for battered women and for men taking anger-management classes. Now forty-six, she has remarried and has two teenage stepsons—and is careful not to keep a gun in the home.

"There's no second-guessing it," she says today. "There's no doubt in my mind that he was going to kill me eventually. He told me, 'Your ass is mine when the time is right.' "[1]

You can't discuss women and guns without addressing domestic violence, and the effect guns in the home have on battered women stuck in a repeating loop of emotional, financial, and physical abuse. Four million women a year are abused by their husbands or partners, 30 percent of them regularly. Male intimates inflict more injuries on women *than auto accidents, muggings, and rape combined*. Twenty-two to 35 percent of all emergency room visits by women are for injuries caused by domestic assault.[2]

Every day three American women are murdered by an abusive mate.

The threat of injury or death by firearm is often a fact of life for a battered woman as an abusive partner holds a loaded handgun to her head or to that of a child or relative. One woman told me her husband kept a loaded shotgun beneath his side of the marital bed. It's a familiar, terrifying ritual that reinforces a woman's sense of impotence against male rage. In one major study of forty-two battered women who killed their partners, 58.5 percent said they were physically abused as children; 76 percent were emotionally abused; 54.8 percent sexually abused; and 47.6 sexually assaulted by family members.[3] By the time a formerly battered girl is embroiled in a violent adult relationship, she has grown accustomed to male fury and her inability to stem it or flee.

Police intervention may not help, writes Angela Browne in her 1989 book, *When Battered Women Kill*—a powerful and detailed study of forty-two women from fifteen states who committed murder—because the aggression usually escalates as a result of outside intervention, and is difficult to deter. The police may simply suggest the man "cool down."

Women who finally try to flee an abusive husband or partner face a number of obstacles: summoning the courage to go, finding a place to live for themselves and their children, hiring a lawyer, requesting a temporary restraining order, filling out paperwork to demonstrate there has been physical harm or threat of harm. The application is shown to a judge, who may, or may not, grant the order. The perpetrator is served notice and both parties must appear in court, generally within two weeks. A final protection order (known as a Protection From Abuse or PFA) cannot be obtained for emotional or verbal abuse.

Not every woman wants a restraining order, explains Kelley Hughes, who has counseled hundreds of abused women in Lewiston, Maine, since 1997. "We ask the victim. She knows him best and can generally speak to whether or not she thinks this will be useful. If she believes that it is a safeguard, great. If not, it's a piece of paper and isn't worth the risk. It's very situational.

"There is a lot of pressure [on women] to get a PFA," says Hughes. Family and friends, exasperated and fearful, just want the problem *solved*. "It all comes from a good place. We want victims to be safe. I believe in order to do that we need to be listening to her, especially when she tells us a PFA isn't going to keep him away.

"Women are often scared throughout this process," says Hughes, who is development director for the Abused Women's Advocacy project, a transitional housing program for abused women. "Because domestic violence is an issue of power and control, and [leaving or asking for an order of protection] is an assertion of control on the part of the victim, it's a very dangerous time for her. Safety planning is a must."

Should a woman, now even more endangered by her own boldness, get a gun of her own? "Honestly, I don't think arming her is the answer," Hughes says. "In so many cases of victim murder it's a murder/suicide. He doesn't value his life—and he is most likely going to take her with him when he goes. He is not swayed by threats of returned violence."

In her study of battered women who kill, and the men they were involved with, Angela Browne found that the majority of these men, 61 percent, had indeed talked of committing suicide. "Injuring and nearly killing one's partner is in itself a self-destructive act. In the eventual homicide incidents, many of the men *dared* their partners to kill them or ran against the gun as the women were firing."

Manhattan criminal defense attorney Michael Dowd, who has represented twenty-four women who killed their abusers (winning

acquittals for 80 percent of them), agrees that it is almost impossible to deter these men. In taking these women's testimony, Dowd
was consistently dismayed by the men's tenacity, their determination to enact their will. "Killing the women becomes an almost
maniacal obsession. They'll stop at nothing, including killing
themselves, to get what they want, to kill the woman who has
rejected them. Suicide bombers now frighten us most as a society—that's how these women feel, that the abuser is impervious
to the notion that in killing her he'll die himself. That's scary."

A battered woman having a gun "only encourages feelings of
false safety," adds Hughes. "I believe the only way she is going to
be truly safe is if this is a whole community effort: if the laws tell
him he can't have guns when a PFA is in place, if the police
enforce this, if the neighbor of the perp[etrator] is telling him he's
out of line when he talks about hurting her. Obviously, we are not
there yet, so in the meantime we offer her a relatively secure shelter, alarm systems, relocation, and other safety plans."

By 2000, all states allowed police officers to make an arrest for
domestic violence if they feel there is probable cause, and twenty-
one states and D.C. make such arrests mandatory.

Yet the effectiveness of arrest remains unresolved. One problem with mandatory arrest policies is that both parties may allege
that the other was the aggressor, requiring an officer to arrest
both, including an innocent victim who may have been acting in
self-defense. States have accommodated this by allowing an office
to arrest only the primary aggressor—a somewhat complex matter
of judgment, experience, and training.

A 1989 study found that police officers make their decisions
based on at least four factors: (1) what the officer understands the
law to be; (2) the beliefs s/he has about battered women; (3) the
amount of work involved in making the arrest versus the repri-
mand for not doing so; and (4) political issues within the department.

The net effect? Even when states enact mandatory or preferred
arrest laws, the number of arrests may not significantly increase.

While blacks suffer the highest rate of gun deaths nationally,

Hispanic women living in the Southwest had the highest rates of gun-related death (which correlated with the highest rates of domestic abuse: 180 cases per 1,000 couples compared to 166 per 1,000 among black couples and 117 per 1,000 among whites). In Chicago, in 63 percent of Hispanic homicides, men killed their female partner.[4]

Alma Lopez of Los Angeles spoke no English and had no documents. As a result, she felt trapped for a decade in a cycle of constant physical and emotional abuse. Her husband insulted her, hit her, refused to give her money, and wouldn't let her have any friends. She thought this was normal because she'd grown up watching her mother endure similar humiliation. She only fled after he'd knocked her unconscious, forcing her to seek medical treatment at a local hospital, where a counselor from the Los Angeles Commission Against Assault Against Women explained her legal rights. Today, remarried and far from her violent past, Lopez works as a volunteer counselor for other abused Hispanic women.[5]

In 1992, the L.A. Commission Against Assault Against Women created a service dedicated specifically to the needs of Latina women, including a hot line with Spanish volunteers, and every year the Latina program receives more than twenty-five hundred calls.[6]

Even after fleeing an abusive home, some women, like twenty-year-old Tameka Gabriel of Brooklyn, New York, can't find help because of a technicality. One night in January 2001, her father beat her with his fists—she was taken to the hospital with two black eyes and a swollen face. At the hospital, she was given a handbook with the phone numbers of agencies that help battered women. Despite calling hot lines and going directly to the agencies, Gabriel found little aid. "Everybody turned away from me because it wasn't a boyfriend, it was my father. I was walking around in circles for a long time."

"Technically speaking, Gabriel had a family to return to. She didn't fit the category," said Reina Ramos, the Children's Aid Society caseworker who finally helped her get an apartment of her own.[7]

Women who marry battering men have great difficulty explaining, to themselves and to others, their descent into a private hell. When she appears to enjoy many options, including easy flight, it's even tougher. Oscar-winning actress Halle Berry married Atlanta Braves star David Justice, endured three rocky years, then divorced in 1997. She filed a restraining order against him. In spring 2001, she told the *New York Times*, "Maybe there was something about me that sparked the bad side of him."

She later told *Vogue*, "We were so wrong for each other that I feel like just being myself sometimes made him really angry, and that anger would get out of control." Berry had also dated a man who hit her so hard she lost 80 percent of hearing in one ear.

"I'm not a victim," she told *Vogue*. "I chose those situations."[8] Rich, beautiful, professionally successful—how, indeed, *could* a woman with Berry's gifts and talents choose such humiliation?

A woman so outwardly successful who eventually kills her abuser also faces an incredulous judicial system, says Manhattan criminal defense attorney Michael Dowd. "Some women will get special consideration, but all too often it's the superficial indices of independence that do her great harm. It's very hard for people to understand that a financially independent woman could be in an abusive relationship. It's intuitively inconsistent." Now that battered women, arguably, have more options—fleeing to a shelter, obtaining a restraining order, "shall-arrest" states where police must arrest an abusive man—women who fail to use them won't be viewed sympathetically by a judge or jury, he says. Upper-class women are also less likely to report their abuse, he says; experts agree that some prefer the razor-edged luxury of their homes and their social status as a rich man's wife to admitting the truth, fleeing to a public shelter, and facing a new, poor, uncertain future without him.

Dowd thinks successful women are even more likely to hide their abuse than others. "I think they're very much more vulnerable. It's so important for them to keep up the facade of success. It makes them even more ashamed. It destroys their public persona of the strong, independent woman."

Berry is hardly alone in having experienced physical abuse at the hands of a lover—in the United States, women are more likely to be attacked, injured, raped, or killed by a current or former male partner *than by all other types of assailants combined.*[9] Intimate-partner violence in 1995 cost the United States more than $23 billion: $18.5 billion in direct costs from the criminal justice system, $4 billion in health care and mental health care costs, and nearly $1 billion in lost productivity.[10] The Federal Gun Control Act forbids the sale or transfer of a gun to a "prohibited person," a category that includes convicted felons, those convicted of a domestic violence misdemeanor, and those under a restraining order. Only twenty-three states restrict access to guns by those under a restraining order (which is issued by a state court), twelve others forbid buyers convicted of domestic violence misdemeanors from buying a gun. But relying on databases for a background check does not guarantee a woman's safety: in 1998 only thirty-two states had the ability to conduct checks for domestic violence misdemeanors and thirty-five states for restraining orders. In Minnesota and Pennsylvania, searching for domestic violence data was impossible, and it was difficult in Washington and West Virginia.[11] It is also unclear how effectively these state and federal FBI databases share information. Criminals could potentially escape detection, even with two layers of oversight built into the system.

Are existing laws even enforced? Only two states, New Jersey and New Hampshire, permit the court to order a search and seizure order for weapons when issuing a restraining order.

Few battered women, or their families, have successfully sued local police for inadequate protection. In June 1985, Tracey Thurman became the first woman to win a civil suit as a battered wife when she sued the police department in Torrington, Connecticut. A judge decided the police had violated her civil rights in ignoring her repeated complaints against her husband.

Yet in July 2002, a federal judge dismissed a suit against Westchester County district attorney Jeanine Pirro filed by a woman who said that officials failed to carry out an order of protection before her ex-boyfriend shot her. The woman, Joy Thomas, twenty, of Mount Vernon, New York, was shot in the head on her way to class on February 7, 2000, by Olonzo David, who then fatally shot himself. The judge, Colleen McMahon, found the county not liable under federal law and gave the other defendants, which included the city of Mount Vernon, twenty days to seek a similar dismissal.

In December 2002, Caine Cassidy shot at his ex-girlfriend Angela Riddick, driving through Mount Vernon, critically wounding her before killing himself. The shooting, as is typically the case, ended a series of escalating incidents, illustrative of the many tangled threads that slow or deter arresting, prosecuting, and convicting a man who beats his intimate partner. Two key issues collide—a woman's reluctance to have an abuser arrested and the abuser's fixation upon doing her harm. Riddick had argued in July 2002 with Cassidy, who punched her in the mouth, splitting her lip. Because they were not married, police could not automatically arrest the man—as they otherwise had to under state law. She declined to press criminal charges against him.

"They don't want their boyfriends to have a record," said Beth Feder, a lawyer with a local domestic violence agency.[12] Thanks to a series of miscommunications between the victim, the perpetrator, police, and district attorney, Cassidy was let out on $1,500 bail in December after shooting at Riddick's car, by a judge completely ignorant of his violent history. Mount Vernon police said they'd merely worked with what she gave them.

"She said there was a relationship," said Captain Robert Kelly. "She didn't say, 'He beat me up.' "[13]

Like female gun owners, women who have been battered, escaped their abusers, and rebuilt their lives are quietly and invisibly everywhere. Some recover and remarry happily.

I met several, each time by accident. In a Texas library, I chatted about my book with a woman who coolly recounted decades of abuse at the hands of her first husband, a prominent member of the community, the head of a university medical center. She was a beautiful, well-spoken redhead, probably in her late fifties, with aquamarine eyes the color of a Caribbean sea. Her chic cotton sweater-set matched her eyes perfectly. Her hair was well coiffed, her manicure fresh.

As she poured out her story, unprompted, it was difficult, and painful, to listen, to match this elegant, composed, and gentle woman with such emotional and physical devastation. The many details she shared were harrowing, from the loaded .44 Magnum he repeatedly held to her head to the sawed-off shotgun he kept beneath his side of the bed. Her family insisted she stay with him, refusing to give her any shelter or financial help. She had married at fifteen, been married seventeen years, and had two children. She discovered her husband, and his father, had abused her seven-year-old daughter.

Why, I asked, did *she* never get a gun, easy enough to do in Texas? Her answer was unhesitating: "I was better than that!"

Her narrative seared me, suddenly and unexpectedly putting a face to the statistics and surveys I was reading. How many women like her are out there? I returned to the stacks—to pore over row upon row of books devoted solely to violence against women. As this random encounter reminded me, there is no shortage of material.

When I sat down to interview one business owner in the gun industry, she calmly suggested I speak up a bit. The room was quiet enough—but her right ear, she said, had lost much of its hearing from the beatings her first husband had meted out.

A fifty-seven-year-old widow now lives alone in a bungalow in a wooded suburb north of New Orleans, on the north side of Lake Pontchartrain. With long, strawberry-blond hair and kohl-rimmed blue eyes, she's an attractive woman with an eighth-grade education, who now lives on her late second husband's military pension.

"I didn't believe in having guns in the house originally. My first husband," she says calmly, "was too violent. As soon as he had enough to drink, most of the time he would hold a loaded gun up to my head. He'd force me to sit still and not leave the room. He would use it to torture me, basically."

She was twenty-seven, living in Tucson, her children eight and three. There were no women's shelters back then. "It *did* occur to me to protect myself, but it would have been one more thing for him to use against me. If I'd used it I would go to jail for life."

Her husband was friends with many local policemen. "I had no one to go to."

I met Debra Jackson, a heavyset black woman, on a street corner in downtown New Orleans on a sunny, hot, late-May afternoon. After years of her own domestic hell, she struck back—chopping four fingers off her husband's left hand with a meat cleaver. She went to trial and was acquitted on the testimony of a white female neighbor. She now carries a loaded .38 in her pocket every day to work; Jackson runs a food distribution program on a street where she had already seen ten murders that year.

Does she think battered women should arm themselves? No, she said. With their nerves shattered, their judgment impaired, a gun would probably do them more harm than good.

Women who have been battered for many years are indeed often too frightened to arm themselves, says Larry Preston-Williams, a former New Orleans police officer who runs a private investigation firm. Wade Schindler, a gun instructor in New Orleans for twenty-two years, has battered women referred to him by psychiatrists and social workers. "By the time these women get to me, they've done everything they're supposed to do, everything the courts allow them to—and the stalker is still there." A retired police commander and professor of criminology at Tulane University, Schindler has taught more than seven hundred women to shoot. Most of his clients are middle-class white women who can afford a Louisiana state permit ($100 for four years), and his classes, which range in cost from $150 for four classroom hours and four more of shooting instruction to a $335 session that quadruples their classroom and shooting time.

"The one thing they have in common is they're all frightened. They're angry that they have to do it [get a gun], but this is the only equalizer they have," he says.

In a 1992 book, *Empowering and Healing the Battered Woman,* author Mary Ann Dutton argues, "When violence is of life-threatening proportions, the use of a weapon in self-defense may be a woman's only viable alternative . . . for some, the choices become to be killed, to kill oneself, or to fight back, potentially killing the batterer."[14]

What finally impels a woman to kill an abusive partner?

According to Angela Browne, author of *When Battered Women Kill,* seven factors push them over the edge:

1. they were abused more often;
2. they were severely injured;
3. how often men forced or threatened sexual acts against them;
4. how often he used drugs;
5. how often he used alcohol;
6. he threatened to kill her, and
7. the woman threatened her own suicide. In addition, these men more frequently raped or otherwise sexually assaulted their partners and many more of them had made threats to kill than men whose partners did not kill them.

Rather than firing in impulsive anger or fear, theirs was the reply to years, if not decades, of assault and escalating attacks.

"The women's behavior seemed to be primarily in reaction to the level of threat and violence coming in."[15]

Battered women live in hell—and often one that remains terrifyingly private, no matter how many visits they pay to their local emergency room. No one knows what makes one woman snap and decide to kill an abusive man while another flees or endures even more. "Because society's standards on violence against wives are ambiguous, and because abused women rarely discuss their victimization with others, most battered women are quite dependent on 'internal' anchors to determine the latitude of behaviors they will accept. . . . They [are] involved in a constant process of assimilation and readjustment. Survival becomes the criterion."[16]

"When it comes to the crucial issue of reasonably perceiving deadly danger, battered women may have broken wings but they have the eye of the eagle," writes Donald Alexander, a professor of political science at the University of Madison, Wisconsin.[17] "Because battering often builds to a lethal crescendo, a woman may feel the need to fight back *not* in the moment of one attack [immediacy] but in anticipation of the next and final one [imminence]," he writes. Ann Jones's landmark book on the subject is chillingly titled *Next Time, She'll Be Dead*.

The night a woman finally kills her abuser resembles the classic Passover question asked at seder: "Why is this night different from all other nights?" It is, says defense attorney Michael Dowd, because a woman *knows* she is about to be killed. "These women have become very sophisticated observers of violence. They are very adept at perceiving a different level of threat." Like combat veterans who once jumped at the sound of gunfire, battered women can delineate the finest distinctions between routine assault and the lethal, unstoppable culmination that will end their life. "They *know* what makes this night different. The man's eyes are dead and cold. Something alerts them."

Woman-on-Woman Crime

It's unusual, but it happens.

Yolanda Saldivar made history on March 31, 1995, when she shot and killed the popular Tejana singer Selena Quintanilla-Perez, who was then twenty-three, with one shot from a .38-caliber revolver. The shot was fired as the two argued in a motel room. The former nurse from San Antonio, Texas, was sentenced to life in prison.[18]

She is now prisoner number 733126, allowed to spend only one hour a day outside her nine-by-six-foot cell in Gatesville, Texas. Saldivar was the founder and president of Selena's fan club, managed the singer's clothing boutique in San Antonio, and was involved in a boutique belonging to the singer in Corpus Christi.

The gun, which was lost after the trial, was found in June 2002 in a court reporter's home and finally smashed with a sledgehammer and thrown into Corpus Christi Bay on the orders of a state judge. "It's time finally to bring closure to such tragedy," said Judge Jose Longoria of district court.[19]

Yet Selena's fans still flock to her boutique, her bayfront statue, her neighborhood, and her grave in Corpus Christi. Hundreds came from as far away as Mexico in 1999 to mark the fourth anniversary of her death.[20]

On May 19, 1992, Amy Fisher, then seventeen, shot the wife, Mary Jo, of her thirty-eight-year-old lover, Joey Buttafuoco, in the neck on the doorstep of Mary Jo's Long Island home with a .25-caliber handgun. The woman survived and Fisher went to jail for almost seven years, winning parole thanks to the efforts of Mary Jo, who argued for her early release and, living now in Los Angeles, is still married to her husband.

Homicide

Women, like men, usually kill on Saturday night. By the end of a full day off, tempers have had time to percolate, escalate, and culminate in murder. (Tuesday night is the second-most-popular choice, and Friday the least.) "Murder is a leisure-time, or weekend, activity."[21]

Most women kill (70.4 percent of murders) in the home, where the victim and offender usually lived together (42.3 percent).

While a 1958 study found the kitchen a favorite spot for murder, in 1978 and again in 1989, it was the bedroom. A survey of 296 murders committed in 1983 in six major U.S. cities found the living room, family room, or den to be the most dangerous.

A 1996 study compared murders in three Southern cities—Atlanta, Baltimore, and Houston—with New York, Chicago, and

Los Angeles (chosen because their homicide rates were equal to or higher than the national average).

Women who drank before committing murder killed on weekends (59.4 percent), while those who used drugs committed murder on weekdays (66.7 percent). In 294 of 296 cases studied, the mean time of the murder was 1:39 A.M. Women kill at night—62.3 percent of the homicides took place between 8:00 P.M. and 7:59 A.M.

A major regional disparity also became clear: Southern women were far more likely to shoot to kill—60.1 percent versus 39.9 percent of Northern women (perhaps because guns are more easy to obtain in the three Southern states studied). African-American women in the Southern states were particularly prone to select firearms over other methods of killing (67.9 percent); of the women who used long guns, such as rifles or shotguns, 68.4 were in Southern cities.

Southern female killers were also slightly more likely to have been drinking—while the men they shot were more likely to have provoked the shooting.

Yet after passions have cooled, the body is removed, and a woman enters the criminal justice system, things get a lot tougher—especially for Southern women. "There was tremendous diversity in the criminal justice process across the six study cities. . . . Only Chicago and New York City . . . seemed to conform to an appropriate model of justice. Cities in the South were more punitive . . . were significantly more likely to extend the more serious final charge of murder/manslaughter and longer prison and probation times to women who killed. The South is clearly not the place for a woman to be arrested for murder."

The only way to know if a woman has truly killed in self-defense, the author argued, is to make sure the height and weight of both offenders and victims are recorded in police reports, to determine whether female offenders, particularly in domestic homicide cases, really *are* at a physical disadvantage that requires "equalization" through the use of a weapon.

In more than half of the cases studied, the victim had been

shot only once, and a number of them bled to death before medical help arrived. Single wounds (57 percent) were found more frequently than multiple wounds (43 percent), particularly among African-American victims (58.6 percent). Women who used alcohol or drugs prior to the murder were more likely to inflict multiple wounds. In 70.9 percent of offenders who used drugs, there had been a prior arrest—versus 39.8 percent for nonusers.

Forty-four percent of the women studied were sent to prison, with 78.9 percent of them getting less than ten years and 21.1 percent more than a ten-year sentence.

Shooting Famous Men

A few shootings by women, usually because of the male victim's celebrity, have not only made national headlines, but resonated for decades later as books, films, and made-for-TV movies.

In the 1950s, Ann Woodward married the richest and handsomest bachelor in New York, a man wealthy enough to take her tiger hunting with maharajas in India and to own Nashua, the top racehorse of the day. One night in 1955, they quarreled in their Long Island home. She shot him twice as he stood naked in the hallway after a shower, saying she had mistaken him for an intruder. She was never tried for the shooting. It was the scandal of the times, and *Life* magazine ran an eleven-page story calling it "the shooting of the century."[22]

The 1980 murder of Scarsdale cardiologist Herman Tarnower, author of a best-selling diet book, by Jean Harris (the prim and starchy principal of the exclusive Madeira School, a D.C. private school for girls), dominated headlines that year, assuming "the proportions of a national melodrama," wrote then reporter Walter Isaacson in *Time*.[23] Feminism was in full flower, with *Ms.* magazine barely six years old, the chants of Helen Reddy's popular anthem "I Am Woman" still fresh. Yet here was a woman breaking all the new rules: *"Shocking* is hardly the word for such a stereotypically groveling woman in 1981," wrote one female reporter.

Harris had been dating Tarnower for fourteen years, but he refused to marry her. Instead, the sixty-nine-year-old doctor began an affair with his thirty-eight-year-old assistant, Lynne Tryforos—enraging Harris, who was then fifty-seven. "I have to do something besides shriek with pain," she wrote to him in a ten-page letter—and on March 10, 1980, at his six-and-a-half-acre estate in Purchase, New York, a wealthy northern suburb of New York City, she pulled the trigger of a .38 revolver five times.

Harris was sentenced to fifteen years to life for second-degree murder and served twelve. Nine books, three by Harris, were written about the case, and a 1981 film was made about it.

Long before the days of confessional talk shows and "reality" television, the trial offered a saga of compelling interest to Americans, "a tale of betrayal, snobbery, lust, self-pity, and degradation," wrote Elizabeth Peer in *Newsweek*. "To some who believe she is guilty, but don't mind a bit, Harris had actually done what most women only fantasize—punish a two-timing male with rich and satisfying finality."[24]

On June 3, 1968, at 2:30 P.M., Valerie Solanas went to the Factory, a studio in downtown Manhattan, to see artist Andy Warhol, who she suspected was planning to use her work without paying her. At 4:15 P.M. Warhol arrived; while waiting for the elevator, he noticed her wearing a thick turtleneck sweater underneath a trench coat on a hot summer day, and twisting a brown paper bag in her hands.

Inside the Factory, Solanas took a .32 automatic from the paper bag and fired at Warhol three times. One bullet entered his right side, exiting the left side of his back. Warhol later told friends, "It hurt so much, I wished I was dead." Taken to a nearby hospital, he in fact was clinically dead for one and a half minutes before doctors revived him. The bullet went through his lung, then ricocheted through his esophagus, gallbladder, liver, spleen, and intestines before exiting his left side, leaving a large hole. Doctors operated for five and a half hours, removing his spleen.

Said Solanas, "I just wanted him to pay attention to me. Talking to him was like talking to a chair."

Carol Carr, of Griffin, Georgia, saw murdering her two sons in 2002 as an act of mercy. The sixty-four-year-old woman killed Michael R. Scott, forty-two, and Andy B. Scott, forty-one, as they lay in their beds in a nursing home. Both men were in the advanced stages of Huntington's disease and were unable to communicate; the same disease had killed their father. Carr's surviving son, James Scott, forty, also suffers from the disease.[25] Sentenced to five years in prison, Carr was due to be released in March 2004 after serving one month more than was the minimum possible. A condition of her parole was that she not live with or become responsible for the care of her surviving son.

Do women shooters receive more lenient treatment than men? Some say yes. Others argue that women simply rarely commit homicides that merit the death penalty. Although women commit one in every eight homicides, they commit less than one in twenty heinous enough to deserve execution. Women killers are also much less likely than men to face sentencing with prior records of violent felonies, which ups their odds of receiving a death sentence.[26]

At the close of 1999, fifty women were on death row in seventeen state prisons, and one was on death row in a federal prison. They ranged in age from twenty-three to seventy, including grandmothers, housewives, and a black former New Orleans police officer, Antoinette Frank, who shot and killed her police partner.

Depression and Suicide

In May 2002, the U.S. Preventive Services Task Force, an independent arm of the federal Agency for Healthcare Research and Quality, suggested that every primary-care physician routinely screen all patients for depression. In 1996, the panel found insufficient evidence for this approach, but a review of fourteen studies showed that screening works, said Dr. Alton Berg, chairman of the task force. The studies suggest that screening could help an additional 9 percent of primary-care patients overcome depression in six months.

Most important to any home containing a firearm and ammunition, early detection of depression could reduce the single most significant problem of keeping firearms in the home, suicide.

Typically, of all firearm-related deaths in the United States, 50 percent are suicides.

Firearms are the most common means of suicide in the United States for both genders and all age groups. While women often use other methods to signal their despair (such as overdosing on pills or cutting their wrists), once they have decided to end their life, they choose firearms as frequently as men do, for the same reason—in 80 to 90 percent of cases, they succeed in killing themselves.

"Depression is not the be-all and end-all," cautions Dr. Alan Berman, head of the American Association of Suicidology, a national, thirty-six-year-old group of researchers, survivors, crisis workers, and health professionals. "There are millions of depressed people who are *not* suicidal." But Berman, who has studied suicide for thirty years, is adamant on one point: "As depression descends into hopelessness, the firearm begins to emit a siren call."

Anyone who fears his or her loved one is considering suicide must immediately remove all access to a firearm. "Make sure, first and foremost, there is no immediately accessible method that can be used for suicide. That will buy us [mental health workers] more time," advises Berman. Because the decision to pull the trigger can be impulsive, removing the firearm delays suicide, sometimes for good. "If you thwart an immediate impulse, it takes some time for them to decide on an alternative," Berman explains. "That delay can allow for a change of mind and for other events to happen," events that might lessen the feeling there is no other option but death. "Suicidal people are not good or very creative problem-solvers."

The decision to commit suicide is complex and still poorly understood, and its warning signs can be missed, he cautions. "People are often in denial about how depressed someone really is or they're feeling angry, anxious, hostile, guilty. The symptoms can be hidden. Some clues are not all that evident."

Several disturbing trends appear in the suicide rate. One is the 11 percent increase between 1980 and 1998 in suicide among men aged forty to forty-four and 10 percent in suicide among men aged forty-five to forty-nine. Sixty-one percent of men who kill themselves use a gun.

As more women are buying and owning more guns than ever before, they're also using them more often to kill themselves. "In the past, men and women in the United States favored different methods of committing suicide. Males traditionally utilize firearms, while women use less lethal means such as poison. While this is still true, an increasing percentage of females end their lives by fatally shooting themselves. . . . Since females attempt suicide so frequently, any increase in the use of firearms will result in a dramatic increase in female suicide fatalities."[27]

Pat Flounders, fifty-one, of East Stroudsburg, Pennsylvania, killed herself with a single shot to the head after the deaths of her husband of twenty-one years in the World Trade Center attacks and their dog several weeks later. A worried neighbor had hidden her handgun but revealed its location after deciding Flounders could safely have access to it. "She was totally, totally devastated, but she would only reach out to people she knew. She was not interested in any intervention from a professional," said state representative Kelly Lewis, a personal friend.[28]

Young women are also reaching for guns to commit suicide; in 1970, according to one study, guns were responsible for 32.3 percent of suicides committed by females ages fifteen to twenty-four. By 1984, firearm-related deaths accounted for 51.3 percent of suicides within that same age group.[29] Between 1960 and 1980, the number of women committing suicide by all methods other than firearms increased 16 percent—*while the number of females committing suicide using firearms more than doubled.*[30]

On October 22, 1999, Carla June Hochalter shot and killed herself six months after her seventeen-year-old daughter, Anne Marie, was critically wounded and partly paralyzed by the shootings at Columbine High School. Hochalter walked into a suburban pawn shop, asked to see a handgun, loaded it, and killed herself.

If someone is determined to commit suicide and has access to a loaded gun, disaster awaits. Wealth and social position offer no protection to privileged women; suicide is too democratic. Upper-class women from families of enormous power and influence are just as likely as their less-affluent counterparts to hear the unmistakable sound of gunfire within their own homes, to suffer for many years suicide's public face, and its private legacy of pain and guilt.

Women are still often seen as the emotional caretaker of their family. Suicide, especially by firearm, blows such myths apart. What does it say about a woman's judgment, her attentiveness to her family's emotional needs, her marital or mothering skills? Knowing her home contains a firearm capable of lethal results, balancing the scale between trusting her partner and children with caution and prudence, could she possibly even prevent or forestall a suicide?

Who, indeed, shares responsibility for that impossibly heavy burden?

Katharine Graham, the late publisher and owner of the *Washington Post,* lived a life from earliest childhood of great material privilege. She lost Phil, her beloved husband of twenty-three years, to self-inflicted gun violence.

"The man who leaves life by the most violent suicide is still at least more honest than those who choose suicide-while-living by defining away all that is human in life," wrote Phil Graham, former *Post* publisher, in an unsent letter to his son.[31] After many confusing and exhausting years of mood swings, Graham had finally been diagnosed as manic-depressive and hospitalized. "Had we known of [the letter, it] might have led us all to a different decision about whether he was ready to have a day away from the hospital," Katharine Graham wrote in her 1997 memoir, *Personal History.*

But her husband *did* come home to their country house. "There was a sharp difference of opinion among the doctors . . . about whether this was a good idea, but no one ever asked if there was liquor or sleeping pills at the farm, nor did I think to mention the guns we had there. I, who certainly knew the farm was stocked with guns that Phil used for sport, was completely deluded by his seeming progress, lack of visible depression, and determination to get well."[32]

After lunch, he excused himself, disappeared into a downstairs bathroom, and shot himself. "It was so profoundly shocking and traumatizing—he was so obviously dead and the wounds so ghastly to look at—that I just ran into the next room and buried my head in my hands, trying to absorb that this had really happened . . ."[33]

Graham blamed herself: "I stupidly was not worried enough. It had never occurred to me that he must have planned the whole day at Glen Welby to get to his guns as a way of freeing himself forever from the watchful eyes of the doctors—and the world. He left no note of any kind."

Lisa Silverman, her neck ringed with pearls the size of gum balls, appears carefree in a photo in *New York* magazine beside her tanned, handsome husband, New York City financier Jeffrey Silverman. She looks like a woman who has it all. But the image accompanied not a happy story about Silverman's business accomplishments but his ugly end—an apparent suicide. In August 2002, he shot himself in the chest on a road near their former Greenwich, Connecticut, estate.

Silverman, at fifty-two, appeared successful: a gorgeous and accomplished third wife seventeen years his junior and with young twins, opulent homes in Greenwich, Palm Beach, and Manhattan, and a wealthy family who had already helped him out financially.

He left behind six children by three wives.

Susan Bowden-White, a former television news reporter for WMAR in Baltimore, lost not only a son to suicide, but her first husband. Using guns, both took their lives in the family home where she still lives.

"I can narrow my feelings to the warning. . . . You're taking a terrible risk," having a gun at home, she says.

In 1974, Bowden-White, who is now remarried, had separated from her husband, an ex-marine who kept a Luger in their bedside drawer. One day, distraught and pleading with her for reconciliation, he appeared at their home. With little warning he went upstairs, hugged their fourteen-year-old son, Jody, and pulled the trigger on himself. Three years later, despondent over a failed romance, Jody went upstairs in the same house and pulled the trigger of his father's gun, an antique .22 rifle.

"We'd lived through John's death somehow," Bowden-White recalls. "I thought we'd be okay. I was a strong woman, determined, maybe we could be closer as a family," she says, her voice still choked with emotion decades later. "I never *ever* thought this could happen again. I wouldn't let myself think it could. But it did."

To ease her pain and guilt, Bowden-White wrote a book in 1985, *Everything to Live For,* and has spoken to many groups about suicide. She also testified in 1996 before Congress in favor of gun control, although with mixed feelings. "We're a long long way from trying to regulate [gun ownership] and I'm not sure we should. But I strongly and passionately believe if those guns had not been in my home, my son would be alive today."

Rates of suicide among teenage boys using firearms climbed by more than a third from the late 1970s until the early 1990s before falling to 10.4 per 100,000 in 1997. The rate for young black men nearly quadrupled between 1979 and 1994 before falling in the 1990s. Suicide by gun among fifteen-to-ninteen-year-old black males rose to a peak of 13.9 per 100,000 in 1994 from 3.6 per 100,000 in 1979; in 1997, the most recent year studied, the rate was 8.4 per 100,000.

Gunshot Victims

American girls and women are shot and killed every day, whether high-profile professionals or anonymous residents of the inner city.

Nan Wyatt, the forty-four-year-old host of a top-rated morning show on KMOX, a St. Louis, Missouri, radio station since

1996, was shot and killed on February 18, 2003, with a .357-caliber handgun by her husband, Thomas J. Erbland Jr., forty-three. Erbland called police and confessed to the crime that night; he admitted planning the murder and carrying it out. Erbland had been out of work and discovered that his wife was planning to divorce him. "He's a nice, friendly guy . . . laid-back, sociable, and outgoing," said neighbor Carol Loesche, who had socialized with the couple. Wyatt left behind a seven-year-old son, Drake.[34]

Ghandi King, a young black mother in her early twenties, was shot while walking home with her uncle after July 4th celebrations in Detroit, the middle finger of her left hand a bloody pulp. A gang of kids between eighteen and twenty-four were hanging around her home when she heard what she thought were fireworks. The youths started firing at her for fun, she says.

She and her uncle tried to run but couldn't get away, and Ghandi fell behind a car. The back window was shot out while she crouched on the ground, terrified. A bullet ricocheted under the car and hit her in the hand. "My whole hand was burning. It hurt so bad I couldn't even cry. I'm just lucky to be alive," she said—her brother was shot dead a few years earlier for "messin' with a girl he shouldn't have."[35]

"9/11? We have it going on every day. Look at how many babies we don't have. We had 9/11 before 9/11," says Paula Drew-Williams, facilitator of the weekly meeting of Save Our Sons and Daughters, an eighteen-year-old Detroit support group for the mothers of murder victims.

The group, known as So Sad, tries to comfort mothers whose children have been shot and killed in drive-by shootings, gang incidents, and other violent crimes. Sharon Nowell Neal, forty-eight, lost a nine-month-old granddaughter, Taijuana, and a three-year-old son, Nathan, fifteen years apart.

In 2002, the number of children sixteen and under killed in Detroit jumped to twenty-five from nineteen in 2001; the 31 percent increase gave the city a child homicide rate of 9 per 100,000, higher than Chicago, Los Angeles, Boston, San Diego, or Miami.

New Orleans had sixteen children killed that year, double the previous year's eight, giving it a rate of 13 per 100,000; D.C. had twelve child deaths, a rate of 11 per 100,000.

As grim as those numbers are, they represent a significant improvement—in 1986, 365 children were shot in Detroit, 43 of them fatally. One a day.[36]

"What happened to these people will never leave them. As much as the rest of us might remember and sympathize or, as a community, share in the experience, it is a personal experience, deeply and differently and singularly shattering."[37]

Monica Selvig was eight years old when she was shot on a Monday morning in January 1979 outside her school by sixteen-year-old Brenda Spencer, firing a .22-caliber rifle randomly at children across the street. Spencer shot eight children, and killed two school employees.

The bullet tore through Selvig's stomach and exited about a half inch from her spine. "In my mind, what happened to me is like a story I can't connect with." She told a reporter in 1999 that she has constant nightmares and, all these years later, still cannot sleep. In her dreams, "at all the places I go . . . I go there and I'm shot. I don't know what safe is."

Christy Buell was a nine-year-old fourth-grader also shot that day; she was hit twice by Spencer, in the abdomen and lower back, was hospitalized for a month, and spent eighteen months recuperating.[38] "There's no other way to say it," she said in a 1989 interview. "I'll never get over it."

On October 15, 1993, artist Stephanie Cress had enjoyed dinner out in Oakland, California, with her husband, Jim. Because of random gun violence, her life was about to change forever.

"We got home around nine P.M., and when we pulled into our driveway and got out of the car, a guy with a semiautomatic handgun and a ski mask came up behind me, demanding money. We had, between us, about eight dollars. The guy became angry that Jim had very little money, instructed him to get down on the ground, and then pointed the gun at him.

"He shot me once and then Jim four times—twice in the

heart, once in the lungs, and once in the abdomen," killing him. Neither victim was armed and they did not own guns.

Undercover officers scoured the streets for two weeks trying to identify the shooter, and police offered a large reward, to no avail. Neither he nor the driver of the getaway car were caught; police told Cress the man had been in various Oakland neighborhoods robbing and shooting victims for several months prior to the incident.

For a year and a half after the murder, despite crippling fears, Cress stayed in the duplex she owned. "The murder of my husband and a large case of post-traumatic stress disorder (PTSD) was about all I could handle." As though she were contaminated with a contagious and lethal disease, she watched friends withdraw just when she needed them most. "Many of my neighbors either sold their houses and moved, and many of my social supports were also seriously affected by the violence and just disappeared. My family had a hard time giving support."

Alone, terrified, and broke, Cress nonetheless had to remake her life. Then a student in graduate school relying on her husband for financial support, she lost her health insurance and income, relying on a fund for crime victims to pay for her health and mental health services until she could return to work full-time. Although she managed to finish her MFA, after losing the structure of the graduate program, which ended six months after the robbery-murder, Cress became seriously depressed and immobilized by the PTSD, eventually losing her duplex to foreclosure. She still faced a huge IRS debt and no health insurance.

"Now, I have only a few of the PTSD symptoms," she told me in January 2003. "I was troubled by overwhelming anxiety, fear, flashbacks, and social isolation for several years. Through a lot of work, I really only have a symptom called a hyperstartle—I jump from a sudden and huge adrenaline rush and heart pounding— but it has lessened to the point where I can laugh and calm down in five minutes as opposed to more than two hours."

Cress returned to school yet again, obtained a master of social work degree, and is now a licensed clinical social worker with a private practice in San Francisco and a specialty in trauma recovery. She also moved to Concord, California, about twenty miles from Oakland, a place she gratefully describes as slower, calmer, and less violent.

Now fifty-four, Cress has also remarried, admitting candidly that it took her five years to "get up the courage to make that commitment again. I'm glad I did because he is worth the psychological risk and is a very nice guy." He has, she added, "been very teachable about trauma and PTSD."

For Susan Gonzalez, then thirty-eight, terror arrived the night that three masked gunmen in camouflage kicked the front door of her mobile home, in a rural area near the airport in Jacksonville, Florida, off its hinges and started firing. Two 9mm bullets tore into her chest, one bruising her heart, and exited her back, causing enormous blood loss. "The first bullet pushed me back a little from the force. It was a burning sensation as it went through my body."

Transported by helicopter to a nearby trauma unit, she required delicate lung surgery, which the doctor described to her "as peeling blood off the lung as you would peel an orange. I have an eighteen-inch scar down and across my back like a shark bit me." While she was able to leave the hospital the first time after seven days, lung complications required her to return for another twenty-one days.

But it is not the physical scars alone that mark her for life. "They fixed me the best they could," she says, "but I live in pain every day from this physically and emotionally. The trauma of dealing with all of this has been very hard. I am on pins and needles all the time. I lay awake at nights praying that nothing would happen, that their friends were not coming back.

"Something like this can destroy a family medically, emotionally, and financially."[39]

Chapter 6
A Member of
the Family

———◆◆◆———

No matter who owns it, when a gun—and its potential for violence and control—enters a home, power shifts.

"Men are threatened by it, for sure," says Sandra Williams, laughing. A black, forty-seven-year-old, nineteen-year veteran of the New York City Police Department, she has been married for more than twenty years to a fire department official, no stranger himself to a quasi-military culture and its trappings. Williams says her competence with firearms has always discomfited her husband. "It's always been a bone of contention, even today." A gun bestows lethal power, and that doesn't sit well with many men," says Williams. "My self-esteem isn't derived from my position at work, but I think my husband projected onto me what it would make him feel." She said she felt the tension "in work, after work, especially when I was on patrol. He was always in competition with me.

"Maybe it's a stereotype—that women are too emotional, too unstable, to have a gun, so some guys might fear that a woman who has a gun might use it in an argument. I don't *believe* this fear is real, but . . ." Is it tougher for an armed black woman? Williams laughs again. "I think it can be an issue for any woman. Guys think they should have the most power."

Men who carry a gun for a living, accustomed to the ultimate potential power of taking a life, bring it home and often misuse it.

Women married to men in the military face higher-than-average rates of abuse; when it comes to severe physical aggression, rates for army wives are three times higher than for women with civilian husbands. This escalated in the summer of 2002 when four veterans of the war in Afghanistan killed their wives at Fort Bragg. "Fort Bragg is a culture unto itself," says army chaplain John Wetherly. "They know they're the first to go. It takes training to be aggressive. You have to be trained to be an institutional killer, so you build a culture around it."[1]

For military wives, the presence of guns in their home—and the training that makes their husbands effective killers—can make for a lethal combination. It was unclear, though, whether the four killings were influenced by the men's use of the antimalaria drug Lariam, which can cause severe psychosis.

"If a woman seeks safety in a civilian shelter, nobody picks up the phone and calls her husband's boss," says Christine Hansen, a former army brat herself who is director of the Miles Foundation, a private, nonprofit support and advocacy organization for victims of violence associated with the military. "In the military, the abuser's fate is decided by someone with a vested interest. The mission—unit cohesion and readiness—is put before victim safety or offender accountability. The murders at Fort Bragg are not necessarily an anomaly. They illustrate the extent of the problem, and it's a problem that's crying out for solutions."[2]

Police wives face their own fears, also knowing they share their homes with a man capable of killing and trained to do so. "Officers learn to interrogate when suspicious, to intimidate or match aggression when challenged, and to dominate when threatened," writes California police officer Lonald D. Lott in a law enforcement journal.[3] "These actions are necessary for survival and control. However, when combined with the unfavorable conditions of police work—undesirable shifts, rotating work schedules, days off spent in court, exposure to pain and suffering, and violent confrontations—even exceptional police officers can become very poor spouses, parents, and friends."

Lott cited a study of 385 police officers attending a training and law enforcement program: 40 percent of the officers reported at least one episode of physical aggression during a conflict with their spouse or companion in the previous year, and as many as twenty episodes a year. Some officers reported brandishing or using their weapon.

Guns raise havoc in civilian life when one partner is much more deeply attached to firearms than the other and/or handles them unsafely. When it belongs to a man who hasn't shared the fact of its existence, and the home contains children, the consequences can be significant.

Novelist Susan Straight married her high school sweetheart, Dwayne, a man who grew up with guns but who, he had once reassured her, would never have one in his own home. Without telling her, he changed his mind. "Thirteen years later, a shotgun fell on my head as I searched the closet for baby clothes, and my heart leapt in fear, like a small animal tethered to my breastbone. Dwayne hadn't told me about the shotgun, never mentioned we were armed. I suddenly imagined him holding the gun, cocking that baby. Shuck, shuck."

Dwayne had once been held at gunpoint by a criminal. "Bravery and size and loyalty don't match up with bullets," she conceded. She confronted him about the gun, and he insisted it was his job, as a good husband and father, to keep them safe in an increasingly dangerous city. But things grew more complicated. "I saw him fall in love with the guns themselves, the seduction of the barrels and oil and wooden stocks with carving, the power of caliber. He bought a handgun, then another, and spent hours comparing weapons with our next-door neighbor and my brother."

Straight was horrified for several reasons, including her husband's race; she feared what might happen to him, a black man, if he was pulled over while driving with a gun in the car. "Then I found a handgun on the dresser under a knit cap, within easy reach of our daughters. There was a gun in the camper when we took vacations, a gun in the glove compartment of the car. . . . We had three children, and suddenly he had ten guns. I didn't feel protected. I felt like I was living with a different man, one who didn't play basketball and read *Sports Illustrated* like before, [but] one who baked his guns clean and read *Guns & Ammo*. Our house and garage and vehicle, my spouse, carried instruments of death. The 9mm handgun on the dresser, shockingly heavy to me, could have been picked up, dropped, fired, by fingers smaller than mine. And I couldn't forgive that."[4]

The marriage ended.

A love of hunting and of guns creates a powerful and unresolvable ongoing tension in the marriage of New Orleans corporate lawyers Lynn Luker and Steve Williamson. They're a handsome and charming couple, professionally successful, socially well-connected, with a mansion in uptown New Orleans whose beveled-glass front doors glitter at night like diamonds. They have two children, Grace, nine, and Jack, thirteen.

Lynn, a tall, pale-skinned woman with a dramatic Louise Brooks bob of thick black hair, was raised in a Southern, upper-class household where guns and alcohol were regularly combined. Her father, when drunk, threatened a family member with a gun, she says. "See this scar?" she says, extending a delicate white hand to reveal a scar in the fold of flesh between her left thumb and forefinger. "I got that when I tried to wrestle a gun away from my father one night. He was trying to shoot my brother." Not surprisingly, Lynn's distaste for guns in her own home is visceral.

Steve, trim and boyish-looking despite a thick thatch of white hair, has been a hunter all his life. The front parlor of their turn-of-the-century home—which Luker dismisses as "the killing room"—contains a dozen stuffed and mounted trophies: duck, the head of a nine-hundred-pound elk, even antelope. Pillows are covered in zebra and springbok fur. A turkey fan, the spread tail-feathers, adorns one wood-paneled wall. In the summer of 2002, Steve took Jack on his first African safari, to hunt dik-dik, a small antelope.

"I've gone hunting," says Luker. But she abhors killing animals and is dubious of others' ability to handle weapons safely. "I think hunters are *personally* meticulous, but other people are much less careful." A hardheaded woman capable of ferocious argument, Lynn wept when she described a nephew who had threatened to commit suicide using one of her husband's guns.

"One of the things we go round and round about is security. My very strong wish is that all guns are locked up in a gun safe. I've found them on top of the refrigerator. I know Jack understands they're not toys, but I worry. The idea is not to test the children's judgment."

Steve wasn't sure how many guns he owned, guessing forty or fifty: ten to twelve handguns, twelve shotguns, and a number of rifles. "I have everything you can name," he said proudly. "Including a loaded .45 stashed where I can get to it if someone kicks in the door." New Orleans's population is 30 percent low-income, with desperately poor neighborhoods mere blocks from mansions, so his fear is not inconceivable. They have already had two cars stolen. "If people want to steal expensive stuff, this is where you come," he says. Public housing sits a few miles away from their landscaped back garden and swimming pool, and like those in many other neighborhoods in this crime-ridden city, the couple pays $500 a year to a private police patrol.

One day they opened their SUV after watching their kids' baseball game—and a man jumped out, carrying one of their guns kept in the car. He had gotten locked inside the vehicle and fled as soon as they opened the doors.

The two see the incident quite differently. Steve smoothly dismisses the danger: "It had a double-action slide with a safety." "Bullshit!" replies Lynn. "He could have shot our kids with our own gun." It's clear the issue won't disappear from this family, nor will it resolve itself—Steve's attachment to gun ownership is as deep and strong as his wife's fear and antipathy.

"It's a dangerous thing to have around," says Cassandra Sefelt, a fifty-seven-year-old widow who lives alone in a suburb of New Orleans, and who owns a .38 Smith & Wesson revolver that she keeps loaded and in her nightstand. She makes sure to keep it hidden from her thirty-three- and thirty-eight-year-old sons. Like many gun owners, she doesn't want novices near her firearms.

Others make it a point to teach their children and grandchildren as much as possible about guns, thereby, they hope, demystifying them and stripping firearms of any Hollywood-inspired glamour and allure. "We taught our grandkids right from the start," says Doris McClellan, a seventy-four-year-old writer and former schoolteacher who lives near Colorado City, Texas. "They're both excellent marksmen." But she is cautious with those unfamiliar with firearms: "When my niece's children come over, we keep them away from our guns. We won't let them have anything to do with them. Her kids are so curious. They don't know what they're doing." Rather than unload and reload their many firearms, a collection of long guns, pistols, and revolvers, McClellan hides them in locked rooms during such visits.

How many guns *does* she have? McClellan, a chatty and outgoing woman clams up. "I have no idea! But I wouldn't tell you if I did."

How guns are handled in the home—both literally and emotionally—affects the likelihood of an accident or suicide; wise gun owners make sure their children cannot reach their firearms or ammunition. Kathy McNeely, a thirty-nine-year-old police officer and firearms instructor in New Brighton, Minnesota, uses a Smith & Wesson 4046, which she leaves at work. She works as a resource officer with local elementary schools. Her husband is also a police officer and leaves his service weapon at home in a locked combination gun safe.

She says her children are comfortable around guns. "My youngest likes that his parents are police officers, although he has never asked to see the guns. Both kids have BB guns and have done some target shooting." Yet her mother was sufficiently uneasy having firearms in her home that she handed down several family-owned guns to her children.

McNeely is adamant about keeping her family safe. "I believe that guns should not be used as conversation pieces. I wouldn't allow anyone to handle my gun. Mental health and stability are factors—I'd remove guns from my home if someone living here were unstable. I've seen too many suicides with weapons that were available in the home."

When her family remodeled their home near Provo, Utah, Pat Nielsen said she was extra careful to keep all her guns in one room, safely away from her eleven-year-old son. "I always want to make sure they're away. We're in the process of getting a gun safe," she said. Both she and her husband have taken a hunter safety course and both feel confident their kids are safe. Guns are essential to her feeling of personal security, she said. She decided to get a gun for self-defense after hearing Texas legislator Suzanna Hupp speak on television about her parents' shooting death. "It made me want to get my concealed-carry weapons permit. If I was ever in that [kind of] situation, I'd want to be prepared."

Shyrelle Makin, eighteen, came to the 2002 Grand American national trapshooting competition in Vandalia, Ohio, from the small town of American Fork, thirty miles south of Salt Lake City. I heard about her within hours of my arrival, not so much because she had brought her fifteen-day-old son, Colby, to the event, but because she was an unmarried mother; the sport is extremely leery of any potentially bad press. He lay happily swaddled and shaded on a bench while she competed. A shooter for six years, it was her first visit to the national event, but she had shot trap, skeet, and clays and had hunted pheasant, elk, and deer, even dressing (gutting) them herself.

"I can remember shooting when I was five or six. We really didn't get into shotgun shooting until I was twelve." The baby's father, twenty-year-old Luke Phelps, said he also enjoys shooting.

"My whole family's into it, and so's his. We all shoot together." Makin said she shot even while eight months pregnant and was back at the range within weeks after giving birth. "It's just something I've been around all my life."

As much as guns' presence in a home can divide some families with fear and anxiety, they also bring many American families together, physically and emotionally, as they enjoy the camaraderie, skill-building, and the outdoors together. For them, shooting is one more shared pleasure, as unremarkable and as normal a shared activity as eating pizza or watching television.

Justin Trimback, of Pittsview, Alabama, came to the trapshooting championship with his two daughters, Autumn, fourteen, and Amanda, fifteen. "Their mother encourages it. It's a level playing field, where men and women compete equally." The girls learned to shoot when they were ten and thirteen, when the family lived in Melbourne, Florida, and joined a local gun club. "The retirees took to them like grandkids," he said.

Trimback had nothing but good things to say about his young daughters shooting. "It teaches them a lot about life, about winning and losing. If you want to succeed in life, you have to excel at it. They're both a lot more confident socially now." Both girls play softball, yet trapshooting remains a favorite for both. "I've never pushed them to do this."

Kay Clark, who runs one of the country's most respected gun-customizing firms, is adamant that her eighteen-year-old daughter carry a Smith & Wesson .38 Special with her when she makes the journey from her home in northwest Louisiana to her father's home in Oklahoma. "There's no way I'm going to let her drive that road without a gun in the car." The trip takes her across northeast Texas, a place where a car breakdown could easily strand her with no cell-phone service. Carrying a gun in the car is legal in her home state, although not in Texas or Oklahoma. Clark doesn't care. "I'd much rather have to deal with the law than to see her in a coffin." In that part of the United States, she adds, "I never saw a vehicle that didn't have a gun in it."

"We have two sons and live close to nature, and guns have become a natural part of the lifestyle, like the furniture," says one woman. "It's sort of an ego trip—now I beat my husband, sons, and all their male friends at target shooting and tease them. . . . We share it a lot with the men as a hobby and an ongoing rivalry. It puts us at an equal level, gives other women a basis for a relationship with the men in their lives. It makes us a closer family— we talk the same language. I don't feel excluded from my husband

and sons' lives. If I was busy doing the Donna Reed thing, I'd never see them."[5]

How safe is a home that contains a firearm? According to the Centers for Disease Control and Prevention, firearms are the third leading cause of death among American children, behind motor vehicle accidents and cancer.

Why are we still accepting this?

Most women become mothers, focused from birth or adoption onward on protecting and safeguarding their children whenever and wherever possible. They buy tamperproof bottles of aspirin, gate staircases, cover electrical outlets, and lock kitchen cabinets filled with deadly cleaning products. Yet teaching themselves and their children about guns—certainly in households where the object, if not the subject itself, is taboo—remains paramount. No matter your personal repugnance at owning one, teach your childen well. Ignorant children or teens treat guns with the carelessness they would a toy or action-figure accessory. Your child may only have seen a firearm on a television or a theater screen; especially for smaller children, it's simply not real. *They don't get it.* No matter how gory and brutal, video games allowing endless replays with every kill don't begin to convey the noise, smell, power—and finality—of the real thing.

Even if you personally sniff with distaste at the mention of firearms, as many women do, your child may not be safe from one in a friend's home, on the street, or at school. When it comes to guns, ignorance is not bliss—it usually proves deadly.

In 2000, eighty-six American children ages fourteen and under died from unintentional firearm-related injuries; children aged ten to fourteen accounted for 57 percent of them. In 2001, nearly fourteen hundred children fourteen and under were treated in hospital emergency rooms for unintentional firearm-related injuries, 21 percent of these severe enough to require hospitalization. The unintentional firearm injury rate among children fourteen and under—clearly a reflection of the 200 million guns in private hands—is *nine times higher* in the United States than in twenty-five other industrialized countries.

Most of these accidents happen when kids are alone and unsupervised—between 4 P.M. and 5 P.M., on weekends, during the summer months (June to August) and the holiday season (November to December). More than 70 percent of accidents involve handguns.

In parts of the country where guns are more prevalent, a child will more likely injure or kill himself accidentally—children living in the South have an unintentional shooting rate *five times* that of children in the Northeast. Rural areas have higher rates of gun ownership and see correspondingly higher rates of accidental injury. In rural areas, most children hurt themselves outdoors with a rifle or shotgun, while shootings in urban areas tend to happen indoors with handguns. Male children are far more likely to die in this fashion—80 percent of the total deaths—while black children ages fourteen and under are one and a half times more likely to die than white children.

If you have kids, and a gun, talk to them clearly about its power and what happens when it is fired. Even if you don't own a firearm or plan to, have the discussion anyway. Determine what they know, and what they *think* they know, about how firearms work. Pistols and revolvers function very differently, as do rifles and shotguns. Do you know—*do your kids know*—that a pistol whose magazine (a "clip" in movie parlance) is empty may remain loaded, a single cartridge left in its chamber?

If you have a gun, show them the difference between a loaded and unloaded firearm; if not, learn and explain it. Set and keep clear rules regarding a gun's use, with equally clear consequences for disobedience. Keep guns and ammunition locked away from their hands when adults are absent.

Unless deeply demystifed (and even then), guns are sexy, alluring tokens of adulthood. A child intent on getting and using a gun is a child at risk. A substance-abusing and/or depressed child in a home containing a firearm invites disaster. Ignoring your child's problems, no matter how intractable, won't protect you from the consequences of their actions. An uneducated child finding a firearm in your handbag or briefcase or basement or linen closet, certainly with no knowledge you even had one, is also at risk. The more you know your children, and their friends, the better your chances. The more attention you pay to storing your firearm and ammunition, the better are your chances of preventing this peculiarly American domestic tragedy.

One of President Bush's pet programs is Project ChildSafe, a national home-focused gun-safety initiative that started in 1999 with a $5-million grant from the Department of Justice. (Originally called Project HomeSafe, an initiative begun by the National Shooting Sports Foundation and funded by the gun industry, while governor of Texas, Bush made it one of his presidential campaign promises to expand it nationally.)

The project now receives $50 million, a congressional appropriation, to provide gun safety kits across the country. In its first two years, the group distributed 2.4 million kits—which include a cable gun-lock rendering a trigger inoperable and a safety brochure detailing how to safely handle and store a weapon. But that figure represents only *1 percent* of America's 200 million guns in civilian hands; the budget was boosted tenfold, but the kits will still reach only 10 percent of households containing a gun.

The initiative uses Mobile Education Units, seventeen-foot vans that roll into such public places as a parking lot at Wal-Mart (the nation's largest firearms retailer), a state fair, or a parade, reports Bill Brassard, managing director of Safety Programs for the National Shooting Sports Foundation, a gun industry lobby group. Fifteen trucks have now toured the United States, visiting eleven hundred communities in fifty states, from Oakland, California, Las Vegas; and Pittsburgh, Pennsylvania; to Orlando, Florida, and Augusta, Georgia. Materials are also distributed in Spanish.

Federal law prohibits a gun registry. Guns may change hands many times after their initial sale—which is the only sale that now requires a federal background check, and only in sales by federally licensed dealers. As a result, no one knows who owns guns, nor how safely they handle them. "You cannot legislate or regulate responsibility. That's where we come in." Brassard concedes that the cable lock won't work on all guns, nor will a pamphlet guarantee gun safety in the home. "It's an effort to raise awareness and to change behavior. Safety needs to be top-of-mind." Brassard hopes to expand the program by distributing DVDs or VHS videos on safety, perhaps even a quarterly email reminder. "People need to think of gun safety twenty-four/seven."

Women gun owners are of special concern, he says. Because they are "nontraditional" buyers (buying handguns for self-defense, not long guns for sports), "they don't access or want access to hunter safety programs." Many of these women live in urban or suburban areas, "a generation or two removed from learning about guns" from a family member who hunted or shot skeet, trap, or clays. For these women, education is paramount, and a reliable, affordable, and trustworthy source more elusive.

"If you need a loaded gun in your home, you have a lot of homework to do, a lot of training to do. You think your mission is accomplished because you just bought a gun? You're just beginning," cautions Brassard. Every gun owner must practice, and practice often, because "skills tend to deteriorate." Most important, says Brassard, anyone bringing a gun into their home needs "superior stress-management skills. If you can't rein in your emotions, don't own a firearm."

In October 1999 a new group, Common Sense About Kids and Guns, announced it would work to raise awareness of ways to reduce gun deaths and injuries among children and teenagers. The nonpartisan, nonprofit group is headed by Victoria Reggie Kennedy, cofounder and president, and wife of Senator Edward Kennedy (D-MA.) "We hope to make unloading, locking, and storing guns properly as automatic as buckling a safety belt," she said.

Members of the coalition group include the gun-industry groups National Shooting Sports Foundation and the Sporting Arms and

Ammunition Manufacturers Institute, the U.S. Conference of Mayors, and the American Academy of Pediatrics.

Nearly one-third of gun owners admit to storing their weapons unlocked and loaded—and at least a quarter of these gun owners have children under eighteen living at home, the group says. While some handguns are more difficult to fire, others have a lighter trigger, several studies showed, making it easy for a young child to fire one by accident.

Does teaching children safety work?

It depends whom you ask. "Gun safety programs aimed at young people do not work and have done little to reduce the toll of two thousand children killed or injured by guns in the United States every year," wrote Helen Rumbelow in the *Washington Post*.[6] Her story was based on a 2002 study, "Children, Youth and Gun Violence," a report written for the *Future of Children*, a journal of the David and Lucile Packard Foundation. The report says the best way to make guns "childproof" is to add built-in safety devices.

The National Shooting Sports Foundation, which represents gun manufacturers, disagreed: "The significant decline in youth deaths and injuries in the last decade indicates that gun safety education programs are working. From 1993 to 1998, the death rate from firearms for youths under twenty declined *nearly 50 percent*, according to the National Center for Health Statistics, a nonpartisan government agency."

Michael D. Barnes, president of the Brady Center and the Brady Campaign (formerly Handgun Control Inc.), says the group abandoned its child education program because research showed it wasn't working.

"Boys aged ten to nineteen have the highest gun-accident death rate. . . . I am not sure I would own a gun if I had teenagers," warns Paxton Quigley, who has taught thousands of women to shoot and thinks every woman should own a gun.[7]

Whatever decision you make about keeping a gun in a home

where there are children, *know the law*—at least eighteen states have enacted child-access-prevention laws, which hold adults criminally liable for failure either to store loaded firearms in a place inaccessible to children or to use safety devices to lock guns. Nine states and several local jurisdictions have passed laws and ordinances requiring a gun lock with the purchase of every handgun.

Chapter 7
A Gun for Fun

————◆►≺×≻◄◆————

AMERICANS UNFAMILIAR WITH FIREARMS OFTEN ASSOCIATE THEM immediately and primarily with crime and violence, not pleasure. Guns used for sport shooting? Most think first, if not exclusively, of hunting—not of skeet, clays, or trap, disciplines that demand skill in hitting fast-moving, inanimate clay targets, not in killing, skinning, and eviscerating bird or beast. Single-action cowboy shooting requires quick reflexes, as do pistol shooting, biathlon, and other sports involving firearms.

These nonviolent activities place women on a level playing field with men. At the range, men and women compete not on the basis of comparative strength or speed, but calm, focus, aim, skill, and practice. Women shooters, everyone agrees, enjoy several inherent advantages: they're more willing to be coached and are more able to separate their egos from a weak result so they stay calmer (which ups their total scores). Because many arrive as total neophytes, they're eager to be taught, while men, even young boys, often think they know it all, frustrating instructors and coaches, who first have to strip them of dangerous habits before teaching them anew.

Yet the shooting sports, apart from specialty cable channels and sports or shooting magazines, receive virtually no mass media coverage, which perpetuates their low profile—you can't admire or even consider trying an activity you've never seen or heard of.

Women who shoot for pleasure or sport remain virtually invisible in the popular media. Interviewed for usatoday.com, Carol Oyster, coauthor of *Gun Women*, was asked by a listener from Dallas, Texas, how gun clubs and manufacturers could "get the word out" that women train and shoot?

"I think the ideal thing would be for the media to give the safe and appropriate use of firearms more attention. An example would be that the very first gold medal in the 1998 Olympics was won by an American woman in the shooting sports. That has only been represented by the gun-affiliated media; it certainly wasn't on NBC! I suspect that if the medal had been won in another sport, the networks would have been crowing about the U.S. taking the first gold."

"The shooting public has brought these problems on themselves," says Tom King, president of the New York State Rifle and Pistol Association. "Gunners are on the defensive. The sport is hidden, unknown, male. It's held in places that are private and isolated.

"The average club member is well educated and sees shooting as a release from daily pressures. It's something relaxing. But they've allowed themselves to become marginalized [from public debate] because we wanted it that way."

Enthusiasts who hope to keep their sports quiet and exclusive instead often end up, metaphorically speaking, shooting themselves in the foot. They end up looking paranoid, elitist, or just plain weird. What devotees of another sport are so routinely, casually stigmatized? You have avid golfers, tennis buffs, ski bums, yachties—and gun nuts.

The salvation of the shooting sports—at least in less gun-friendly states such as New York—lies in the elegant, upscale outdoors game of sporting clays, King says. "It's golf with a gun. It's about the gentler aspects of the sport."

A product of the English shooting sports establishment begun several decades ago, sporting clays consists of a number of shooting stations laid out in a loop or circuit through which each shooter passes. Each station passes a natural landscape to present the shooter with a different shooting scenario. Targets are thrown as singles or in pairs, simulating different hunting situations—such as ducks passing high overhead, teal springing straight up from the underbrush, quail or pheasant being flushed from cover. When the targets are called for, the shooter, who starts with the shotgun loaded but off the shoulder, is allowed one shot at each target. Because the shot distances vary on a given course from close to far, shotguns with interchangeable choke tubes are popular, allowing the shooter to match the choke to the shot just as a golfer matches the right club to the shot.[1] An estimated 326,000 women participated in clays in 1998, a 51 percent increase from 1990 to 1997.[2]

Skeet, from the Swedish word for "shoot," is an American invention dating from the early 1900s. The skeet field is laid out in a wide arc with eight shooting stations; squads of five shooters each fire from one station before rotating to the next, taking one shot at each target during a round of twenty-five birds. Skeet targets are thrown as a mix of singles and doubles from the two houses located at each side of the field; the targets tend to cross more in front of the shooter rather than move away from them, as in trap. Skeet has been a part of the modern Olympic program since 1968.[3] In 1998, about 343,000 women participated in trap and skeet—a decrease of 22 percent since 1990 from 437,000.[4]

Chloe Polemis, a senior at New York University, jokes that she is "the only New York City private-school girl who got a shotgun for her sixteenth birthday," a $1,500 20-gauge Beretta over and under. A passionate skeet shooter, Polemis first picked up a gun when she was twelve, accompanying her father, who went trap-shooting every Sunday morning in upstate New York. "My father always encouraged me to try shooting, but for the first two years I felt completely uncomfortable. It took two years before I actually started to shoot. I was fourteen, and I felt like it legitimized me in the eyes of many of the people in the group. Whereas I had been just the little girl who hung around while all the men shot, now I was the kid outshooting many of the men."

She discovered that she loved it. "It was empowering, therapeutic, exciting, but most of all it was fun. It gave me a ritual, something different that I was good at, something to look forward to on Sundays. Plus it gave me time with my father and a chance to get to know all of these other people."

"As much as I enjoy trap, skeet gave me more of a challenge. Plus, I love actually going out and trekking around, rather than just standing in a line with six other shooters. Skeet is more interactive, less passive. In a large group, it tends to be very social. When my father and I go, it's more instructional."

A city girl, Polemis also loves that shooting takes her outdoors. "We usually go in the fall, which in upstate New York is the most beautiful thing in the entire world. You're in the woods, it smells like dirt and leaves, and you get that nice chill in the air."

Polemis says she knows of no other women who shoot skeet and is amused by the reactions it provokes. "Initially, men are taken aback by the fact that I shoot, but once they get over the initial shock, they tend to think it's interesting or cool. It's definitely a conversation-starter."

Trap dates back to nineteenth-century England and originally used live birds held in wooden or wire traps as the targets. The birds were released on call by pulling a rope to free them (which is why modern shooters still use the archaic word *trap* [for round disks that shatter when hit] and a microphone into which the shooter says "Pull" to initiate the target's release). Live birds have been replaced by breakable disks thrown away from the shooter either in singles or doubles from a small machine located in a small house or bunker near ground level in the center of the field.

In American trap, the targets are fired at by squads of five shooters rotating through five shooting stations arranged side by side in a fan. Each shooter fires one shot at each target, then moves on to the next station, to complete a round of twenty-five targets. Shooters stand as close as sixteen yards to as far back as twenty-seven yards; the targets are shot to a height of fifty yards in singles or forty-five yards in doubles. In International or Olympic-style events, they are thrown at much higher speeds, over much wider angles, and to much greater distances. International trap has been a part of the modern Olympics since 1900; double trap was added in 1996.[5]

Kim Rhode, the Olympic gold medalist at the 1996 games—the youngest winner ever—is a tiny, slim blonde who shoots an average of one thousand rounds a day during eight to nine hours of training. "Anyone who tells you they don't miss, lies," she told a group of trap enthusiasts in August 2002 at the Grand American, the annual international championships held in Vandalia, Ohio, that drew thirty-one hundred shooters.

A premed student in California, Rhode was in training for the 2004 Olympics when we met. Easygoing and down-to-earth, she empathized with the fans clustering around her that afternoon. "It's a very frustrating game. One little slip of the mind, one little mistake, and it's all over." Renee Supancheck, an eighteen-year-old from David City, Nebraska, was brave enough to step forward for a little one-on-one help in front of the crowd. "It made me nervous, but it was nice to have someone coach me," she said. Rhode happily showed anyone who wanted to see them the gold medal on its dark green ribbon and her bronze medal on a turquoise ribbon.

Kyndra Hogan, a slim, petite, blond twenty-two-year-old from Springfield, Oregon, is the second-best trapshooter in the United States; I met her in August 2002 at the Grand American. Like many American women who take up the shooting sports, Hogan began by hunting with her father. She was eight the first time she shot and began competing at eleven. Even as a little girl, guns were as unremarkable and amusing to her as a Game Boy or Barbie doll. "We had fake little guns to learn gun safety," she recalls affectionately. She'd head out to the duck blinds as early as 3 A.M. to set up decoys and "just hang out with Dad."

When Hogan took hunter-safety programs, she knew few other girls participating. "My friends thought it was interesting. I have a friend who's a vegetarian, but she understands what I do."

Echoing women of all ages who shoot, Hogan says some men are nonplussed by her competence with firearms. "It can be intimidating to guys, especially if you can beat them!" Her skill has taken her to competitions around the world, from Peru to Egypt.

Hogan treasures her Perazzi MX 2000, a shotgun worth about $15,000. "Shooting really gets into your blood. It's fun. You meet a lot of people. You create a network that's hard to leave." She takes great pride in her achievement with guns. "I'm representing my country. Most people are rather positive and open about it—I'm shooting for them. It's an Olympic sport. How can you not support an Olympic sport?"

She competes in double trap, in which only one spot is available on the Olympic team, competing with five other women for the opportunity. While "it's designed to be a very mental game," Hogan also trains lifting weights and doing cardiovascular workouts.

Nursing student Nancy Johnson won the first-ever U.S. gold medal for small-bore rifle shooting at the Sydney Olympic Games in 2000. "Shooting is what gave me the ability to find out what I was capable of, and to focus and maintain my self-discipline."[6]

Patricia Black, a trim sixty-three-year-old with short blond hair from Fairborn, Ohio, was competing in Vandalia wearing a floral T-shirt, aqua vest, white leather gloves, and diamond studs. For her, shooting was simply the latest of her many athletic pursuits. "I'd always been a sportswoman, and it was something I wanted to do." She'd enjoyed basketball, softball, and bowling. "Shooting is a fun sport. It's addictive."

We spoke as she rested between rounds. "You don't want to know the score. I haven't been shooting much," she joked. Black managed a gun club for five years, ironically allowing her no time to practice, hitting perhaps three thousand targets in three years. "Some people do that in a month." Her first husband taught her to shoot in 1965; from 1977 to 1987 she worked at the Grand American every summer releasing the clay targets. "They were long, hard hours," she recalls—at $1.75 an hour. She met her second husband at a gun club.

* * *

Like the bubbles in a glass of Veuve Clicquot, issues of wealth and social class quickly rise to the surface of American gun ownership, whether for self-defense or pleasure. The shooting sports, especially, like other high-end sports such as golf and yachting, demand a significant time commitment to gain proficiency (for which you need leisure time), decent equipment (for which you need money), and safe, comfortable, private, and spacious facilities for practicing (for which you need easy access to a suburban or country range).

Outside the world of gun ownership, and sometimes within it, handguns are most often associated with the urban, grim, déclassé, bloodstained world of crime and self-defense. While some handgun owners eagerly spend their evenings and weekends practicing quick reloading and defensive skills (and some compete in speed/kill competitions), the ugly reality of shooting another human isn't what one usually associates with exquisitely detailed $80,000 Perazzi, J. Purdey & Son, or Holland & Holland custommade rifles and shotguns.

The shooting sports instead offer the aristocratic comforts of privacy and luxury. One private club on Long Island, New York, is so silently exclusive it immediately ejects any member who mentions it to a journalist; members come from some of the country's oldest and wealthiest families. Hunters congregate on large private estates, theirs or others', vacationing on elegant, commercially owned hunting ranches in Argentina, Texas, Mexico, or Europe with others who can afford to spend $5,000 and up for a few days' fresh air and a chance to test their skills. Those selling to this elite market know to target it carefully. "Refinement still comes with a double-barreled name," says one advertisement for Holland & Holland in *New York* magazine. The 169-year-old British firm has operated a retail store in a five-story town house on Manhattan's Fifty-seventh Street, in a row of high-end luxury stores, since 1996. In addition to guns—one of which, the 577 NE Royal Deluxe Double Rifle 25″, sells for $140,000—the store has an art gallery and sells books, luggage, and clothing.

In 1989, Holland & Holland, a private company, was bought by another luxury brand name, Chanel Ltd., the UK affiliate of the French apparel, cosmetics, and perfume company, for $16.89 million. The previous year Holland & Holland had shown pretax profits of $444,850 on sales of $7.9 million. "We are buying a traditional British company with fine-quality products," said Tim Coles, managing director of Chanel Ltd. "It just so happens those products are guns."[7]

At the World Side-by-Side Championships in Millbrook, a Hudson Valley weekend enclave for wealthy Manhattanites, gun enthusiasts spared "no expense to realize an idealized vision of the great era of game-hunting and bird-shooting that ended with the First World War. In the world of shooting, what separates the Land Rover gentry from the Dodge dudes is the choice of weapon. Here, it's a custom-made side-by-side shotgun, preferably crafted in the turn-of-the-century style with curved hammers reminiscent of a flintlock and detailed hand engraving. The best guns are British models—new or old—that cost anywhere in the five figures. This fall weekend, the elite British gunmaker Purdey casually takes an order at its booth for a pair of shotguns; a nice round $100,000 makes the deal worth the trip from London."[8]

It's a long way from public pistol ranges, some of them grim, cramped, and grimy, where cops and security guards and fearful civilians spend hours honing their skills on paper targets, some of which portray snarling male thugs. A range is open to anyone who can afford to join, paying usually $400 to $600 a year; anyone with a pistol permit can take the stall next to you.

"There is definitely a class division in the attitudes of Americans when it comes to guns," says skeet shooter Chloe Polemis. "Most people assume gun owners are a paranoid, white, rural fringe element. I personally don't fall into that category and wouldn't want to be grouped into it. It's a shame that more people don't realize the many different activities and people that are involved in guns and shooting."

Shooting skeet, trap, or clays, or hunting for small game such as pheasant, turkey, or grouse, places participants in the outdoors, usually surrounded by others of their economic or social class. Some gun manufacturers carefully nurture this image of luxury and tradition, European elegance and history, as much as the weapon they design and sell. A glossy advertising supplement, added in the fall of 2002 to six upscale Hearst magazines, including *Town & Country* and the women's magazines *Marie Claire* and *Harper's Bazaar,* included a fresh spin on a familiar Italian-designer name, Beretta.

Describing their new clothing line, the writer might have been limning the guns' appeal: "Beretta marries aristocratic chic with country ruggedness." The company, founded in 1526, is the oldest weapons manufacturer in Italy, their trademark the Beretta 92FS pistol (used by the American armed forces and federal agents). American film heroes—Mel Gibson in *Lethal Weapon* and Tom Cruise in *Minority Report*—carry Berettas. In 1994, the company opened a store on Madison Avenue, home of some of the toniest and pricest shopping in the United States.

"We immediately realized there was an international clientele eager for Beretta products," says Franco Gussalli Beretta, the company's managing director. The store expanded from its initial stock of hunting rifles and hunting attire to clothing, lamps, glasses, towels, robes, and books. In 1997, a second store opened in Dallas, at Highlands Park Village. Beretta says Madonna and her husband, Guy Ritchie, are clients. Big bankers in both Europe and the United States are among Beretta's most devoted clients, and hunting offers as much a chance to enjoy the sport as for business networking.[9]

The autumn 2002 cover of *The Double Gun Journal,* which has won six National Magazine Awards, less resembles a magazine than a private nineteenth-century journal, its thick brown cover mimicking leather, a detailed, gold-embossed dog portrait in the center. Published quarterly, it costs $12.95 an issue. Every page is edged with a gold border, including the advertisements. The cover of *Gray's Sporting Journal,* $6.95 an issue, for November/December 2002 was equally upscale, a painting of an African landscape.

For a while, one wealthy, well-known American—Madonna—enjoyed pheasant shooting, a typical pastime for upper-class Britons with large private estates; hers, Ashcombe, in Wiltshire, is worth $15 million. She initially embraced the sport, but later termed it "barbaric," apparently disappointing her British husband, Guy Ritchie. "Guy thinks it's ridiculous," a friend told the *Daily Mail*. "He thinks it's mad to own such a beautiful estate and not be allowed to shoot there."[10]

Like many female hunters, Madonna had savored the peace and quiet of the outdoors—perhaps more than the shooting itself. "When you're shooting, you are standing in the forest for really long periods of time, so you end up looking at the leaves and the sky and the trees and you have a lot of time to meditate," she told BBC Radio One. "I eat birds. You have more of a respect for the things you eat when you go through, or see, the process of killing them. . . . I like knowing what I'm eating, and knowing the process."

Rachel Lussier, a thirty-seven-year-old graphic artist in Stamford, Connecticut, has been an avid biathlete—a summer sport that combines alternating events of running and shooting—for more than fifteen years. "It is one sport where men and women are nearly physically equal and struggle with the exact same issues of discipline, mental concentration, and focus. It's very intriguing."

She grew up in Michigan, in a large family of six girls and three boys. "My dad and brothers would sometimes go hunting in the fall. I never really had any great desire to participate in that activity. Hunting was definitely more of a male-oriented activity.

"All of the nine children in the family had a healthy respect towards firearms and how they should and shouldn't be used. Mom, in general, did not take issue with having rifles in the house. She never felt she had to worry about us kids getting into them. She also grew up in a household where hunting was a relatively common event. There were no more than three to five rifles in our household that I can recall while growing up, .22s and shotguns primarily."

Lussier was always athletic, playing softball as a child. She began running cross-country in high school, doing biathlons in her midtwenties. "It was an opportunity to call upon my hand-eye coordination skills again in a sports event. It was like I had missed using that ability from my very early years playing softball. After doing my first biathlon, I was hooked. The sport added a completely new set of dimensions and complexity to the footraces that I was accustomed to. Running involves general motor skills, while shooting requires fine motor skills—trying to find a balance between the two is a challenge."

She was surprised, not happily, to discover how divisive shooting is, even for sport. She bristled at having to join the National Rifle Association to join her local range for a place to practice with her $1,600 rifle; her dues help the small range defray the high cost of insurance. She's quick to distance herself from the NRA's political activities. But she's equally dismayed by the disdain she often encounters, especially from other women, for her new, beloved sport.

"Most women, friends and family alike, tend to have a negative reaction. Maybe women are cautious and fearful because they have been segregated historically from guns and the gun culture. Somehow the violent connotation of guns comes foremost in most people's minds, especially women. I don't even think they are aware that they are automatically assuming something negative.

"Men tend to respond with surprise, respect, and even admiration. My husband thought it was kind of cool."

And because gun ownership is so politically divisive, finding sponsors for biathlons is virtually impossible, she says. "Potential sponsors just don't want to go near the issue, partly out of fear, partly out of ignorance. Misconceptions [about guns] and the fear of not being politically correct are very intertwined." A race official told her several companies had refused to associate their products with the sport.

"In Germany, winter biathlon is a state-supported event! People over there are crazy for the sport, and the state will purchase TV time so that the public can view it—kind of like televising the World Series here!"

Despite her enthusiasm, Lussier easily admits her sport can be risky.

"When I purchased the rifle, it felt like I had a personal responsibility beyond just the investment that I had just made. When I went to compete in my first biathlon, I really had no shooting experience whatsoever. The USBA and the race organizers are very thorough about getting new people started. Each first-time participant is required to go through a training and safety course that is conducted before each race, which not only emphasizes the importance of safety and the power of a firearm, but also gives the first-timer a chance to shoot, receive a little coaching, and get better oriented to the layout of the race and what to expect.

"What struck me, and still makes an impression on me, is how safety-oriented and responsible the race officials were. I see this same level of commitment from some of the guys at the range where I shoot."

Lussier thinks sports shooters, especially, get a bad rap, often unfairly. "For the most part, most experienced shooters that I have encountered are quite responsible and respectful of the power of a firearm. I don't know why I should be so surprised at the fact that there are a lot of responsible shooters out there. Was I influenced to think that all gun owners take unnecessary risks? Where did that come from?"

She wishes there were more evenhanded conversations about guns in America. "I think education starts to dispel the myths and romance about guns and provides people and kids with practical understanding and respect for firearms. There seem to be a lot of public misconceptions about people who own guns and shoot. Why do most of the nonshooting public think gun owners are a bunch of yahoos like a scene out of *Deliverance*?"

In fact, says Lussier, her local shooting community "is quite diverse—policemen, contractors, lawyers, professionals. All pretty nice guys, real characters! I am one of just a few women at the shooting club, and now that most of the guys are pretty comfortable with me, it's like being a fly on the wall in a men's club."

For Beth Livingston, a married, thirty-nine-year-old mother of two in Bozeman, Montana, winter biathlon is her love. "Shooting guns and skiing: How much more fun can it get?" Livingston, who is paraplegic, requiring her to sit-ski, returned to skiing in 1990, a year after her accident. She did her first Paralympics at Salt Lake City in 2002, the first time the United States fielded a team in that sport, with five shooters. An avid hunter, Livingston had shot a fourteen-point elk a few months before competing. "I've always loved shooting and I'm a crack shot," she says.[11]

Custom-gun maker Kay Clark teaches and competes in IPSC, also known as run and gun, a form of pistol shooting originally developed for military training. "It's pretty physical. You might have to climb a wall or jump a fence. We turned it into a sport. It's practical and it's fun." Handgun target-shooting is also popular among American women; in 1998, 3,138,000 participated, a 19 percent increase over 1989 figures.[12] Rifle target shooters numbered 1,956,000 in 1998.[13]

Beverly Ruddock, assistant sales manager at Manhattan's Beretta store, travels most weekends to upstate New York, her revolvers and rifle safely stowed in her car—along with her petticoats. For four years, she's enjoyed the sport of single-action cowboy shooting, a sport in which everyone wears period clothes and takes an alias; born in Birmingham, England, she's "English Bev." A trim beauty in her midforties, at work she's the picture of metropolitan chic. Her eyes light up as she describes her sport, the latest in a long line she's tried, after field hockey, basketball, soccer, and javelin. The sport involves shooting at targets using revolvers, a shotgun, and a rifle. Shooters form into "posses" to compete against one another. "It's a challenge to switch from revolvers to shotgun and rifle. The sighting is different, the stance is different, the distances are different." She discovered the sport through her fiancé, now her husband; together they drive long distances to compete with shooters of all ages and income levels. It is, she says frankly, one of the most populist and down-to-earth of the shooting sports, and one attracting a wide range of participants. Some participants she's met hunt because they need the food to feed their families.

Hunting

American women have been hunting, and enjoying it, for centuries.

"I started to head to a little spring to get water for my coffee when I saw a couple of jack rabbits playing, so I went back for my little shotgun. I shot one of the rabbits, so I felt like Leatherstocking because I had killed but one when I might have gotten two. It was fat and young and it was but the work of a moment to dress it and hang it up on a tree," wrote Elinor Pruitt Stewart on September 28, 1909, from her homestead in Burnt Fork, Wyoming.

Today more than a million women hunt in the United States, about 9 percent of the nation's 14 million hunters, up from 6 percent in 1950. Women have become the fastest-growing group of hunters, a surge that has affected "everything from the design and marketing of guns and hunting apparel to the way couples get along with each other—or quarrel—during deer-hunting season."[14]

Yet a woman willing to kill is someone who many others, especially women, find disturbing, says Mary Zeiss Stange, chair of the women's studies department at Skidmore, an avid hunter and author of *Woman the Hunter*.

"To the extent that hunting has served both patriarchy and feminism as a root metaphor for men's activity in the world, Woman the Hunter is a necessarily disruptive figure. She upsets the equilibrium of the conventional interpretations of both sides. This no doubt helps to account for the virtual invisibility of women hunters in most popular literature (positive and negative) about hunting and in the various strains of feminist discourse."

Since female hunters, like men, are aggressive and kill animals, argues Stange, they challenge traditional ecofeminist principles of women's identity with nature, "their 'innate' passivity and nonviolence."[15]

Traditionally women were taught to hunt, as men were, by their male relatives. Today, many women enter the sport through Becoming an Outdoorswoman (BOW), a national organization founded in 1991 in Wisconsin to help women of all ages become competent and comfortable in the outdoors. BOW was conceived by Dr. Christine L. Thomas, a natural resources professor at the University of Wisconsin at Stevens Point; women, she found, were less squeamish about hunting than simply mystified. "We find most of the perceived barriers boil down to 'How do I do it?' "[16]

"Real Men Love Outdoors Women" reads the bumper sticker on Dawn Fairling's bulletin board. Fairling, a state wildlife educator in New Castle, Delaware, visits schools to enlist girls into the pleasures of shooting and hunting. "There are more and more single-parent households these days, so we want women to discover the old male traditions in which you and your kid can be together in the woods." In the years 1997 to 2002, the BOW program in Delaware licensed seven hundred women to hunt. "Before, the number was zero," she says.[17]

Kathy Andrews is the Illinois coordinator for the state's ten-year-old program. At two weekend retreats each year, the Illinois BOW program offers women courses in hunting, fishing, and other outdoor activities such as wilderness camping. Hundreds of women have taken part over the years. "We've had women eighteen to seventy-five participating," says Andrews. "One woman walked away from the weekend saying, 'You've changed my life.' And other women feel the same way. And that's how it grows."

Those horrified by the idea of women hunting—shooting, killing, gutting, and enjoying it—are even more dismayed by the natural outgrowth of their interest, the next generation. "We've found that a lot of our women are in our program because they want more confidence so they can teach their kids about outdoor activities," says Andrews. "If a woman understands the concepts behind hunting and gains confidence and experience, she'll bring kids into it."[18]

For New Orleans housewife Maurer Culpeper, hunting and shooting have been a lifelong pursuit and pleasure. She's shot squirrels, ducks, rabbits, and every year makes several trips out of state. In 2002, she and her husband, a lawyer, traveled to Mexico to hunt.

She uses shotguns, either 12-gauge for duck or 28-gauge for quail. "I like to be out in nature, basically. It's something my husband and I have done for a quarter of a century." Her son hunts, but not her daughter. "It's something she's not interested in. I was always a tomboy. It's something I did with my father and grandfather. It's a family tradition."

Culpeper fired her first gun when she was three: "I've been at it ever since." Like many women who try shooting long guns, her first experiences were painful and uncomfortable thanks to the recoil and too big guns. "Only in the late eighties did I get a gun that fit me properly." Culpeper and her husband love shooting clays, heading out to Goodby, Louisiana, once a week to practice. "It helps you sharpen your shooting skills and gives you a better sense of range. When you shoot clay targets, you know what killing power your gun has. I like to retrieve [a dead bird], not wound." Unlike skeet or trap, clays are meant to simulate a hunting situation, moving at the speed and distance of a live bird.

As much as Culpeper loves to shoot, she finds it a predominantly male sport. "Most of my friends are male. There aren't as many women as I would like to see. Shooting is a great sport because it doesn't matter how big or how athletic you are. It's nice to be able to compete on an equal footing."

"For me, it's not a macho thing, it's bonding time," says Katherine A. Fiduccia, a forty-two-year-old freelance videotape editor in Warwick, New York, who took up hunting after she met the man she later married, a longtime outdoorsman.[19]

For Laurie Pettigrew, a forty-seven-year-old coordinator for New Jersey's workshops for prospective outdoorswomen, hunting is about far more than killing animals. "The point for me, and I think for most women, is not to kill. There are people out there and that's why they do it, they want this big trophy animal, but I think for most people it's being out there, being a part of your surroundings. I love to be able to go out in the woods and sit quietly and watch what's going on. When you come home without anything, it's still not a bad day."[20]

Kate Gittinger, a thirty nine-year-old accountant in Hooksett, New Hampshire, hunts deer, turkey, and snowshoe rabbits "at every opportunity." Gittinger owns several handguns, a muzzle-loader, a rifle, and a shotgun; she learned to shoot trap at the age of ten from a local male family friend and was the only woman in her hunter-safety class. She hunts "almost every day from September to December." Up an hour before daylight, she suits up in camouflage and positions herself either in a tree stand or at the base of a large tree. "I never cease to be amazed at the changing colors and moods of the woods. I'm always at peace there. The chipmunks and squirrels are always busy, the owls and hawks going about their business. It's fascinating to watch!" Although she comes from a nonhunting background, family and friends are supportive of her sport. "They enjoy listening to the passion in my voice as I tell tales. My best friend is a vegetarian, pleased I can do anything I care to."

For Erin Hunter, a forty-one-year-old general contractor in Vermont, hunting has been a part of her life since her late twenties. She grew up in a hunting family and her father taught her to shoot when she was young. She owns several rifles and shotguns, which she has used to hunt bear, deer, and turkey. She has hunted elk in Montana. "It is such amazing country out there. Plus they are great eating! Same with caribou. The area is so different and the style of hunting unique to the animal. The appeal is both in the wildness—you don't see caribou and elk in the suburbs—and the uniqueness of the animal.

"How often do I hunt? As often as I can. I hunt in Vermont and try to hunt in New York at my brother-in-law's. Most, if not all, of my guns were chosen for hunting. Originally, I figured I would have one gun so I wanted something all-around. I chose the .30-'06 because it is sufficient for most big game and the bullets are readily available when traveling. I had one custom-made for me. With it I've taken several deer, a bear, a turkey in Virginia, a groundhog, and a muskrat."

Like every sport, hunting has its arcane traditions and jargon, specialized clothing and gear, and a shared culture in which the lucky few win special bragging rights. A woman bagging a sample sale pair of Manolos couldn't be any happier than Mary Zeiss Stange the day she finally won "treasure, in the form of an either-sex elk permit for Montana's hunting district 622. Annually, sixteen hundred hunters applied for these nontransferable permits, of which a mere thirty were issued via lottery. I had hit the jackpot."[21] The rarity and exclusivity of certain permits, and the skill, determination, practice, and travel across difficult terrain to use them, combine to make hunting a powerfully attractive sport to women, as it has been for centuries to men.

Ask Mollie VanDevender of Jackson, Mississippi, a forty-eight-year-old, size-2 brunette who was, in 1975, Miss Mississippi. She proudly displays her trophies of a lion, a leopard, and a zebra in her custom-built home, so elegant it was featured in the June 2002 issue of *House Beautiful*. While her designer included such traditional touches as striped pale pink walls, a tufted velvet ottoman, and silk lampshades, he also incorporated her sport, with a compass stained into the limestone entrance floor pointing to four painted panels depicting the four continents on which she hunts. In the sunroom, with its black-and-white-striped tented ceiling and black-and-white tile floor, a black-and-white zebra head (which she shot in Tanzania) seems equally at home as the huge fern towering in a corner.

She grew up in a family of four girls and never hunted, "although I was from a country town in Mississippi." Motherhood did it. "It was after my third child was born. I needed an outlet! It was pretty busy at my house," she says wryly. She began by going duck hunting with her husband, getting up at dawn and sitting in a duck blind with him. "I was so intrigued by the woods waking up in the morning, the birds and the light and the silence. The peace-fulness of it all! It just evolved after that."

After buying two hunting camps, VanDevender learned from a biologist that their land would only sustain a limited number of healthy deer. "I was able to rationalize shooting because of that." Within a few years, VanDevender took her new skills to Africa, where she has since shot between twenty and thirty species, all of which she has brought home as trophies.

"I became very passionate about hunting. I'm very competi-tive," she says, so much so that, even traveling on safari with her husband, sister, and sons, she prefers to shoot alone, with only her trackers, skinners, and professional hunter beside her. "We all like to get our own game."

She's also obsessive about tracking game she has wounded but not killed, once following an antelope for six hours, which she never found. She won't kill any endangered species and must apply for permission from wildlife authorities to bring home what-ever trophies she gets. Permits are costly, up to $5,000 for a lion permit that allowed her to kill one cat.

She got hers one golden afternoon in Tanzania. "It was just the most beautiful setting, the tall, golden grass, the sun setting—all monochromatic." She shot the feline, high-fived her trackers with excitement, and went closer to inspect her kill. She burst into tears. "Oh, my gosh, he was so beautiful! He was so huge. His paw was twice as big as my hand." Bagging a lion, a menace to cattle in the area, was cause for great celebration, she discovered; as their truck returned to camp, the trackers sang a triumphal song signaling their achievement, and VanDevender was hoisted in a chair and paraded around the camp.

The roller coaster of emotion is one she has felt many times when hunting: "When you shoot a magnificent animal, you're just overwhelmed." She has bagged three of the Big Five (leopard, lion, and Cape buffalo) and looks forward to the final two, an ele-phant and a white rhino. Hunting, she says, offers an extraordi-nary array of pleasures: the thrill of tracking, the landscape's beauty, the stamina required to sit still and quiet for up to twelve hours in a blind, the camaraderie of friends and family, the rustic nostalgia of drying her hair by the heat of a campfire and living in tents without electricity, the sheer adrenaline rush of sighting and shooting a camouflaged or racing beast.

She knows others might find her passion repugnant, and so she rarely mentions or discusses it.

"It's in my soul," she says simply. "I don't know how it got there."

Chapter 8
In the Line of Fire

◆─❖─◆

The DINING ROOM AT THE PENINSULA HOTEL IN MIDTOWN Manhattan was quiet that bright, clear morning as New York City mayor Rudolph Giuliani sat down for a meeting with friend and colleague William Simon. They had just begun eating breakfast, two of the mayor's bodyguards, as usual, sitting a few tables away. "We were saying it was such a beautiful day we should play hooky and go shoot some golf," recalls Patty Varone, for nine years Giuliani's primary bodyguard.

Her cell phone rang. She hated to interrupt her boss.

She walked over to their table, leaned low, and quietly began explaining the situation to Denny Young, the mayor's right-hand man. Giuliani stopped his conversation.

"What?" asked the mayor. "What happened?"

She hesitated for a second, loath to interrupt. "A plane has flown into the World Trade Center, sir."

Ask Varone, a tall, redheaded, husky-voiced detective first class, what she remembers of 9/11, and she shakes her head.

"What *don't* I remember?"

Giuliani's motorcade speeding down Fifth Avenue, Varone, as always, sitting in the mayor's limousine, their advance man already on the scene, the backup car, with two more detectives, close behind. Doctors standing expectantly by their gurneys outside St. Vincent's Hospital.

Their cell phones, already, weren't working properly, and she feared the worst—had her partner, the advance man, been killed?

The second plane hit as they were en route. They pulled up to the site.

"It's crashing all around us. It was raining garbage from the sky—paper, glass, debris. People were hanging out the windows screaming. Flames are shooting out of the building." All around them, the sickening, unforgettable thud of bodies hitting pavement.

Was anywhere safe? Like all dignitaries with police protection, the mayor normally only entered buildings after they had been checked and secured—none here had. "We were worried that the other buildings were rigged to explode. We knew we were under attack. We couldn't just rush him into 7 World Trade because we didn't know if it was secure."

Her job, as always, was to protect the mayor's life, something—for once—Varone considered highly unlikely. "I really didn't think we were going to survive that day. There was so much going on all around us. There were too many people. I was afraid that we weren't going to be able to do our job."

As Giuliani took command, talking to five people at once, including the White House, the first tower came down. They had taken refuge in a nearby office building and were now trapped; the door they had entered was now piled so high with debris it was impossible to open.

"All we could see was white smoke, even inside the building." Varone and her fellow officers didn't know where to go or even which way was safe. "It's fine. Let's do it," urged the mayor, and they followed two maintenance workers who led them through a maze of corridors and stairways until they found a way out.

Exiting, Varone ran into someone she loved and respected, a calm and friendly face in the midst of hell: Father Mychal Judge, the New York City Fire Department's hugely popular chaplain. He gave her a reassuring hug and kiss, his usual optimism firmly in place despite the nightmare erupting around them. "We'll manage," he told her. "We always get through it."

Minutes later he was dead, killed by falling debris.

Privately, Varone talks quickly, easily, and comfortably. Professionally, her job is to stay calm and in control. Only once, in three hours of lively conversation, did she pause, struggling to keep her composure, as she described realizing how many fellow officers were lost that day, men and women she knew well.

"You knew the numbers were high. But for a while we didn't know the names. When you find out, then you lose it."

The daughter of an Irish mother and an Italian father, a butcher with his own shop in Brooklyn and father of six—Varone never wanted to be a cop. She studied education in college and took the police exam in 1979 on a lark. "I can't say it was a burning desire." No one in her family was in law enforcement. "I thought it would be exciting, fascinating, different—but it's as mundane as anything else."

In 1981, she graduated from the New York Police Academy, assigned to the "67," a high-crime Brooklyn precinct largely Haitian and Jamaican, then to the "78," another Brooklyn house. She moved to the Major Case Squad after five years, working on burglaries, bank robberies, and kidnappings. She enjoyed the work, and the new skills she was learning, but was curious when a friend suggested she interview for the mayor's police detail. She joined the Intelligence Division, home to all officers who work in what is formally called dignitary protection, officers more commonly called bodyguards.

Her new position required extensive special training: in first aid, in driving techniques, and in defensive shooting. Should the motorcade be attacked, for example, she learned how to accelerate quickly to eighty miles per hour, brake suddenly, and do a U-turn. "If something happens to the principal [dignitary], you can't wait for the ambulance to get there. Dignitary protection is a whole different avenue. You learn to see the world differently, to think differently."

A typical workday, with barely one day's notice as to the locations and events, consisted of two "doubles"—a 6:30 A.M. to 11 P.M. shift two days in a row, followed by four days off. After the mayor left office, published a best-selling memoir, went on the international lecture circuit, and got engaged, Varone's two days often stretched to four or five without a break. She once flew to Portugal for a day and a half, and to California from New York for an afternoon. Between jet lag and fatigue, Varone—a stunningly fit forty-nine-year-old who looks ten years younger thanks to a healthy diet and running six to nine miles a day—was exhausted. A woman so high-energy she used to run, play racquetball, and play softball in the same day, Varone once fell into bed for forty-four straight hours to recover.

Although Giuliani left office after the election of Michael Bloomberg in November 2001, he enjoyed round-the-clock police protection for another fifteen months—at a cost of up to $100,000 per year per officer. His detail included sixteen officers, with Varone the only woman. She earned a base salary of $76,000, plus overtime.

Wearing a Smith & Wesson five-shot revolver or a Glock 9mm with a fifteen-round magazine, Varone spent nine years of her working life never more than twenty feet from Giuliani. Where she stood depended on the layout of the room, whether it was public or private, a closed reception with a guest list or a less controllable book-signing, a night at the opera, a law school graduation, a water-main break, or a Yankees game. "If it was a crowded restaurant, we'd stay a lot closer. We had to gauge it. Can we get to him if he needs us?"

Toughest part of the job? "Getting dressed!" She laughs. "Belt loops and pockets. I needed belt loops and pockets." For reasons of comfort, modesty, and ease of movement, she wore only pantsuits and, often, man-tailored cotton shirts—for their pockets. Like every police officer, Varone still had to carry handcuffs, pen and notebook, cell phone, a gun. She often wore everything on a heavy belt *over* her dress belt, easier to remove when she went to the toilet. Flat shoes, no jewelry, no makeup. (She wears a diamond on a gold chain beneath her shirt.) "I have to be comfortable. I have to be ready to run."

Often, people who couldn't imagine a woman in so essential a job had no idea she was there. Men would saunter up to hit on her, wondering aloud why the mayor hadn't brought security with him.

Between the hours, nonstop travel, and her own demanding career success, dating during those years was especially difficult. Divorced after eleven years without children, she's great-looking, easy to talk to, tells terrific stories. She's stylish and athletic and has met everyone from the pope to Presidents Bush and Clinton. "A lot of men are intimidated by me and what I do. This is a small part of what I am." (She reads, runs, listens to music, and plays for hours with her dozen nephews and nieces.)

But she says she had one of the best jobs a female officer could wish for and, when we met in Manhattan a few days before Christmas 2002, said she planned to retire from that position. "He's given me responsibility beyond my wildest dreams. He respects me. He treats me like gold. This is the top of the mountain."

Women who work in law enforcement, whether police, security, FBI, the Secret Service, or other positions, enter a world that is 87 percent male. They operate, manage, and promote, and are managed and promoted, within a military hierarchy and mind-set, a world where macho strength is celebrated and where a weak or hesitant partner is perceived, fairly enough, as a lethal liability. Women in this world feel compelled, sometimes even after decades on the job, to prove themselves. Many of these women come from families with a male relative already working in the field, giving them insights into what's expected and the toll of long hours on family life. For that reason, many also marry or date fellow officers and agents who encourage and support their non-traditional ambitions; civilians, they say, are often threatened by female competence with firearms and the risks a woman faces in putting on a gun every day to go to work.

For one black New York City policewoman, honored for her bravery, things didn't turn out quite the way she expected after the TV lights and tape recorders were turned off.

On February 5, 1994, Officer Arlene Beckles, then twenty-nine, was off duty and a patron in Salon La Mode beauty parlor in downtown Brooklyn when, using her service weapon, she shot three gunmen—one fatally—who came in to rob the place. She escaped death when one of the wounded men put his gun to her head and pulled the trigger, twice. Each time, the gun jammed.

"Beauty Parlor Bandits Meet Their Match," "Hair-Raiser; 110-lb. Cop Makes 3 Collars in Bloody Salon Shoot-Out," read newspaper headlines. She was promoted to detective, and days later then-mayor Rudolph Giuliani officiated at her wedding, to fellow police officer Steve Imparato.

The happy ending proved instead the start of new nightmares. In 1996, Beckles was suspended from duty—the police department said she was calling in sick too often, while Detective Beckles said that persistent pain in her back and knee injuries from the 1994 altercation had led to the sick days. Later, she said that severe anxiety and depression stemming from the trauma of the confrontation had left her unable to perform police work.

She retired in 2000, but received only half of her $55,000-a-year salary—an ordinary, taxable disability pension—instead of the three-quarter-salary, untaxed, line-of-duty disability pension. At the time of writing, Detective Beckles, embittered and angry, was still fighting to win the extra pay. A police medical and pension review board said her "depressive syndrome" was, instead, linked to the failure of her marriage.

Unable to hold a job, she told a *New York Times* reporter she thought it unlikely that "guns placed to your head, nightmares, flashbacks, did not have anything to do with it." It had been a long, hard fall from grace, she said. "I just cannot understand why they would decide to treat me that way."[1] (As a matter of policy, NYPD officers fired upon in the line of duty, even if physically unharmed, are all immediately sent to a physician for assessment. If deemed unfit for active duty, even if they say they feel fine, they're reassigned until considered sufficiently healthy to continue regular duties.)

For female, and male, police officers, the gun is normally as unremarkable and quotidian a part of their uniform as their notebook and nightstick. Kathy McNeely, a thirty-nine-year-old police officer in New Brighton, Minnesota—a town of twenty-five thousand just outside Minneapolis–St. Paul—began carrying a Smith & Wesson 4046 every day when she joined the force in April 1991. She grew up in "a big hunting family," and her brothers own several guns.

"There are twenty-seven officers—and currently four women—working in this department. I had been a medical lab technician when I went through police training. The job was changing and I had always been interested in all aspects of police work." Her father and brother were officers. "I was ready for the change and the challenge police work offered."

Like every female working in law enforcement, McNeely entered a male-dominated world with a firm, unbreakable chain of command, and with hazing and harassment from male colleagues and superiors inevitable.

"When I was first hired, all my field training officers were male. It was not a great fourteen weeks of training. Another female was hired a week after me, and we would compare notes," she recalls. "If I had known then what I know now about harassment and discrimination . . . One male didn't think police work was for women. He would take me behind some dark building and ask if I would feel safe driving behind there alone. They would constantly ask if I was sure police work was for me.

"I handle calls differently, perhaps because women are raised differently," adds McNeely, who has a four-year degree focusing on psychology, crisis intervention, and counseling and is returning for a degree in sociology. "I think we are better able to see what it might be like for others, stepping into their shoes and dealing with it that way."

She prefers a less confrontational approach. "I don't need to piss someone off in order for them to comply with what I'm asking them to do. I've learned that if you treat even the nastiest person as if they were human and with respect, they will usually do what you ask. It doesn't work all the time but most of the time it does. You can't take what they say personally, or you won't last too long."

At the start of her career, McNeely faced discrimination not just from fellow officers and management, but from those she had been hired to serve and protect.

"I think women have to work twice as hard to gain the respect of the public. When going on calls with partners that first year, it never failed that the person who called would look to the male officer to give their report. It is much different now. Criminals are okay most of the time, but you get the occasional name-caller. There was only one criminal that really did not like women. He had just beaten up his wife and girlfriend. They lived in the same apartment! He wasn't very happy when he saw two female officers there to arrest him."

Physically, emotionally, and intellectually, McNeely enjoys her work, but it took a while to relax into her authority and to gain acceptance from her colleagues.

"I am comfortable with the gun. The gun belt is heavy and adds a lot of strain to the hip area, but I am teaching in the [public] schools now and only wear the gun. There is a big responsibility having the gun. Everyone knows you have it and are expected to be the first one to respond to a situation because of it. Being a firearms instructor has definitely been a plus. I would not have a problem pulling my gun and using it."

Like most officers, McNeely has drawn her weapon a number of times: defusing potential suicides, in hostage situations, and in domestic disputes. She has, like most police officers, never fired it in the line of duty.

Women soldiers serving in the U.S. armed forces are still not allowed to fight in direct ground combat—but they are nonetheless required to learn how to aim, fire, load, and care for their rifles. Those women who choose to become marines arrive, as all would-be marines do, at Parris Island, a marsh-covered sea island in the shallow waters of the Atlantic, where marines have trained since 1915. Halfway through training, they arrive at the rifle range given a matter of days to master their M16A2s, to shoot with accuracy at distances of up to a quarter mile. Many young recruits have grown up with the assumption women were part of the military; they were in grade school during the Persian Gulf War, when thirty-seven thousand women were deployed. (Five were killed in action and two taken prisoner.)

Women in the armed forces remain a tiny minority—14.3 percent—and make up only 6 percent of marines. Candice Fleming, a fashion junkie from Arlington, Virginia, whose pre-enlistment steering-wheel cover read "Princess," decided to become a marine after years of her father's teasing her that, because she was "just a girl," she couldn't.

"Hours after Candice Fleming [and three other women] arrived at Parris Island—before they had a full night's sleep or a shower or a hot meal—they were issued M16A2 rifles designed for the rigors of combat. For the next twelve weeks, the guns would become like another appendage to their bodies, slung over their right shoulders as they marched and hiked and even attended classes. At night, the guns hung down from their bedposts, locked down for security. The gun was the centerpiece of their new culture."[2]

It was not until 1980 that women fired rifles as part of their marine training, and even though they may never use them in ground combat, the weapons are meant to become second nature. On the rifle range, women are expected to meet exactly the same standards as men, take the same tests, and score the same scores.

Women's role in the military began to grow in 1973 when the draft ended and recruiters looked to females to fill the ranks. In 1976, the service academies began accepting women. The air force opened its flight program to women, but in early 2003 widespread revelations of rape and harassment of female cadets at the Air Force Academy made national front-page headlines, and four senior officials were fired. Many women had tried to protest their treatment, found no redress, and quit training. As many women penetrating the professional male-warrior culture have learned, admission clearly doesn't equal acceptance. In 1988, the Pentagon opened thirty-one thousand positions to women but set criteria for keeping them out of combat; in 1994, those distinctions were elimimated when the "risk rule" was repealed.

As American soldiers went to war with Iraq in March 2003, two hundred thousand women were on active duty (out of a force of 1.4 million). Overall, women represent 15.5 percent of the army, 13.3 percent of the navy, and 18.3 percent of the air force. The price of their rising importance is a new burden of fear and grief for their families. After an early ambush in Operation Iraqi Freedom, when eight members of the 507th Maintenance Company were listed as "whereabouts unknown," two were women, nineteen-year-old Pfc. Jessica Lynch and Pfc. Lori Ann Piestewa of Tuba City, Arizona. They were trained for noncombat roles and sent to supply soldiers on the front lines, but after taking a wrong turn, were trapped by two buses, Iraqi irregular forces, and tanks. (Lynch was rescued in a dramatic mission while Piestewa was killed.)

Specialist Shoshanna Johnson, a single mother of a two-year-old and an army cook, was captured early in Operation Iraqi Freedom and later released with injuries. Women are barred from combat roles, but serving in a support role placed her in equal danger—she was the only female among seven POWs. "It bothered me a lot worse than if it would have been a man," said Laura Sargent, a senior airman preparing to ship out. "I'm thinking,

'Well, women don't really go into combat,' and then you look at TV and think, 'Yeah, they do. That could be me someday.' "[3]

In contrast to the 1991 Gulf War—in which two women soldiers were killed when a Scud missile hit their tent far from the battlefield—women now fly combat missions and serve on fighter ships; they are barred from submarines, Special Forces, and the army's infantry, armor, and artillery divisions. The Clinton administration's decision in 1994 to lift the "risk rule" opened 90 percent of military positions to women, including in hostile zones, which is how Johnson ended up in a convoy that was ambushed. By its second week, the Iraq war had already involved more women in combat, and commanding combat missions, than ever before. "There is no front line in combat anymore, so we have to change our thinking," said Carol Mutter, chairwoman of the Defense Advisory Committee on Women in the Service. "The enemy wants to go after the supply chain, and that's where you will find women, in those rear areas, in combat-support areas."[4]

At home, women now serve as corrections officers guarding some of the most dangerous male inmates in prisons across the country. Inside prison, they don't carry weapons in case they're attacked or kidnapped and the guns used against them, but when transporting prisoners to and from prison they do. The first female to work in a men's prison was Rachel Perijo, at the Baltimore Men's Penitentiary in 1882, although not until the 1970s did women start to serve alongside men in men's prisons. Today, all states and the Federal Bureau of Prisons now employ women as corrections officers at every security level in both men's and women's institutions.[5]

Carol Sarlo, a white, 240-pound, five-foot-seven-inch forty-nine-year-old, has been working as a CO at Rikers Island near Manhattan since 1990; New York City has fourteen jails, including one for adolescents and one for women. "The women are much worse than the men. They're quicker with their mouths.

They can be extremely violent and think they won't get hit back. One of them bit an officer.

"It's not a job you aspire to, but one you fall into," Sarlo admits. "I was in dead-end jobs. I was too old to become a cop. Besides, they want older people. You bring a certain maturity, a different approach. It cuts down on the violence in the jail."

She doesn't dwell on the dangers of her job. "I put it in my head that I might get hurt, then I get past it. I've got the bulk to take care of myself. I took out an inmate who was six foot six by kicking his legs out from under him. I've had to get down and dirty."

Sarlo earns a healthy $67,000 a year, plus overtime; if she rises to captain, she'll earn $75,000, $90,000 as assistant deputy warden, $115,000 as deputy warden, and up to $135,000 as warden. "It's about the money," she says candidly. "I'm exposed to TB, to hepatitis B, to AIDS. You don't really learn the job until you put on a uniform and walk the tiers [the different cell floors]. You leave your sensibilities at home."

She carries her service weapon—a Smith & Wesson 9mm with three fifteen-round magazines—on hospital runs and when transporting prisoners to court and to outposts (nonprison wards). "You *can* have a problem in the hospital. Hospitals have no search procedures or magnetometers, and you don't know who's coming to visit them. It can get really dirty. We can get murdered." One prisoner, she says, killed a fellow CO when he grabbed the officer's gun and shot him with it.

Inside the prison, she carries a standard set of equipment, including a memo book, flashlight, handcuffs, pepper spray, and a "911," a sharp J-shaped piece of metal designed to cut down a prisoner who has hanged himself. She wears a vest designed to protect her from stab wounds: "It feels like having a girdle on your chest." However uncomfortable, the vest is crucial: "We have a lot of injuries. We do a job no one wants to acknowledge. We don't get the kind of press the police department does."

Sarlo privately owns two handguns, for which she paid $500 apiece. She carries one with her in the city when she is not working. "I like having a gun. It does give you an edge. You stand a better chance on the street if someone has a knife or gun. I *have* had my life threatened. I have run into former prisoners on the street. We process thirty thousand a year, and they remember you."

She's well aware of the added legal responsibility a gun imposes on her. Even showing the gun is considered a "use of force." "I take great pains to conceal my weapon. It's tough in the summer."

Sarlo lives with her sister, a former air force officer, who is as comfortable as Sarlo is with weapons in the home; her lover of two years is also fine with them. "The only thing that worries her is that if something happens to us on the street, I'm not going to run away." Sarlo practices her shooting every couple of months.

As a lesbian, she says she receives no disapproval from friends and lovers regarding her gun ownership. Feminists, she says, are another story. "These are the same women who want me drafted! You can't have it both ways! You can't want to be a strong woman and fall back on feminist dogma. It drives me crazy!"

Sandra Williams was a double minority, a black and a woman, when she became a New York City police officer in September 1980. Williams, a warm, direct, native New Yorker, says she never gave her unusual career choice much thought. Her mother wanted her to be a "nurse/teacher/wife/mother," and Williams faced enormous opposition from her family over her unorthodox choice. Encouraged by her fiancé, now her husband, a fire department official, she decided to apply, motivated by the salary, benefits, and full pension after twenty years' service. "I like people. I wouldn't be stuck inside behind a desk. That was intriguing to me."

She started her training in three of New York's toughest neighborhoods, thickets of high crime, violence, and drug activity—the 28, Central Harlem; the 32, a region north of Harlem; and the 25, Spanish Harlem. "There were very few women back then, and very few women on patrol," Williams recalls. In those first months, she heard a sniper on a rooftop firing around them but was so green she didn't recognize the *ping!* of a ricocheting bullet. Only when a street-smart civilian in front of them dove to the pavement for protection did she appreciate the danger they were in.

Although Williams grew up in the Bronx, seeing crime and criminals on the street as a civilian and having to deal with them directly proved very different, she says. The first time she had to pat down a heroin addict, who was wearing many layers of clothing on a winter's day, he jumped back in fear and surprise. She, in turn, was scared enough to put her hand on her still-holstered Smith & Wesson .38 revolver. As he reached for his waistband, she feared he was drawing a weapon. Instead, his pants plunged to the sidewalk. "I saw ulcers on his legs that were so deep I could have put my fist into them."

Williams worked for nineteen years in the NYPD, retiring in 1999 at a salary of $70,000 as a sergeant. In those years she worked in Internal Affairs, and for eight years training fellow officers at the Police Academy on "sensitivity issues" such as sexual harassment, racism, and ethical awareness.

She faced down gunfire and potential serious injury several times. Once, on a call of a "man with a gun" in an apartment building in the Bronx, Williams and six other police officers found themselves dodging bullets when the man opened his door. "You get so many of those calls you often go in tactically unprepared," she says. "I had only three years' experience by then, but I was considered the senior person." Once the man opened fire, "it went crazy! You're just afraid in that situation, and you count on your training to get you through it. When my partner arrived, my knees buckled."

On another occasion, on an eighty-degree midsummer night, she was left alone—facing an angry crowd of one hundred—guarding the entrance to an alleyway where fellow cops were making an arrest. A young Hispanic man with a knife began to taunt her: "I'll take that gun and put it up your ass." Williams stayed calm, but was intimidated by him and by the restless, swelling crowd. "He was too big and too angry to fight with." His friend told him to back off as she warned, "One more step and I'll fire." He backed off.

"Had I been a man, it would have become a *mano a mano* situation," she says. She knew she had to shoot, and so did her provocateur's friend.

Williams enjoyed being a police officer, even if she knew, always, she was held to a higher standard of behavior and excellence than her male colleagues. "It might have been more true back then, but it's still true today. If a woman requested a shift change, it was completely focused on her being female. All of the significance of her choices was placed on her gender." Like most former officers, she kept her service weapon. Police and city officials like knowing there is an auxiliary of retired officers. "You're still trained. You're still responsible."

Although none of the women I interviewed have killed in the line of duty, the possibility was rarely far from their thoughts. "I would always dread the thought of killing someone," says Patty Varone. "I think any woman who killed would feel worse than a man would. It's the way we're brought up.

"Cops are given God's power, the power to take someone's life in a millisecond. When you're in a life-or-death situation, you have to act quickly. It's a fine balance."

Women are gaining ground as municipal and state police officers, yet they remain a minority in the much smaller, more competitive, and therefore more elite services of the Federal Bureau of Investigation and the U.S. Secret Service; only 11 percent of FBI agents are women and 17.3 percent of Secret Service agents. Uniformed Secret Service officers, who work only in D.C. to guard embassies and chanceries, the White House, and the families of the president and vice president, make up 6.5 percent with an additional 10.84 percent working across the nation as agents.

The Secret Service has five thousand field operatives, including one thousand officers in the Uniformed Division and approximately three thousand special agents. To join, you need a four-year college degree, must be an American citizen between twenty-one and thirty-seven, and must pass a background and polygraph check and undergo intensive training.

While schedules of protective details, such as those for the president, vice president, and former presidents, are dictated by the protectees, "we limit the time our agents spend on protective details," says Marc Connolly, a spokesman for the agency. "These are typically four-to-five-year assignments, and during those years, agents may rotate through different responsibilities in that division." Unlike the barrel-chested bodyguards typically pictured with movie stars and pop-music idols, agents on the presidential detail, like all others, are part of a large, rotating pool of professionals. They work for the Secret Service, not the White House, and receive assignments, promotions, or demotions accordingly.

Like a Ford assembly line, the president has three shifts of agents, each working for eight hours. Agents carry a Sig Sauer .357 pistol; the agency upgraded from a Sig Sauer 9mm a few years ago. While several women are members of the security detail for President George Bush and First Lady Laura Bush, the Service declined to say how many.

Like Patty Varone, former Secret Service agent Mary Ann Gordon, the first woman ever assigned to a presidential detail, helplessly witnessed one of America's most frightening moments, an attempted assassination on her watch. Gordon was working on March 30, 1981, the day that John W. Hinckley opened fire on President Ronald Reagan, "one of the most controversial days in the annals of the Secret Service."[6]

That day, Gordon drove along the motorcade route to and from the Hilton, accompanied by a member of the Washington, D.C., Police Department; it was her job to coordinate presidential motorcades not only with local police but with U.S. Park Police, who would secure the route and handle traffic control. She was reassigned to a nonprotective job and has since retired.

The first female agent to die in the line of duty was, ironically, killed in a random shooting unrelated to her assignment. Special Agents Lloyd Bulman and Julie Cross had been assigned to watch a site near the Los Angeles airport for a gang of counterfeiters. Around 9 P.M. on June 4, 1980, two men suddenly appeared behind their car and opened fire with shotguns. Cross was killed, while Bulman survived. It took nine years to find her killer; Andre Alexander was handed a death sentence in 1995.

A second female Secret Service agent, Cynthia L. Brown, was killed in the Oklahoma City bombing.

Like a football player, fifty-one-year-old Cathy Schroeder was proud to tell me her number is 93—the 93rd woman to become an agent of the Federal Bureau of Investigation. The FBI only began admitting women in 1972; Schroeder graduated the academy in 1976. It was, she easily admits, her life's dream.

"I absolutely, positively knew I wanted to be an FBI agent after the first year I was in college." Growing up, Schroeder had a much admired family friend who was an agent and, working a summer job, met a few more. Her father was one of eight hundred police officers selected nationwide to attend the prestigious FBI National Academy, so she knew something about what she was getting into.

Yet her father fought hard against her choice, telling her she could make a much better living as an accountant, her first choice and her college major. "He knew I would meet a lot of resistance and opposition as a female. I would face long hours. He wanted to be sure I wasn't in it for the glamour or the money."

Yet Schroeder has managed to accumulate both. At the very top of her pay scale, eligible for retirement, she earns an $84,751 base salary, plus a 25 percent bonus for overtime (known as availability pay). She was appointed, in her third assignment, firearms instructor for new agents, training everyone who came through Quantico, Virginia, for four and a half years. In the sixteen weeks of training, it was her job to take new agents "from zero to qualification." She was assigned as principal firearms instructor for the entire division of 225 agents and was also the training coordinator for the division; in a field always heavily male-dominated, it was a coup. She worked at the Olympics in Atlanta and in Salt Lake City, also considered plum assignments.

She became a firearms instructor under the tutelage of her husband, Lyle, a former Michigan state police officer who is now retired. They met when Schroeder worked in Detroit as a white-collar crime agent, sixteen months as an undercover agent, and six years on a Special Operations Group, mostly high-level surveillance. Her husband knew that marrying Schroeder, whose passion for the job remains undimmed, meant moving whenever and wherever her job required. "When you sign on to the Bureau, they own you. Whatever the 'needs of the Bureau' are, that's where you go. We discussed it at length." Lyle said anywhere warm with a golf course would suit him fine, and they married in 1981. They have no children, although Schroeder said many female agents do and, since 1985, can even work part-time.

She had always wanted to work in a Violent Crime squad, which she joined in 2002 in Atlanta. She handles as many as twenty cases at once, most of them related to bank robberies. When we spoke, she was hoping to soon clear twelve cases by one thief and seven by another. The hours are long and unpredictable, and often include weekends. She said no women working Violent Crime in her squad have children—"You're not even home long enough to conceive a child!" she joked.

Schroeder laughs easily and often, one sure way to stay sane in a business filled with violence. It's a stressful job, no matter where you're posted and in what squad. "You have to be confident that the training will help you in a dangerous situation, but you're always thinking, always what-iffing." De-stressing—whether through jokes, working out, a few beers—is essential. "If you didn't have it, this job would wear you right down to a nub. No matter who you are, you've got to have a thick skin and a sense of humor." Not surprisingly, the agency requires all agents to retire at fifty-seven.

Few female role models are out there for FBI agents and there are few realistic media depictions of their work. Every year fifty thousand applicants vie for nine hundred positions; they must be between twenty-three and thirty-five, have a college degree, and be willing to relocate wherever they are needed; since the terrorist attacks of 9/11 those with language, computer and scientific skills are in great demand. Starting salary in 2003 was $41,634 (plus 25 percent overtime).

Schroeder arrived at the academy to teach just as *Silence of the Lambs,* the 1991 film starring Jodie Foster as federal agent Clarice Starling, came out. The agents-in-training were given free tickets to a local theater and hooted as they recognized several real-life colleagues cast in the film. (For the record, Schroeder says, no agent-in-training would, as Starling was while chasing a serial killer, ever be given so much responsibility so soon, nor would she ever be sent into the field alone. The investigative methods and backup resources used in the film, such as working with top-level scientists, *were* realistic, she says.)

For Lorraine Hogan, being a tiny minority suits her just fine.

Her skin is fine-pored porcelain, tiny laugh lines crinkling the edges of her pale blue eyes. Her knitted, cream-colored cap is Ralph Lauren, the toes of her soft leather boots fashionably narrow. Sitting in a Greenwich Village café with her Louis Vuitton clutch and bronze-colored cell phone, Hogan looks like one more fashionable tourist, sipping her coffee at four on a winter's afternoon.

Yet, tucked into the waistband of her straw-colored trousers, set so far back on her right hip as to be invisible, sits a loaded Smith & Wesson .38 pistol.

"I don't always wear it, certainly not if I'm going shopping and I'm going to be carrying a bunch of bags." But, when it gets dark at four-thirty and she's nicely dressed and wearing gold jewelry, and it's a long subway ride home to Brooklyn, why not carry? In a city whose style tribes are marked by their visible status symbols, a legally concealed weapon is, for some, the rarest and most coveted of all.

Hogan, forty-six, is a retired corrections officer who now

works as a freelance bodyguard for Beau Dietl and Associates, one of Manhattan's top three private security firms. She has an officer's shield and a pistol permit allowing her to carry her loaded weapon. The permit is a small, folded piece of white paper, with a page of rules and regulations in five-point type and room on the back to list up to eight weapons by make, model, serial number, caliber, and type. It must be renewed every two years and can be revoked at any time. It carries her signature, color photo, and fingerprint.

She's never had to fire her weapon or even draw it to fend off a threat. Only once did it forestall an ugly confrontation—but not when she worked as a guard at Rikers Island. She was walking home alone at 3:30 A.M. in Chelsea, a middle-class section of Manhattan filled with restaurants and shops, when she noticed three men following her. One sidled up to her and asked for the time. "Time for you to leave me alone," she replied. The men moved on. "I'm pretty sure they saw the bulge, that they knew I had a gun."

She was earning $60,000 a year when she retired in 2000 after twenty years. She now collects $30,000 a year in pension and supplements her income working an average of three days a week for Beau Dietl for an hourly rate. She is extraordinarily rare in the world of New York City private security. How many are women?

"One percent—me!" She laughs. "No, two percent. I worked once with another female at an event."

Typically, she's called a day or two in advance for work, often as security at parties, functions, and fund-raisers. Working with a partner, she takes a position within the room—by the door or a lavatory, for example—and watches civilians with experienced eyes. For safety reasons, Hogan turns down 10 to 20 percent of her assignments.

"I ask them what the location is, who the site manager is, and who else I'll be working with. Because I'm female, I want to be sure someone good has my back if something happens. Sometimes I'm more comfortable with a former corrections officer than with a former police officer. The police officers don't pay as much attention as they should to watching their prisoners or cuffing them. It has a lot to do with training. You have to listen to those cuffs closing. You have to leave two fingers' space around their wrist. And you always have to assume that people will try to escape as soon as they can."

After twenty years around criminals, little rattles her. On one recent assignment, sent to a midtown site to determine whether construction workers were drinking on the job, several of them spoke only to her male partner, but she took it in stride. "You could cut the tension with a knife. I was the invisible woman!" It was smarter to stay calm, keep the client happy, and get a callback for more work than to engage, she says. "I'm there in a professional capacity. I'm there representing the firm. That's what's most important."

Hogan agrees that being female has helped her do a dangerous job better. "Sometimes the presence of a woman makes a hell of a difference when a situation arises in a jail. The male ego comes into play. They lack common sense. It's a macho thing." Women officers, on or off the job, are more skilled at defusing a situation rather than escalating it.

Socially, though, these determined women agree, men just can't figure them out. Dating is never easy. How can a woman who dresses so beautifully be trained to kill? What corporate war stories of his could ever match, or top, hers? Is she packing a gun beneath that elegant blazer? Would she ever pull it on him?

Hogan's expertise has unnerved so many would-be romantic partners she's almost given up dating anyone but cops. They, at least, understand what she does, why she does it, and why she loves it. But regular guys just can't handle a curvaceous, soft-spoken blonde who packs heat. She tells them instead she's a personal assistant, a personal shopper, or an interior decorator.

Chapter 9
Guns Mean Business

Head south on Route 83, drive through Eden, and you'll end up at Gwynne Lundgren's ranch, on a rolling, quiet, two-lane Texas road. She greets you with a breezy confidence tempered by an old-fashioned formality. When she strides across her land, in what appears to be her natural gait, you scramble, panting, to keep up. Long-eared hares bounce up out of the deep grass as she moves through it. She knows its every inch. She still swims in the fast-moving San Saba River, full of lethal water moccasins, as she has since early childhood.

Lean, elegantly lovely, red-haired, long-legged, she looks at forty-five like a Jane Austen character in gum boots. This dusty land contains her history, her roots, and her future. Unmarried, with no children, Lundgren loves this earth and the cherished independence it provides. She sleeps in a building that was once the one-room schoolhouse where her grandmother learned her lessons. She coolly shoos rattlesnakes away when they slither up the drainpipes into her bathroom sink. On the dusty front seat of her truck sits a Coach purse, Revo sunglasses, and a .22 revolver in a tooled leather holster.

Lundgren earns her living—more than $100,000 a year—hosting hunters. They are almost always men, men she has never met before and to whom she must remain ever-gracious and hospitable. She lives a twenty-mile drive from the nearest police station; keeping her handgun close by is prudent, a worst-case backup should politesse fail her. Lundgren is a rarity in her male-dominated industry, admitting with an easy laugh that of all the hunting operators meeting their clients at the regional airport in San Angelo, she's always the only woman.

They come in the fall to shoot deer and in spring to shoot turkey. Sometimes late at night, after they have sipped fine wine in Waterford crystal and enjoyed thick steaks, the doctors and accountants and corporate executives from big cities and suburban enclaves eagerly suit up once more in their camouflage, slide into a pair of bucket seats in the back of a pickup truck, and head out into the starry silence to shoot "varmints."

While Lundgren earns her living from the killing of animals, she draws careful boundaries around what her guests do and what she believes is fair game.

"I would never kill for its own sake!" she says, horrified. "When we grew up, we would only kill for food." Lundgren, a graduate of Texas A&M University, minored in wildlife and considers the hunting on her land wildlife management. Every year she hires a biologist to count the number of deer to decide how many to cull. The deer and turkey no longer have natural predators; hunting is an efficient way to maintain balance, she says. In 2003, the 129-year-old, six-thousand-acre ranch had about thirty excess does. "The habitat of the ranch is improving so we have more and more deer."

She's an intriguing blend of sophisticate and frontierswoman, as at home at the elegant Manhattan salesroom of high-end British gunmaker Holland & Holland, with whom she is affiliated, as negotiating with government officials in Istanbul; she also raises Angora goats whose wool is used in the cloth for finely tailored Italian suits.

Her life mingles rugged isolation with sensual luxury. In the living room of her home, which she shares with visiting hunters from around the world, lush Oriental rugs, tweed-upholstered wing chairs, and deep sofas covered in leather and velvet face an enormous stone fireplace. Mixed nuts are offered in gleaming crystal bowls. Betty, the maid, stands ready to serve in her black uniform and crisp white apron. Lundgren welcomes six guests at a time, each of whom pays $1,250 for three days' hunting. They arrive every four days during April, rising at four-thirty for breakfast and heading into the dark, cold woods by six to await the sunrise and the turkeys, who, at that hour, are gobbling quietly to one another in the treetops.

"I attract an older hunter, those who are more interested in wildlife than killing," she says. "I don't attract the 'blasters,' " hunters who fire fast, loud, and often at anything that moves. Twenty-five percent of her hunters come from overseas, and about 10 percent are women, a few of whom come alone.

Lundgren started her operation in 1998, only one of two such ranches in the U.S. affiliated with Holland & Holland, and advertises in hunting magazines under the deliberately androgynous name G. K. Lundgren. Despite its upscale nature, Lundgren says it's "very difficult" to run her business. "Dealing with the hunting clientele is tough. It's harder to get business when the economy is bad." Outfitters, like many in the travel industry, lost customers after 9/11 because of many clients' newfound reluctance to fly, and many of Lundgren's clients come to Texas from the Northeast. When she started, she expected most of her clients to come from Europe, but "they're still committed to hunting in Africa."

As in any business, Lundgren relies on word of mouth and repeat customers; many of her hunters return year after year. "This ranch has the biggest deer herds I have ever seen," wrote Nate Fisher of Alexander, North Carolina, in Lundgren's guest book. "The Oak Knoll Ranch is as close to heaven as any hunter can get."

* * *

While it remains male-dominated, women work in almost all sectors of the American gun industry; about a third of the thirteen thousand exhibitors at the 2002 Shot Show, the annual trade show, were female. In 2002, for the first time, a hundred of them attended a luncheon for women in the business.

Many work in their own small stores across the country, the "mom-and-pop" dealers such as Norsela Cole, fifty-two, a gun dealer since 1991 in Commack, New York, a town on Long Island. I met Cole, a stylish woman with bouffant, ash-blond hair, a plaid blazer, black jeans, and a French manicure, at a gun show in Springfield, Massachusetts. With every table in the room stacked with long guns like cordwood, and middle-aged white men milling about in battered jackets and baseball caps, we were drops of estrogen in a sea of testosterone. While many of those I spoke to were nervous sharing information, Cole was relaxed and comfortable talking candidly to a journalist.

Twenty percent of her clients are female, most in their thirties and forties and most in a relationship with a man who also enjoys shooting. More than three-quarters of the women come into her store accompanied by a man, a son, or a husband. "It's a relatively new thing for them. Women are just getting into it."

She sells about five hundred guns every year, three hundred of them to other dealers. "We're unique because we do a lot of collectible guns." Cole says she earns more than $100,000 a year and is proud of her livelihood. She's annoyed when people, as they do, berate her choice. "A large part of our economy relies on guns, even locally." Once an avid reader of *People* magazine, Cole says she reluctantly canceled her subscription after the magazine ran a gun-control advertisement.

In an industry today dominated by a few large players, some— such as Beretta, Glock, and Taurus—with foreign owners, an all-American firearms company with history and tradition carries weight. Two women who carry on an established family name and reputation are Kay Clark of Louisiana and Elizabeth Saunders of

Waco, Texas, who run companies founded, respectively, by their father and husband.

Some women work for major manufacturers in public relations, advertising, sales, marketing, and distribution. Former instructor Cathy Graham crisscrossed the country for five years, from 1997 to 2002, training law enforcement officers how to use their 9mm Glocks, now standard for many police departments. Sharon Zaiffiro, a legendary markswoman and competitor, is Glock's Range Program coordinator, traveling to shooting ranges across the nation to sell them Glock weapons. She also runs the Glock Shooting Sports Foundation's indoor program. Glock has no women sales reps, although many women work as support staff at their U.S. headquarters in Accokeek, Maryland.

Women like Graham and Zaiffiro represent, at most, a handful of female experts in their business, women who are high profile, highly respected—and who usually teach men how to shoot. Others work on staff for a manufacturer or freelance from home, delicately engraving the metalwork of shotguns with exquisitely detailed designs or checkering the stocks and butts of rifles and shotguns.

Nadine Little is property manager for the Scottsdale Gun Club, in Arizona, described by its owners as the world's largest civilian indoor shooting range. It opened in September 2002 with $750,000 worth of gun merchandise for sale and rent. The $6-million club has thirty-two computerized shooting lanes, two stories, and thirty thousand square feet.[1]

Women work at Beretta's two retail stores in Dallas and Manhattan, and their advertising and communications director is female.

Beverly Ruddock, assistant sales manager for the Beretta store in Manhattan, didn't grow up around guns. A slim, stunning brunette in her midforties who grew up in Birmingham, England, Ruddock used to sell men's clothing. The Beretta store, housed in a four-story sandstone town house owned by Beretta on the west side of Madison Avenue at Sixty-fourth Street, fits unobtrusively into one of the city's most elegant and upscale neighborhoods.

Retail neighbors include Steuben, Hermès, and Lalique. Beretta's storefront shows only clothing and accessories, never the guns it sells from a third-floor showroom invisible from the street, its windows covered and protected with thick, black iron bars. The company, like most firearms manufacturers, is privately owned. It is the largest firearms dealer in the world and the world's oldest industrial manufacturing company, founded in 1526.

Store stock varies widely, from a $995 paisley wool woman's jacket to a $40 pocketknife, a set of big-game-engraved crystal barware, books and hunting prints to safari jackets in cotton and linen for men and women. Customers are evenly divided between those who venture only into the first floor for jewelry, clothing, and accessories, the second floor for hunting clothing, and the third floor, whose every wall is lined with rifles and shotguns. (Because of New York City's handgun laws, unique to that city, Ruddock may only show pistols and revolvers to customers who already own a New York City pistol permit.)

"It's never been a ground-floor business, and never in public view. We don't make it obvious we're selling guns. You've got to get halfway into the store before you even see a gun, and it's locked in a display case," she says. In the showroom, its walls full of trophy heads, an antique, glass-fronted display case contains guns ranging in price from $6,000 to $85,000; prices rise with the detail of engraving, the quality of wood, and the workmanship involved in production. There are guns made mostly of synthetics, for those who don't want to bother cleaning and wiping down their firearm after use, and guns made of camouflage-colored metal. Clients, who are mostly male, tend to know what they want, Ruddock says. Women often come with a husband or fiancé, taking a few visits to get acquainted with the unfamiliar product. "It's a process. In the beginning it's more casual, more of a conversation. It's a new environment for them and you don't want to be overbearing. It takes time to make that sale."

As shooters gain proficiency and begin to specialize—primarily shooting birds or deer or big game—they often upgrade to more expensive guns. "They might just want a simple, rugged, down-to-earth gun," available for as little as $900. The store offers a wide range, all from firms owned by Beretta: riflemakers Tikka, Sako, and Uberti and shotgun makers Benelli and Franchi.

At the other end of the spectrum are small, home-based businesses such as that run by Kathy Forster, a friendly-looking, forty-four-year-old brunette who lives in Portland, Oregon. She practices the art and craft of checkering, incising hundreds of thin, intersecting lines on the wooden stock and stock panels of shotguns that make them easier to hold. At the 2002 American Custom Gunmakers Guild show, a gun she had worked "was one of the highlights of the show," wrote an admiring gun enthusiast in an article for *Shooting Sportsman*.[2] She earned $12,000 in her best year, usually making between $9,000 and $12,000 for her highly skilled labor.

Forster designs each checkering pattern by sketching it right onto the stock with a grease pencil rather than using a predrawn layout. She cuts her initial lines with a hand tool, then switches to an electric tool. After only two passes with the electric tool, Forster picks up one of her carbide hand tools and starts the fine, detailed, nitpicking work. She tightens the stock into a cradle and has a variety of fixtures to accommodate different shapes and sizes of stocks. Sitting in a pneumatically adjustable secretarial chair, Forster wears simple drugstore reading glasses in various magnifications to view the progress. Each job usually takes about twelve hours, although some take up to eighteen hours if the layout is unique or the wood especially challenging to work with.

She became interested in checkering after she began hunting; she uses a custom-made Fox when shooting clays and an original Fox CE when she hunts deer, usually with her husband, David Trathen.

She began checkering professionally in 1985, working for the mass-market gunmaker Kimber, making $5 an hour. "It quickly became apparent this was a good fit and a way to channel my compulsive perfectionistic nature," she says. Forster, who never attended college, enjoyed working with her hands; in three years with the company, she checkered more than two thousand rifle-stocks. She started taking in freelance work in 1987 and since then has built up a steady clientele across the United States. She checkers about forty stocks a year, a third of them shotguns. She also recuts the checkering for a few shotguns a year. About half her clients are hobbyists and the rest semicustom riflemakers and factory custom shops.

"I aim to make the pattern fit in with the stockmaker's concept rather than use the stock as a showcase for my work," she explains. "I think the ideal custom gun should have a cohesive overall design, with all elements adding up to an overall impression of quality. I think I really go the extra mile on the details. I also flow with the lines of the stock so [my design] looks like it belongs there. There is the technical aspect of the work and there's the artistic side. I've been equally good at both."

After she's done working on the guns, Forster rarely ever sees her work again. She did once later see again a museum-quality rifle at a national show. "I was really impressed. I could hardly believe I'd done it!"

Guns have provided a living, a platform, and an evangelical passion for Paxton Quigley, a slim blonde likely in her fifties (she won't discuss her age), one of the first women to strongly and publicly advocate female gun ownership. Her paperback book *Armed and Female* has been in print since 1989, selling more than two hundred thousand copies. Since 1991, she has taught women ages eighteen to seventy-two to shoot, from New York to Florida, Texas to Michigan, in Washington, Arizona, San Francisco, and Los Angeles. From 1990 to 2001 she was also a spokeswoman for Smith & Wesson.

She taught actress Geena Davis to shoot for the film *Thelma & Louise*.

Twenty percent of her students are Asian, only 5 percent black, and "very few" Hispanic, likely, she says, because of the cost of her classes: $185, cash. She doesn't advertise or solicit students but says they come to her through her speeches across the country—to colleges, Junior Leagues, local women's groups. She talks to them about self-defense, with a gun as one of many choices.

"I have a question-and-answer period that's quite lengthy, and I often get the same sorts of questions: how to travel more safely, how to make homes safer. I hear great concern about their children, about kidnap and assault and rape."

She is unapologetically, energetically, and indefatigably pro-gun. "I feel very strongly the best protection for a woman—or a man—is a gun. They should carry, and I'm really an advocate of all states allowing permits to carry." Should *all* women own guns? "Those who can be responsible adults and take safety courses and secure a gun." Quigley likens owning a gun to carrying insurance, a sure way to minimize risk and mitigate damage. She's also optimistic that younger women are more receptive to gun ownership than their mothers or older sisters.

"We grew up in the 1950s and 1960s, an era of assassinations—Martin Luther King, John F. and Robert Kennedy, Malcolm X. We tended to be very antigun as a result. This new generation of women don't have that attachment. These women in their twenties are very independent.

"Being involved in the gun movement has been absolutely *wonderful* for me!" she rhapsodizes. "I've learned what it is to be a strong, self-reliant woman. I've seen how your confidence expands when you know how to shoot and shoot well. I know that I've helped thousands of women. I've had them thanking me. It's been a profound experience."[3]

For Clark Custom Guns, Inc., pedigree and history are entwined with the reputation of their products and workmanship. The company was founded in 1950 by James E. Clark Sr., a national legend as a marksman and gunsmith; the company doesn't make guns but customizes them with trigger and sight adjustments, most often for competitive shooters. "That's our bread and butter," says Kay Clark, his daughter, only one of two women in the United States who heads a firearms company. Today the Princeton, Louisiana firm, at 336 Shootout Lane, is headed by Clark and her brother, Jim Clark Jr.

"We're never going to get rich at it, but it's a comfortable living," she says; typically, the most profitable part of the business is selling gun accessories. Competition is not as stiff for her company, nor as capital-intensive, as for American manufacturers, such as Smith & Wesson or Colt, struggling to keep a foothold and grow in a saturated market. "I would hate to have to start from scratch!" she says.

"You're always scared of making a mistake and getting shot down," Kay says. "Depending on who's in the White House, you never know politically what's coming next. Right now we're riding the top of the wave."

Kay, who is forty-six and a mother of three, is president of Clark Gun and Personal Safety, the retail and training side of the business. She started by teaching the Louisiana state concealed-carry class but found that there was such a demand for advanced training she added a defensive-shooting element. She offers a women-only class and, when we spoke in December 2002, had so far trained seventy-five women. Her $100 one-day class offers two hundred rounds of ammunition and the chance to try fifteen different guns. "That way they can come to the retail store and make an intelligent decision." She has taught women ages twenty to seventy-two and finds that many older women, imprudently, tend to skip training because their fathers or brothers had it.

Clark bought her shooting range in 1996 and says her visibility is growing, partly through local radio advertising. The company is based in northwest Louisiana, near Shreveport. She also offers a weeklong juniors class, for youngsters aged twelve to eighteen; she had trained sixty to eighty when we spoke. The youngsters come from all across the country, including a pair of sisters from Minnesota, and Alabama, New York, and Oregon.

She enjoys the novelty of being female in a male-dominated industry because no one, she says, cares about the gender of the salesman, just the quality of the product.

Until last year, Elizabeth Saunders was the only woman in America to run a gun manufacturing firm, the American Derringer Corporation, founded in 1980 by her late second husband, Robert. The derringer is unique among handguns; with twin barrels, it fires only two cartridges. Because it is so small and light, it's most often marketed as a lady's gun or a backup weapon for law enforcement. When we met at her offices near Waco, Texas, in April 2002, times were already tough. Sales had dropped precipitously, and her company—which had earned $2.4 million in 1994—had not been profitable since 1995. Her son Christopher Reynolds, then a twenty-one-year-old employee, was accidentally killed working in her factory in 1995.

In 2002, the company's liability insurance doubled, from $75,000 to $150,000. Hoping to regain solvency, Saunders dropped the coverage, gambling that she wouldn't need it. She did. In November 2002, she was sued by a Virginia police officer who claimed her product was unsafe and had fired unexpectedly, injuring him. She was hit with a default judgment of $150,000. When we spoke again in March 2003, she had decided to shutter her business.

"What this boils down to is, you're going to have to be a big enough company or you're going to go under." Sales for the first quarter of 2003 had been $244,784.60. "We're just a small company," she protested. "If we make two thousand guns a year, we're flying!"

Once, her glossy, color, eight-page catalog showed Saunders in a pale pink straw hat trimmed in tulle and a high-necked, lace-trimmed, cream satin dress, posing as "Lady Derringer." Products included the M-6 and M-8, with a barrel length of six inches, marketed to ranchers, campers, and other outdoorsmen for shooting snakes. Three models, the M-7, M-10, and M-11 were ultralight, their frame or barrel, or both, made of lightweight aluminum, the barrel merely 4.82 inches long.

Saunders's factory is the size of a suburban garage, hidden behind her office, which fronts onto a wide highway south of Waco. It's easy to miss as there is no sign announcing the company, a deliberate safety measure, she says. She hopes to reopen under the name American Backup Corporation, marketing exclusively to law enforcement in the hope of forestalling lawsuits. She stopped advertising in 2001. "It wasn't doing me any good," she said. "I don't want to sell to consumers. I get nothing but grief."

She alternately anguished about her uncertain future and swore she'd somehow survive. "I'm fifty-two. This is what I've always done. This is what I know how to do. This is more than just a business to me, it's something I really believe in. I *love* guns."

Chapter 10
Both Sides
of the Aisle

In 1994, Mary Leigh Blek was the stay-at-home wife of an attorney, a registered Republican with three children enjoying life in affluent Orange County, California. She could never have imagined becoming a national spokeswoman and organizer, spending her life on airplanes and in committee meetings, endorsing political candidates and speaking at the Harvard School of Public Health. A soft-spoken nurse who gave up her career to become a full-time mother, she trembled when asked to read out the minutes of the PTA meeting. "My husband was the talker in the family," she says with a laugh.

Then their son Matthew, a nineteen-year-old college freshman, was mugged and murdered on a Manhattan street on a summer night in 1994 by two men who shot him in the head with a cheap handgun.

Blek quickly found her voice. "When Matt was killed, self was not important. My self-consciousness disappeared."

Talk to Blek today—in her role as head of the Million Mom March, a national gun-control lobby group—and words pour out of her in a steady, articulate torrent, a Niagara of conviction. "This kind of violence is preventable. I come from a background of public health, and this is an issue that is so clearly one of public health. I'm not in favor of banning all guns. But I want guns made safer. I want them to be better regulated and manufactured. I want to see common-sense gun laws."

On both sides of the gun debate, whether they work on the issues as lawyers, researchers, lobbyists, or legislators, women's passions run as deeply as hers. Many are pulled into the discussion reluctantly, like Blek, by a random act of gun violence. Their learning curve is vertical and the new pressures they face enormous and unrelenting: to raise money, address the media, attract and retain members, understand what legislation is workable, winnable, or worthless. When it comes to addressing one of the country's most divisive issues, polite compromise, de rigueur in some circles, often leads well-meaning women into an ineffectual, invisible quagmire.

Blek first organized locally, finding other parents whose children had been murdered by gun violence. In the spring of 1995, she founded the Bell campaign, named for its symbolism: "You can ring it as a memorial or to celebrate a special occasion such as a marriage—or a legislative victory." When in 1999 Donna Dees-Thomases, the New Jersey–based founder of the Million Mom March, asked the Bell campaign to merge with them, Blek eagerly agreed.

"We needed to replicate our local success nationally. We needed a national organization in order to impact national legislation." In May 2000, Blek became the director of the Million Mom March, a group whose name is now something of a misnomer. It began with a 750,000-person march in D.C. (augmented by tens of thousands more in seventy-two additional cities across the United States). "It was always planned to be an *event*, not an ongoing organization," Blek explains. By May 2000, MMM had forty local chapters, each with a minimum of twenty members. But Blek doesn't know how many members they have. "It's very hard to say. Each chapter can be a local church congregation of eight hundred or an email newsletter that goes out to a thousand people."

She recognizes the ongoing disparity between the size, wealth, visibility, and political power of the relatively young MMM and the Brady Campaign (with which they merged in October 2001), and the 133-year-old National Rifle Association, with its 4.3 million members (a number that has tripled since 1978) and appetite for bare-knuckled public debate. The NRA website's home page opens with an eagle, a waving flag, and other patriotic symbols; the MMM website feels cozy and somewhat folksy, with a Time-Out Chair for those whose views they disagree with.

"The NRA is more than a hundred years old. They are a single-issue group and what they usually say is 'No!' " says Blek. "In contrast, we have a diverse base of constituents and we've been held to pretty strict standards that are research-based. We have not been mobilized.

"Our two barriers to sensible gun laws are denial and apathy. Most people just don't think that gun violence is ever something they will have to deal with personally, so they choose not to think about it. Gun death is very traumatic so most people simply don't want to face it unless they have to. When it comes knocking on your door, you're very bowled over by it."

A third barrier, she agrees, is ignorance—many Americans just don't understand the current city, county, state, or federal gun laws, or their limits. "People already think we have licensing and registration of guns, and we don't. In some states there are limits to the amount you can sue the gun industry for. People don't know this."

Blek knows how hard it is, even after the sniper killings of 2002, even after countless other mini-massacres, to gather allies and spur significant legislation. "We haven't been mobilized and we haven't been strategic. We need to become more powerful and visible. That critical point will come and we will prevail."

When?

"The sooner the better." She laughs. More soberly, she admits, "It will take a while."

Getting politicians deeply committed to her cause is tough, she says. "People who are responsible for making gun policy also care about the environment, heath care, elder care. They also have other interests."

The attacks of September 11 only exacerbated her challenge, as Americans' attention refocused on homeland security and terrorism. In an age of increased fear and insecurity, of random patdowns at the airport and armed guards at national monuments, gun control has sunk to the bottom of the political agenda. "Since 9/11, the public hasn't been aware that we're now a chapter-based organization working on state and local laws, as well as national issues. In time that message will be out there."

Blek plans another Million Mom March on D.C. in 2004, a presidential election year. She wants the "gun show loophole" closed: federally licensed firearms dealers are required to conduct background checks of every buyer, but no such requirement exists for those at home, in flea markets, and at gun shows who sell firearms privately. No one can definitely say how many of these transactions occur each year—but it's one way for criminals to obtain guns while avoiding the notice of law enforcement agencies.[1]

Sarah Brady faced many of the same battles as head of the Brady Campaign (originally named the Center to Prevent Handgun Violence). Her husband, Jim Brady, then press secretary to President Ronald Reagan, had barely begun his new job when, on March 30, 1981, he was shot in the head on a D.C. street corner, leaving him in a wheelchair for life.

Facing the NRA was, for her as well, a David-Goliath struggle. "They would mount huge campaigns that just saturated the media with their message. We, by contrast, couldn't afford anything close to that kind of advertising blitz. For the most part, we had to depend on press conferences and news stories, which meant we had to think of ways to get the press's attention.

That's not an easy thing to do. . . . You really have to work at it."[2]

"Dedication and imagination alone were not going to be enough," writes Brady.[3] Only after a generous supporter gave them the money to run an ad in the *Washington Post* did the Center to Prevent Handgun Violence start to attract national attention.

To her dismay, it ended up taking seven years to get the Brady Bill passed—legislation that required a five-day waiting period to buy a gun and a background check of those buyers. The glacial speed of change, and the ferocity of political opposition, took Brady somewhat by surprise. After some initial setbacks in gathering political support, "for the next couple of years, we worked even harder—lobbying, traveling, speaking, meeting with editorial boards, cultivating support, and spreading the word in every way we could. Our momentum continued to build. Before long, our backing from law enforcement groups was overwhelming. Ours was the first piece of gun legislation that won the support of every one of the major law enforcement organizations, from those representing the rank and file to those representing the chiefs of police."[4]

Brady admits to some of Blek's battle fatigue. When personal tragedy thrust them into the national spotlight, both were women in their late fifties, both of a generation who expected to become, and stay, affluent wives and mothers, their lives focused on the private comforts and pleasures of home and family, not embroiled in ferocious, tireless, exhausting, public political fighting.

After their success in passing the Brady Bill, the battle lost some of its allure, she admits. "Jim, who improved physically with every year that went by, was devoting more and more time to fund-raising, dialing for dollars with a success no one else could match. As for me, I was frankly tired—and a bit dispirited. At the national level, we no longer had the focus we'd had with Brady and assault weapons, and I missed it."[5]

While her name in NRA and gun industry circles carries the

resonance and popularity of Beelzebub, Brady insists she does not oppose gun ownership. "I believe that law-abiding citizens should be able to buy and keep firearms. We should try to keep guns out of the hands of those who should not have them, including criminals, lunatics, and children." Gun owners must also be well-trained in the safe use of firearms and be required to keep weapons secure.[6]

Margaret Childers, a twenty-seven-year-old elementary-school teacher, began working with the Bradys when she was fifteen and a student at Georgetown Day School, a private school in Washington, D.C. She was galvanized to gun-control activism by the random shooting death of a young classmate, Alain Colaco. A popular, talented athlete and scientist, Colaco was shot five times in the head and chest on August 9, 1992, while doing yard work at his family's suburban D.C. home. The killer, Sean Lee Qualls, was a total stranger later diagnosed with a "psychotic disorder."

"I was devastated," recalls Childers. "This generous, intelligent, talented person was gone before I ever got to say good-bye."

Like Blek, Childers describes herself as intensely shy, someone who finds public attention disconcerting. Yet for the next few years, she gave six press conferences, spoke to a congressional subcommittee in a session that received national media coverage, organized fellow students, and did everything she possibly could to support gun control legislation. "Somehow Alain's death, and my passion for this issue, enabled me to summon the courage I needed. I discovered a strength I did not even know I had."

Childers visited several members of Congress—"with a camera crew in tow"—and tried to deliver petitions in support of the Brady Bill to the White House. She became cochair of Students Against Handgun Violence, a program designed to involve and organize youth in secondary and postsecondary institutions across the nation; it has since evolved into a program administered in schools by law enforcement officers.

On November 10, 1993, she sat in the "war room" with Sarah and James Brady during their final lobbying efforts and eventual passage of the Brady Bill, on November 30, 1993, "one of the most exciting days of my life." She was later invited to a ceremony conducted by President Clinton in the White House Rose Garden.

"I do believe that gun control groups can effect change—I have seen it happen. But the NRA is an incredibly powerful force. I don't know what it will take before public demand overpowers the NRA's political influence. But no matter how outmatched, gun control lobbies with the Brady Campaign play an important role. They give voice and hope to all of us who wish to someday see an end to the epidemic of violence."

No matter how passionate or well-intentioned, every gun control activist quickly comes to appreciate the Sisyphean fight ahead. Public apathy, denial, and ignorance, distracted or uninterested politicians, a well-funded gun lobby, the persistent political distractions of terrorism, and a struggling economy all conspire against activists. Tom Diaz, for four years Democratic counsel to the Crime Subcommittee of the U.S. House of Representatives, agrees:

"Given the inherent lethality of firearms, it is no wonder that guns cause so much mayhem in the United States every year. The wonder is that our society has become so inured to firearms violence that we hardly pay attention to the casualties that mount steadily, day after day and year after year. . . . Its anemic gun control movement musters little effective outcry."[7]

Having watched the political process firsthand, Diaz holds little optimism for movement on gun control. "Although individual members of Congress regularly introduce bills proposing to give authority for health and safety regulation for firearms to one or another executive agency, no such bill has seen the light of a public hearing or moved out of committee. (Members of Congress routinely introduce legislation relating to all manner of subjects, including firearms, that they know have no chance of going beyond the files of their colleagues. Nevertheless, both the members and the gun lobby wage vociferous press release wars over such paper tigers. The 'debate' serves both of their interests.)"[8]

Few politicians have the appetite to spend much time studying the gun industry or crime statistics to decide what changes, if any, might truly prove beneficial if enacted into law. In addition to competing political concerns and the need for bipartisan cooperation, the three factors hindering public action—ignorance, denial, and apathy—also affect legislators. "Many public officials know little about firearms and are happy to leave the details to the professionals," writes Diaz.[9]

The first federal firearms law was the War Revenue Act of 1919, which placed a tax on the manufacture of firearms and ammunition to help pay the costs of the First World War. The National Firearms Act of 1934 and the Federal Firearms Act of 1938 together comprised the federal government's first attempt at regulating the industry, largely through a taxation system that required manufacturers, importers, and dealers to register with the Treasury Department to pay a tax and obtain a license. It was effective in raising revenue, but not in limiting commerce in firearms.[10]

"World War II effectively ended federal anticrime concerns until 1965. Rates of criminal homicide, after peaking in 1933, fell during the Great Depression and war years and drifted downward thereafter until the early 1960s," says Franklin E. Zimring, a University of California/Berkeley law professor and expert on gun policy for more than thirty-five years.[11]

The 1960s, with the assassinations of John F. Kennedy in 1963, of Robert Kennedy and Martin Luther King in 1968, rising rates of violent crime (jumping 57 percent between 1960 and 1967, according to the FBI), and an explosion of handguns pushed Congress to pass the Gun Control Act of 1968. Until January 2003, manufacturers, importers, and dealers obtained a federal license from the Treasury Department (although it was administered by the Bureau of Alcohol, Tobacco, and Firearms. What do alcohol, tobacco, and firearms have in common? They are all subject to excise taxes, which is why they came under the Treasury Department's authority). Since January 2003, the renamed Bureau of Alcohol, Tobacco, Firearms and Explosives has been part of the Justice Department.

Gun industry lobbyists and the NRA like to complain there are already more than twenty thousand gun laws in existence—an impressive-sounding number impossible to verify and never proven. The implication is that Americans, and their guns, are already overregulated. The reality is more complex. That twenty thousand figure was first cited in 1965 by Representative John D. Dingell, was repeated more than twenty years ago by then president Ronald Reagan, and is bruited whenever opponents of gun control gather. A more realistic figure, even including federal, state, and local laws, is about four hundred. At time of writing, eighteen House bills and four Senate bills dealing with firearms were before the 108th Congress. These included H.R. 153, which would repeal the Brady Law, H.R. 357, which would prohibit federal or state lawsuits against gun manufacturers or sellers for damages resulting from criminal or unlawful use of a gun, and H.R. 76, which would, among other things, require all gun buyers to purchase a trigger lock.

Gun laws vary widely from state to state. More than twenty years ago, handguns were banned in Chicago and D.C., for example. Law can vary widely *within* each state, from city to city, county to county. To obtain a pistol permit within Manhattan, for example, you apply to the police department, as you would in other New York jurisdictions. But thanks to the Sullivan Laws, enacted in 1911, it's virtually impossible for a civilian to get a concealed-carry permit—while residents upstate in Buffalo or Rochester traveling professionally with valuables such as large amounts of cash or jewelry can. In many jurisdictions, local police chiefs retain considerable power to grant or deny pistol and carry permits, leaving only the courts as a method of appeal.

Let's say you are curious about guns and simply want to try shooting; in Manhattan, without a permit, you can rent and try a .22 rifle at a range. But only a .22, a light caliber and one that in no way reveals the true power and emotional impact of loading and firing a handgun. On the island of Manhattan, without a permit, you cannot touch a handgun—even to buy one. But drive across the Hudson River to Jersey City, a distance of barely ten miles, and accompanied by a licensed gun owner, you can shoot any handgun you can lay your hands on.

The country's current patchwork of city, county, state, and federal laws are already, for many politicians and voters, contradictory, confusing, and full of loopholes. Most Americans, no matter how horrified by gun violence, simply can't keep pace. What sorts of new guns or innovations *are* needed? Are any? What about making modifications, such as adding gun locks so that children and teens can't use guns? How difficult or expensive would it really be?

Even the NRA website warns, "While federal legislation receives much more media attention, state legislatures and city councils make many more decisions regarding your right to own and carry firearms. NRA members and gun owners must take extra care to be aware of antigun laws and ordinances at the state and local level."

Currently thirty-seven states allow the right to carry a concealed weapon, and the issue is under debate in Wisconsin. As of February 2003, the number of concealed-carry permits varied widely: 223,584 in Texas (pop. 21,325,018); 130,187 in Tennessee (pop. 5,740,021); 49,173 in Utah (pop. 2,269,789); 172,347 in Virginia (pop. 7,187,734); and the largest number by far, Florida, with 798,732 (pop. 16,396,515).[12] The list of state laws on handguns and long guns posted on the NRA website looks like a confusing and badly designed bingo card—where no one emerges a clear winner. While thirty-two states have no waiting period to purchase a firearm, in California it's ten days for handguns and long guns, fourteen days for both in Connecticut, seven days for both in Maryland, one day for a handgun in Kansas, and three days in Florida or Illinois. In Illinois, residents of Chicago, Evanston, Oak Park, Morton Grove, Wilmette, and Highland Park can't buy handguns at all.

California bans "unsafe handguns," while Vermont doesn't even demand a permit. Only seven states, California, Connecticut, Maryland, Hawaii, Rhode Island, New York, and Michigan, require a handgun safety course. (Michigan's is a written questionnaire.) Only thirteen states require permits or licenses: Connecticut, D.C., Hawaii, Illinois, Iowa, Massachusetts, Michigan, Minnesota, Missouri, New York, New Jersey, California, and Ohio.

No matter how curious or determined you are to learn about guns and their capacities, gaining access to any unbiased information is extremely difficult. Available data on firearms, violence, and firearms control are "both abundant and spotty," says academic expert Franklin Zimring.[13] "What used to be an undocumented dispute with little data and no specialist experts has become a debate between special interests that are well informed but heavily biased by anti- or pro-control orientations."[14] The gun industry is rarely eager to speak with uninformed or unsympathetic journalists who are not with the gun press. Most gun companies are privately owned, lacking the transparency of shareholders' meetings, annual reports, or SEC oversight. Until political pressure builds to an explosive degree, they're free to conduct business as usual.

While journalists struggle to gather any kind of cant-free information, legislators and voters remain largely out of the loop.

"Many of the major gun-rights and industry organizations [such as the National Shooting Sports Foundation (NSSF), Sporting Arms and Ammunition Manufacturers Institute (SAAMI)] network with each other and most have formal or informal working contacts with state, local, and federal government legislatures and executive agencies. The extent of this networking should not be underestimated," writes Tom Diaz, now a senior policy analyst with the D.C.-based Violence Policy Center. "These organizations are so thoroughly intertwined with gun manufacturers, the gun press, and other components of the firearms industry there is little light between them on most issues. They share common strategies, often share common officers, and frequently meet to plan coordinated action."[15]

"Federal and state wildlife and natural resource agencies can be and often are powerful supporters of gun industry interests, able to provide direct taxpayers' subsidies to assist them. . . . By and large, the gun industry and its constellation of supporting organizations are cooperating more to develop a common strategic plan, in the sense of having agreed-upon strategic goals (such as increasing the number of shooting ranges in the country, and targeting women, children, and minorities as consumers), hashed out in large public symposia and in private meetings in boardrooms and government offices, and implemented by getting the word out through the gun press and taking active stands through the organizations and their network of contacts."[16]

While national gun-control advocacy groups such as Americans for Gun Safety, the Violence Policy Center, and the Brady Campaign are well-known and usually enjoy positive media coverage, it's unclear how effectively they network and leverage off one another. They are most visible only in reaction to a forthcoming bill or act of violence, responding with the same familiar statistics. Unanimity offers strength; with many elements to gun control, disagreement about how doctrinaire a position to take weakens advocates' position, admits Mary Leigh Blek.

"There are no clear priorities among the new gun control activists," writes gun policy analyst Franklin Zimring. "Citizens are for or against gun control as a general sentiment, never mind the details. And most of the new academic experts on guns have done little to push the gun control debate toward specifics and priorities."[17]

Financially, gun control activists are forever overpowered by the manpower and connections of the National Rifle Association, the SAAMI, and the NSSF. The Violence Policy Center, which relies for funding solely on foundations and grants, has an annual budget of $1.6 million for a full-time staff of ten. The Brady Campaign to Prevent Handgun Violence has a full-time staff of forty-three and an annual budget of $8 million; they rely on individual donations from their half million members, not on foundations. The Sporting Arms and Ammunition Manufacturers Institute was formed in 1926 to promulgate standards for firearms makers and has about two dozen members, who focus their attention on technical matters related to design and manufacturing. The National Shooting Sports Foundation was founded in 1961. It has thirty-four staff and twenty-five hundred members, including all the major manufacturers of firearms, ammunition, and associated products, distributors, manufacturers' representatives, shooting ranges, retail stores, and publishers of books and magazines about the industry. Its budget comes from the annual Shot Show, the industry's major trade show held each year.

The National Rifle Association, based in Fairfax, Virginia, has an annual budget of $20 million and a full-time staff of five hundred. The NRA includes a well-organized machine whose grassroots, locally based fund-raising is continuous. The twenty-nine-year-old Institute for Legislative Action, with a staff of eighty and three offices, ensures a steady stream of revenue from committed members. The NRA frequently holds fund-raising dinners across the country, channeling $20 million into the 2000 elections in direct campaign donations, mobilizing, as the website proudly proclaims, "the most aggressive grassroots campaign in NRA history."

A sampling of documents filed with the Federal Election Commission shows the NRA support some politicians have enjoyed: Larry Craig, running for the U.S. Senate in Idaho (and a member of the NRA board of directors), received $5,883.02 on July 26, 2001; Bill Gormley, running for the U.S. Senate in New Jersey, got $22,545.27 on June 6, 2001; and John Cornyn, running for the U.S. Senate from Texas, $11,460.15 on October 15, 2002.

A few female names appear, among them Maine senator Susan

Collins, who got $1,701.84 on October 15, 2002; Virginia state senator Louise Lucas, who received $1,211.55 on June 7, 2001; former state legislator Jo Ann Davis of Virginia, who received $7,544.23 for her congressional race; and Beth Taylor, Martha Yaeger Walker, and Shelley Moore Capito, all of West Virginia, who each received $351.36 on May 1, 2000, for their campaigns for House seats.

(Craig, Miller, Shuster, Cornyn, Collins, Davis, and Moore Capito were elected or reelected. Gormley dropped out of the race. Contrary to popular belief, the NRA supports Democratic candidates when it sees fit; Taylor, Lucas, and Walker are Democrats. Spokesman Andrew Arulanandam, the NRA's director of public affairs, would say only that decisions are "made internally" on whom to support.)

Women, of course, also work for the NRA, among them fiscal officer Mary Rose Adkins, who oversees every donation to a political candidate. Karen Mehall edits their new magazine, *Woman's Outlook,* and Mary Sue Faulkner runs the popular national Women on Target program. Marion Hammer made history from 1995 to 1998 as the NRA's first woman president and today serves on the board of directors and executive council. Phoenix attorney Sandra Forman is the NRA's second vice president and a certified instructor in pistol and personal protection.

Many smaller organizations are devoted to gun rights for specific groups, from pinkpistols.org for gays and lesbians to Liberty Belles, Armed Females of America, and Second Amendment Sisters for women. Second Amendment Sisters, a national gun-rights group, was founded in December 1999 by five women, ranging in age from the thirties to sixties, across the country. "Our organization is entirely grassroots," says Maria Heil, a stay-at-home Pennsylvania mother of four who is the group's spokeswoman. She says they have "tens of thousands" of supporters who have paid $25 to join ($15 for men and those under 18).

"Society has changed. Women need to protect themselves because the way men treat women has changed. Guys are not being brought up with the notion that they have to protect women." Heil thinks women need to defend themselves, but must understand the ramifications of their choice. Heil could afford to take a $700 class that taught her how to handle herself *after* she has shot, but knows this is way out of reach for many women who have armed themselves ignorant of the legal consequences. "We see there's a great need for this education, but it has to be affordable."

The group focuses much of its energy on lobbying in state legislatures to back gun rights. Heil, a self-described "rookie" at lobbying and media relations, often visits D.C. legislators to show the group's support for H.R. 1036, "The Protection of Lawful Commerce in Arms Act," a bill introduced on February 27, 2003, that would prohibit lawsuits against gun manufacturers. With fifty-two cosponsors, the bill easily passed the House, 240 to 180, and at the time of writing was headed to the Senate.

Many female gun owners I spoke to expressed great discomfort with the most extreme and vocal of gun-rights supporters, whose unyielding position feels embarrassingly intransigent and unrealistic, yet—or perhaps thereby—garners the biggest headlines. Heil agrees, "When they hear NRA, they think of white men with guns." More moderate voices, including those of gun owners concerned about gun violence, simply get shouted down. For gun control diehards, owning a gun destroys your credibility to discuss safely using it. Those who don't own one claim moral authority. As long as no one cedes an inch, the dialogue of the deaf continues.

"There are a few reasons I would never consider myself a part of the gun culture of America," says twenty-three-year-old Chloe Polemis, a senior at New York University. "First and foremost, I really feel as though the NRA and many gun supporters within this country are most often lumped into a category of people that I often find frightening and that I rarely agree with politically. The most vocal gun supporters tend to be right-wing, Christian, Republican men, and I have never identified with individuals like that. I do not believe people should have total freedom to buy automatic weapons, high-powered rifles, or anything like that."

Polemis's family, who live in Manhattan, own eight guns, used exclusively for sport. She's quick to distance herself from what she sees as a lunatic fringe. "We are not holed up in a bunker, waiting for the day when we need to protect ourselves. Obviously that's an exaggeration, and most gun owners are not like that, but the stereotype does exist." She appreciates the irony that, legally allowed to own many guns, she nonetheless holds strong feelings against some types of them. "I guess I am in a very conflicting situation."

Nor is the current political climate conducive to a long, thoughtful conversation about gun control: war with Iraq and the worst economy in twenty years dominate front-page headlines. As the nation jumped to orange alert status and residents stocked up on duct tape and plastic sheeting to block out a chemical attack, state legislators in at least twenty-four states, thirteen of them with Republican governors, were confronting yet another unpleasant reality—significant budget shortfalls and the need to cut costs everywhere while raising taxes.

In addition to cutting money for teachers' raises and prescription drugs for the elderly, Governor Mike Huckabee of Arkansas (one of the states with the highest per capita gun ownership) warned, "We'll have to have a massive early release of thousands of inmates"—unlikely to reassure any voter already worried about personal security.[18] On Valentine's Day, 2003, Smith & Wesson announced the introduction of its biggest handgun, a $989 .50-caliber Magnum revolver, powerful enough, according to the company, to bring down a charging bear.[19]

Democrats and Republicans must balance the competing views of urban, suburban, and rural voters, yet suburban women, usually poster girls for gun control, must be wooed. "Republicans know they can't win statewide in swing states like Pennsylvania and Michigan and Illinois and New Jersey if they're on the wrong side of the gun issue," says Michael D. Barnes, president of the Brady Campaign.[20]

What's missing, always, in the national conversation about guns is a lasting sense of outrage, of a citizenry that has reached breaking point. No matter how egregious or bloody the massacre, no matter the unprecedented fear and violence it ignites in a previously quiet middle-class community, the minute the killing is over, our collective memory begins to fade. The individuals affected, and their families and friends and colleagues, are forever scarred emotionally, physically, and professionally, yet the body politic seems afflicted by an odd and incurable amnesia.

In October 2002, a pair of snipers, John Muhammad and Lee Malvo, terrorized D.C. and Maryland residents, killing thirteen and wounding seven. High school football players began practicing indoors. Mothers refused to let their children play outside. Gas stations erected tarps to protect customers from a clear shot while they pumped fuel.

Barely two months after the snipers were apprehended, First Lady Laura Bush made newspaper headlines—not by expressing outrage at the gun violence but by visiting their first and youngest victim, thirteen-year-old Iran Brown. "You look like you're doing great! Bless you, darling," she told the young man during a holiday visit with patients at the Children's National Medical Center. Brown walked through the hospital with her, a "miracle embodied," wrote one reporter.[21]

On the morning of October 7, Brown was left for dead, bleeding on a schoolyard sidewalk with his stomach shot to shreds, screaming for his aunt, who had just left him off at school. "As you opened up his chest, it was just unbelievable. It was like a bomb had gone off in there," said Dr. Kurt Newman, the surgeon who treated him. Doctors removed Iran's spleen and part of his lung and pancreas. After massive blood loss, he spent thirty-six days barely conscious. He suffers pain from a broken rib, a foot-long scar, difficulty breathing. He faces more surgery and medication for the rest of his life.[22]

Brown had become one more unlucky statistic, admired for his reluctant bravery.

The bully pulpit of first lady is best used judiciously, as Hillary Clinton learned in her unsuccessful attempt to push health coverage. Gun control, even the arguably softer issue of responsible gun ownership, presents political quicksand, as elected officials know too well. Assassinations aside—widowing Mary Todd Lincoln, Ida McKinley, Lucretia Randolph Garfield, and Jacqueline Kennedy—rarely are first ladies publicly associated with firearms.

In 1958, at the age of seventy-four, one woman determined to travel alone to the South to speak about civil rights was warned to stay home by the FBI. The Ku Klux Klan had put a $25,000 bounty on Eleanor Roosevelt's head. She took her own handgun and went anyway. She first carried a handgun shortly after she moved into the White House in 1933; after leaving the White House and moving to New York City, she obtained a handgun permit, fearful of death threats from those offended by her newspaper columns. As the niece of Theodore Roosevelt, who walked her down the aisle at her wedding and was perhaps the best-known gun enthusiast in American history, she, not surprisingly, felt comfortable with firearms.

Nancy Reagan, famous largely for her impeccable designer clothing, made headlines in 1981 when it was discovered—hours before a summit meeting between Canada's Prime Minister Pierre Trudeau and President Ronald Reagan—that she owned, and was bringing with her, a personal handgun. A pearl-handled revolver, to be precise. Canadian federal solicitor general Robert Kaplan made clear she would be frisked for weapons upon arrival—bringing guns into Canada is illegal. No exceptions.

Yet, with hasty diplomacy, a showdown was averted.

"The Mounties went from rogue elephant mode into reverse," recalled Kaplan in a 1998 interview. "It was a very sensitive time for them, and the commissioner had already threatened to resign. But we couldn't tell Mrs. Reagan she would be searched for weapons and risk the summit being canceled. Nor did we want the commissioner to quit because we wouldn't allow his officers to search Mrs. Reagan. . . . [The two men] eventually compromised and the Reagans were quietly informed about Canadian law. To this day, only Nancy Reagan knows whether she came to the 1981 summit with a pistol in her purse."[23]

Like Blek and Sarah Brady, Carolyn McCarthy reluctantly joined the ranks of those wounded by gun violence and pushed to ongoing national prominence. On December 7, 1993, Colin Ferguson, a crazed gunman carrying an assault weapon, killed her husband of twenty-eight years, Dennis, and injured her twenty-six-year-old son, Kevin, when he opened fire on them in a Long Island Rail Road commuter train. Kevin's skull was shattered, his chances of survival so poor that McCarthy signed his organ-donation sheet. (Today, although his left arm and leg are still impaired, he works as a broker and is married with two children.)

Today McCarthy is a four-term elected official, the first congresswoman in Long Island's history. After her husband's death, she'd only planned to speak out in favor of gun control, but was galvanized to run for office when she questioned the local Republican congressman, Daniel Frisa, about his plan to repeal a ban on assault weapons. Dissatisfied with his answers, McCarthy, a lifelong Republican, campaigned for the Democrats—and beat Frisa 57 percent to 41 percent. "All we wanted to do was make something good come out of a horrible situation. Well, we did that," she said.[24]

Then fifty-two, she arrived on Capitol Hill a total novice, well aware of the snickers and doubts of seasoned colleagues. "They called me the 'gun lady.' I was naive and full of fire," she recalls.

A less likely trajectory is difficult to imagine. A petite former ICU nurse, McCarthy still lives in the house where she grew up. Thick blond bangs frame her face, and her bright blue eyes catch and hold yours. She smiles easily and often. Her ears are twice-pierced, her fingernails unvarnished, her black leather, lace-up shoes sensible and comfortable. She retains a nurse's blend of warmth and efficiency. Yet, barely three years into her new career, she made a gun-control speech so passionate that Democratic House Leader Dick Gephardt called it the best he'd heard in twenty-two years. While passion propelled her into politics, her pragmatism helps keep her there.

Today she's a veteran of the policy-making process who relishes the backroom deal-making. She happily works with colleagues from the most rural, NRA-dominated districts. "They know I have a lot of patience. I'm extremely sincere. I explain line by line what the bill will be."

Realistically, though, in a Republican-controlled House, Congress, and administration, the odds of getting any gun control bill passed are slim. And McCarthy prides herself on being a pragmatist, someone eager to see her bills *move*, not rotate endlessly in committee. So she builds bridges where she can, working on one bill with Arizona Republican senator John McCain, on another with Michigan Democrat Mike Dingell, a former NRA board member who once shot down a bill of hers. "McCain and I both believe in moving *forward*. Will it be the best bill possible? We hope to get it *passed!*"

Hard-line gun control activists consider such concessions traitorous, as they are quick to remind her.

"I hate the Violence Policy Center!" she says. "Yes, you can print that. They are the worst. They're purists." When her most recent bill, Our Lady of Peace, did not make it to the House floor for a vote, activists hounded her for watering it down, saying it didn't go far enough. "They wanted every single thing in it to remain unchanged. That broke my heart to be called a traitor!" Like Brady and Blek, McCarthy was shoved at midlife into national celebrity and relentless pressure from impatient special interest groups, igniting nonstop scrutiny and criticism she clearly doesn't appreciate. "This is *not* what I was planning to do with my life," she adds with asperity. "This is personal for me, not political. I'm limited on what I can get through. I will do what I have to do *inch by inch.*"

When we met at her office in March 2003, McCarthy was working on several gun control bills. Our Lady of Peace, H.R.

4757 (named for a church where a priest was shot dead by a parishioner), is designed to force states to update their many databases to more accurately reflect current data on felonies, making the standard NICS check more effective. Senator McCain was working with her on another bill to close the "gun show loophole," which currently allows private sellers of firearms to sell them without checking the background of their buyers.

McCarthy says she's seen as a "gun grabber," the dismissive nickname the NRA gives anyone opposed to its policies. "I'm *not* opposed to gun ownership," she says, and even recommends buying a rifle over a handgun for home self-defense for its greater accuracy.

Suzanna Hupp, a tall, auburn-haired, easygoing Texan mother of two, has been a Republican member of the Texas legislature since 1996. Like McCarthy, Blek, and Brady, she too was a complete political novice propelled into politics by gun violence. On October 16, 1991, she was eating lunch with her parents, Al and Suzanna, in the popular chain restaurant Luby's in Lubbock. The couple had recently celebrated their forty-seventh wedding anniversary. A truck smashed through one glass wall, blocking the exits, and thirty-five-year-old George Hennard stepped out.

Hupp watched in terror as he slowly circled the room, randomly selecting twenty-two victims, most of whom he shot in the head at point-blank range. He wounded twenty more, shooting her father in the chest. "I knew he didn't have a chance," she said. Her mother ran forward to cradle him as he died. Hupp managed to escape and ran to her truck, parked across the street, to grab the revolver she kept there. But it was too late. By the time she found her gun and returned to the restaurant, her mother had also been killed.

Her sense of impotence haunts her still.

"I used to carry my gun, a Smith & Wesson .38, illegally, but I could have faced felony charges if I was found with it." She stopped doing so barely three months before her parents were killed. "What are the odds? It's not going to be a bright sunny day in a crowded restaurant. It will be on a dark, deserted highway." She guessed wrong. "I made an incredibly stupid decision to obey a bad law," she says now.

She was thirty-one, filled with remorse, convinced that if she had only had her gun with her, she might have been able to save her parents. Hupp's testimony was instrumental in passing the concealed-carry law in Texas in 1995. Texas Democratic governor Ann Richards had repeatedly vetoed it, but when George W. Bush became governor, he signed it into law.

Urged repeatedly to run for office as she spoke out over and over about her parents' murders, Hupp began to consider the idea. "I always thought my brother would do it," she admits. "You have to *really* want to be here."

She's something of an icon to the NRA and gun-ownership advocates. She did cosponsor SB717, which prevents Texas cities and municipalities from bringing lawsuits against gun manufacturers—such as the thirty-four suits launched by other major cities across the country, starting in 1998 with New Orleans and followed by Boston, Philadelphia, and many others. (At time of writing, fifteen had been thrown out or abandoned, and nineteen were still moving through the courts.)

For some legislators, political office brings perks, prestige, staff, and a six-figure salary. Hupp earns $285 a month, less than her two young, part-time aides, to represent a district of 140,000 voters spread across four and a half counties, half-agricultural and half-military, thanks to the presence of Fort Hood, the largest military installation in the United States. When we met in her Austin office, she wore jeans and cowboy boots, one eye reddened thanks to a stray piece of straw; she lives on a ranch with her husband and two young sons.

She has run for office three times and won't have to run again, as she has no opponent. Last time, Hupp took 63 percent of the vote. "For the most part, people are pretty happy with me." Despite her many years in office, Hupp seems unpretentious, likable, and down-to-earth.

She started carrying a gun when she opened her chiropractic practice, driving alone over long distances. "I thought this was an incredibly logical decision. You stick it in your bag of tricks. To me it's like driving with your seat belt on. Does it change the odds? Yes!"

She has heard all the gun control arguments but remains unpersuaded. "There are thousands of guns in the hands of people who handle them safely, and the creeps who want to commit crimes are looking for easy victims. They want to take people out like shooting fish in a barrel. I know. I've been there!"

That Hupp and McCarthy diverge so completely, despite their same bloody initiation into politics, is not unusual. More than perhaps any other political issue—reflecting how differently guns appear to voters in the elk-hunting mountains of Wyoming, Colorado, and Montana to the duck-hunting wetlands of Louisiana, Alabama, and Florida to crime- and violence-plagued cities like New York, Detroit, Philadelphia, and D.C.—gun control views differ widely from one region to another.

Gun control is a battle waged on many fronts, some highly public, others long, quieter courtroom duels. However low-profile, women are involved at every level, as witnesses, lawyers on both sides, and as lobbyists.

Thirty-four cities have sued the gun industry, including Atlanta, Miami, St. Louis, and Boston; as of this writing, nineteen suits were ongoing, including those of Chicago, Cincinnati, Cleveland, and Newark. The others either gave up, were dismissed by judges, or were, as in the case of New Orleans's lawsuit, preempted by a state law granting immunity to the gun industry.

Marc Morial was in his second and final term as mayor when he decided in October 1998 to launch the first salvo. For years, New Orleans, a city 70 to 75 percent black, has battled an extraordinarily high crime rate. Unemployment, officially 5 percent, is more like 15 percent among blacks, the city's majority. Working with the U.S. conference of mayors, with Willie Brown of San

Francisco, Ed Rendell of Philadelphia, and Richard Daley of Chicago, Morial mapped out his strategy. Since there appeared to be no way to stem the flow of guns, legal or illegal, into their cities, the mayors hoped to humble firearms manufacturers through the million-dollar cost of defending themselves. Profit margins in the industry are razor thin.

"We have nothing to negotiate," said Smith & Wesson president Ed Shultz in May 1999. "There's nothing there, okay? Nothing. Zero. There are no contingency plans. The only contingency plan is when you give them the keys [i.e., go bankrupt]. All they can get is the business that they hate."[25]

"The issue was safety," says Dan Abel, the lead lawyer for the New Orleans lawsuit. The mayors were as fed up with gun accidents as criminal activity and, bolstered by the success of lawsuits against the tobacco industry, decided to use the same legal methodology. In search of a partner with expertise, they called Dennis Henigan, attorney with Handgun Control Inc., the group founded by Sarah Brady.

Did they really think they could win? "Yes!" insists Abel. "We all grew up hunting and fishing, but the matter wasn't ownership of guns, but safety." The plan was to put the matter to a jury. "If a gun could be manufactured to be childproof, who wouldn't buy it?"

The first surprise for the gun manufacturers came from their insurance companies, who denied them coverage from the lawsuits, arguing the language that would cover them wasn't in their policies. "We picked the ones we thought had the most products—Colt, Smith & Wesson, Glock, Ruger, Browning," says Abel. "Our argument was that if guns could be made safer, they *should* be made safer."

The New Orleans suit took two years of work, involved forty-five law firms and two hundred lawyers. The gun industry didn't have a lot of money to chase—total profits for the entire industry, for guns alone, were $118 million a year. The suit abruptly ended, though, when the Louisiana state legislature passed a bill in June 1999 making it illegal for the city of New Orleans to sue gun manufacturers. "A gun lock would have cost fifty cents to a dollar per gun," says Abel. "We never even got to argue the merits of the case."[26]

"The problem with all the national gun legislation is that it won't stop violence," said Louisiana governor Mike Foster. "The way to stop violence is to put people in jail who use guns. There's just not enough prosecution."[27]

Christine Cox, a New Orleans public relations consultant in the tobacco suits who closely followed the gun lawsuits, attended a Senate committee hearing in Baton Rouge. "They saw Morial as a black, grandstanding Democrat, whose concern was of no benefit to the state. They could never get past the fact they thought it was a political agenda being followed."

Today Cox, forty-two, doubts significant progress can be made on the issue of gun control for some time. "We're still too ambivalent in this country about guns, about whether or not we should carry. We might have won this [lawsuit] ten years from now, but I don't think the political climate is ready yet. It's a multitiered thing," she adds. Because gun laws are made federally, state by state, county by county, and even city by city, progress is haphazard, an ongoing game of legislative Whack-a-Mole—for every gun control victory, another pro-gun move is introduced.

Cox is surprised more women aren't involved, and loudly, on the issue of gun control. "It would make a difference if more women were involved in the political process. Women are sensitive to violence in general. They're naturally very protective of their children, more so than men. I just think they'd be more interested in change at this level."

What would it take, I asked her, for gun control to take center stage in American politics?

"Barbara Bush getting shot."

Morial knows that no politician anywhere, and certainly not in New Orleans, can separate gun-related crime from the highly lucrative, jealously guarded drug economy. "Guns are the tools of the trade," he told me, as did former district attorney Harry

Connick Sr., who for twenty-five years fought the same battles. Even sitting in his comfortable living room on a street in a gentrifying neighborhood of New Orleans, Morial said he's as vulnerable as anyone to the city's violence. Typical of the neighborhood, his home has a locked metal gate at the sidewalk. Even he can't imagine strolling for pleasure through his area.[28]

The National Association for the Advancement of Colored People filed its own suit against the gun industry in 1999. In doing so, the group said its goal was "to protect the well-being and security of its membership, which has been disproportionately injured" by illegal handguns. Their chief lawyer, Elisa Barnes, said she expected the most useful material in the lawsuit to come from newly released gun-tracing records from 1996 to 2000. "I think it is the one important moment in this type of litigation." The tracing will show who used the gun after it was sold.

Ms. Barnes was the chief lawyer in the only case against the gun industry as a whole that ended with a verdict for the plaintiffs—but it was overturned in New York State's highest court, the Court of Appeals. In her new attack on the industry, Barnes decided not to seek damages for the families of gun victims but instead seek an injunction that would establish new restrictions on the marketing and distribution of guns. In July 2003, after a six-week trial, a federal judge in Brooklyn dismissed the lawsuit.[29]

No analogous litigation has been brought by a Hispanic group—despite a 2001 report from the Violence Policy Center, "Latinos and Gun Violence," that showed that while only 11 percent of Hispanics own guns, 72 percent of Hispanic homicide victims were killed by a firearm. In California, Hispanics represent 30 percent of the population, but 44 percent of homicide victims, 77.4 percent of whom died as a result of gun violence.

While the highest rate of gun deaths is still claimed by blacks, Hispanic women living in the Southwest had the highest rates of gun-related death (which correlated with the highest rates of domestic abuse: 180 cases per 1,000 couples compared to 166 per 1,000 among black couples and 117 per 1,000 among whites). In

Chicago, in 63 percent of Hispanic homicides, men killed their female partner.

While much attention has been focused on gun violence and death rates among blacks, there are few data on Hispanics, the study said. The study found that Hispanics, like blacks, are far more likely than whites to become victims of gun violence—57 percent of blacks and Hispanics and 43 percent of whites. More than any other group, Hispanics are most likely to be attacked by strangers—65 percent of attacks—versus 58 percent for whites and 54 percent for blacks.

In the 2004 presidential election, how women and Hispanics will vote on issues of gun control is crucial to George Bush. "The white South is now a Republican bastion, and the party's candidates thrive in white working-class suburbs ringing heavily black cities such as Detroit and Chicago," notes political commentator Thomas B. Edsall. "This realignment has helped produce six Republican victories in the past nine presidential contests and Republican control of the Senate and House. Now the Republican Party is seeking ways to keep these gains while also winning new support among constituencies with different agendas, especially Hispanics and working women. . . . GOP operatives know that marginal voting shifts by any key group—blacks, working women, Hispanics, suburbanites—can spell victory or defeat in 2004 and beyond."[30]

The major challenge facing the GOP, says Miami pollster Sergio Bendixen, who has twenty years experience in the field, is that Hispanics vote very differently on gun control depending on how long they have lived in the United States. For most Hispanics, gun control is not even a key issue—falling far down a list of concerns headed by education, employment, and economic parity. "They're much more focused on assimilation."

Hispanics new to the United States often come to this country from Latin American countries fleeing high crime, terrorism, or paramilitary violence. "The last thing they think about is owning a gun," says Bendixen. "They have fairly radical positions on the issue. They want guns outlawed—period. Even gun safety is not a subject of interest to them; if you talk about gun control, you lose them." Sixty to 70 percent of Hispanic women feel this way, 10 to 20 percent more than Hispanic men polled on the issue.

Bendixen worked with the 2001 New Jersey gubernatorial campaign of Democrat Jim McGreevey, where gun control was key to McGreevey's victory. "This was *the* most important issue for Spanish-speaking voters in that election," Bendixen says. McGreevey's opponent, Bret Schundler, had favored introducing a concealed-carry law to the state (although he doubted it would ever survive the legislative process). A statewide poll showed that crime and violence were by far the most pressing issues for New Jersey's Hispanic voters, not the usual complaints of high taxes and the nation's costliest car insurance.

"People were almost offended by the Schundler campaign," says Bendixen, a finding that helped the Democrats create a Spanish-language direct-mail and television campaign with "very very positive results."

Hispanics who have lived in the United States for many years differ substantially in their views from more recent immigrants, he adds. "They definitely feel closer to the general population in their point of view. We see it on abortion, on gay rights. They're much closer to the average American."

The challenge for the GOP is an interesting one: while recent immigrants reject any conversation on guns, it is they who will sway the 2004 elections. "They vote in much higher numbers than U.S.-born Hispanics," says Bendixen—10 to 15 percent more likely. "U.S.-born Hispanics have statistically been one of the lowest groups to turn out, and the English-dominant voter is very hard to reach." Of the country's 7 million Hispanic voters, 50 percent are new immigrants eager to exercise their franchise.

"The Hispanic vote will be the key battlefield for American politics."

Bush's dilemma? The people most likely to share his views on gun control are those least likely to vote, while those most likely to turn out in droves on Election Day hate guns. "The immigrants don't agree with him on many issues, but they love him," says

Bendixen. "He gives speeches in Spanish, he visits Mexico and Peru. . . . The Democrats cannot connect emotionally with these voters. Bush is someone who grew up among Mexican-Americans and who has communicated his respect for Spanish-speaking immigrants on Spanish-language television." (Surveys by Greenberg Quinlan Rosner Research show that the Democratic advantage among Hispanic voters fell to 21 percentage points this year, the lowest level in at least two decades. The Democratic edge over Republicans among Latino voters was twenty nine points in 2000 and twenty six points in 1998.)[31]

The election may well hang on this newly powerful, populous vote, Bendixen says. "It's going to be fascinating to watch."

Chapter 11
The Next Generation

EVEN IF THEY CAN'T LEGALLY BUY ONE, GUNS AFFECT THE HEARTS and minds of many young American women, whether they hunt with their family, dodge bullets from neighborhood drive-bys, or attend college on a riflery scholarship. There's no unanimity among American teenagers on gun use and gun control because, like those of adults, their experiences are so disparate and heterogeneous. Ask a white, middle-class thirteen-year-old from Ohio why she loves to shoot trap and she'll tell you it's cool. Ask a poor, Hispanic twenty-year-old from the Bronx convicted for possession of a stolen weapon and she'll tell you that a gun gave her a power nothing else could. Ask a poised white, nineteen-year-old Mount Holyoke sophomore why she target shoots and she'll say it's relaxing. Ask an eighteen-year-old new mother from small-town Utah why she shot while eight months pregnant and was back at the range within weeks of giving birth and she'll say shooting is as much a part of her identity as her tiny newborn.

Their feelings about guns are as passionate and diverse as those of their parents and teachers.

Like adults, young women's opinions about guns are affected

by many of the same issues: class, race, region, neighborhood, socioeconomic level. For Tiara Simmons, a black, nineteen-year-old college sophomore in New Rochelle, a mixed-income New York City suburb, guns were a normal part of her high school life experience in Mount Vernon, another Manhattan suburb largely lower-income. "It's a little Manhattan up there," she says. Girls and boys alike brought guns to school, sneaking them easily past the metal detectors. "You can hide it well. You can get around it. If the alarm goes off, you show them your belt buckle and blame it on that," she says. "It's not something I saw every day, but it wasn't that shocking." In her school of three thousand students, Simmons says about twenty students each day brought a weapon to school. She did not; a double amputee confined to a wheelchair, she relies on her intuition to stay away from trouble.

Slow police response in bad neighborhoods has left her cynical. In an area she calls Chez Whitey, a few blocks from her home, "they're on the phone with you within the next few minutes" of any disturbance. Where she lives, barely five blocks away, she questions her level of personal safety. "Would they really be there if you need them? They know there's always something going on in that neighborhood. The other day I heard gunshots and I didn't hear sirens until twenty minutes later."

Eboni Aarons grew up in suburban New Jersey completely comfortable around her father's three guns, a 9mm pistol, a .357 Magnum, and a rifle. She described the .357 as "a cute little gun. It was so pretty! I loved cleaning it." Her father, a former military officer in Jamaica, taught her to shoot when she was eight. Yet, at twenty-one, she doesn't own a gun, can't imagine owning one, and knows no women her age who do. Yet she firmly believes in arming herself. Aarons is pretty, vivacious, and articulate, her thick black hair in ringlets, a stylish cream cotton sweater beneath her jean jacket. A full-time college student from a middle-class family, she nonchalantly pulled out a small black nylon case from her jacket pocket to show me her knife and its three-inch blade. "If people know you have a weapon on you, they'll leave you alone."

She used it, once, in a fight with a friend's boyfriend who kept coming on to her. Fed up, she confronted him, and he pulled a knife on her. "When I pulled out my knife, he was so shocked!" Aarons cut him on the hand and the leg, but admits she was lucky—she escaped without injury and he didn't press charges.

Aarons described her knife as "very empowering. I want to *live!* I don't want to be hindered. I'm not going to be able to live my life being afraid to go somewhere. I have no problem whatsoever having a knife. Women are empowering themselves politically, economically, sexually. This is part of the same process. There are so many people willing to rape you, rob you, mug you, for no apparent reason. To feel I'm on a level playing field, I need this."

Owning a gun, though, is a responsibility she's not ready to assume. While she says she knows at least half a dozen men her age who carry illegal weapons, Aarons said she can't imagine having one herself. "A gun is just such a big step! It's something significant."

Fear of school-related gun violence is common for many teens today. But, long before Jonesboro, Paducah, Pearl, and Littleton became the high school killing fields of angry young men, it was a young woman, Brenda Spencer, who fired the first shot. She aimed a .22-caliber rifle out her window on a Monday morning as children arrived at the elementary school across the street from her San Diego home and started shooting.

"It was a lot of fun seeing children shot. I just don't like Mondays. This livens up the day," said Spencer after killing principal Burton Wragg, fifty-three, and custodian Mike Suchar, fifty-six, and wounding eight children. Sentenced to twenty-five years to life, she's serving her time at the California Institute for Women, most recently denied parole in April 2001. "With every school shooting, I feel I'm partially responsible," she said then. "What if they got their idea from what I did?"[1] San Diego district attorney Richard Sachs says Spencer even has a fan club. "She's had letters from teenagers obsessed with what she did. As the first person to shoot at a school, she has gained notoriety."[2]

Spencer set a powerful precedent. Since 1974, American schools have, on thirty-seven occasions, erupted in lethal gun violence—five times in 1999 alone. Forty-one attackers, all males thirteen to eighteen, have vented their rage, frustration, and suicidal isolation in massacres of teachers, administrators, and fellow students. Twenty-seven states have been affected, with the most incidents—five—occurring in California, with three in Kentucky and two each in Arkansas, Georgia, Tennessee, and Missouri.

While young women are usually only the victims or witnesses, Robyn Anderson bought three of the guns used by Dylan Klebold and Eric Harris in their murder of thirteen at Columbine High School in Littleton, Colorado. A study by the Centers for Disease Control and Prevention found that more than half of the guns used in the 1990s in school shootings came from home (38 percent) or from friends (23 percent). Students bought only 7 percent of the guns and only 5.5 percent were stolen.

Two government studies of the school attacks, each of which involved dozens of detailed interviews with students, teachers, mental health experts, law enforcement officials, and even ten of the attackers, reached the chilling conclusion: *There is no way to predict when, or if, such an event will happen. There are no specific characteristics of a student who is a would-be killer.*

What both studies found was an extraordinarily deep well of rage and pain impelling students to murder. Adults too many decades past adolescence and the closed loop of high school life easily dismiss or minimize the private hell of ostracism. Imagine being stuck in a job for two, three, or four years where your colleagues subject you to daily physical or emotional abuse. You'd quit or sue or both. Most kids can't, and adults forget that.

"Bullying was not a factor in every case, and clearly every child who is bullied in school will not pose a risk for targeted violence in school," said one report. "Nevertheless, in a number of the incidents studied, attackers described being bullied in terms that suggested that these experiences approached torment. These attackers told of behaviors that, if they occurred in the workplace, likely would meet legal definitions of harassment and or assault. "[3]

Students who decide to kill at school feel isolated, alone, and often suicidally depressed. But even those who know what's coming don't have an adult they trust enough to turn to for help—*in 81 percent* of the incidents studied, other students knew an attack was being planned, giving them the opportunity and the choice of telling someone in authority. *But they didn't.*

Certainly, if these students had no access to guns, they couldn't go on a shooting rampage; 61 percent of perpetrators used handguns, 49 percent rifles or shotguns. While 76 percent used only one weapon in the shootings, almost half of them, 46 percent, had more than one weapon with them during the attack. But, while access to weapons is key, teachers, school administrators, parents, and fellow students need to consider their complicity.

In nearly two-thirds of incidents (59 percent), more than one other person knew, and in 93 percent of cases, those who knew were peers—a friend, schoolmate, or sibling. In 11 percent, the shooters had assistance from fellow students in planning the attack; in 8 percent, two or more students were involved in its execution.[4]

However "isolated" these young killers appear (and subjectively feel they are), they're in fact deeply embedded in a larger teen culture that—by allowing their deadly plans to reach fruition without interruption or sabotage—tacitly encourages this deadly behavior.

In her 1999 book, *A Tribe Apart,* the result of three years of hanging out with eight middle-class, suburban Maryland high school students, writer and suburban mom Patricia Hersch found an extraordinary loneliness and a profound lack of connection to the larger adult world beyond parents or school authorities. The kids Hersch met didn't trust the few adults they knew. They didn't have a rabbi or minister, an uncle or Boy Scout leader, a close adult friend of any description whose advice mattered.

Instead, they saw parents as selfish and unavailable, preoccupied with their own work and recreation. In many single-parent homes, teens face many hours alone after school. The teens told Hersch that teachers or administrators are equally improbable sources of solace or advice, focused instead on the measurable and impersonal, on test results and discipline, herding kids like cattle from one class to the next. Adults, they said, weren't reliable, responsible possible confidants but inconsistent, distracted, emotionally and physically unavailable arbiters.

"Churches, schools, family, are supposed to give structure to kids," says Curtis Hanson, director of the popular 2002 film *8 Mile*, which featured rap star Eminem. "But now they're all part of a dysfunctional culture. No one's helping kids figure out where they're going—not just in the inner cities, but in the suburbs. Hip-hop comes out of that. It is a voice for people who have no other voice."[5]

So is gun violence.

If the only true measure of success or failure lies within one's tribe, yet you can't find your place there, God help you. What adult will notice or intercede? Offer you protection, comfort, or counsel? How likely, then, *is* any child to betray other tribe members? Can enough trust in adult authority—teachers, parents, administrators, therapists, *anyone*—be (re)established to forestall such violence? What will it take for those in authority to recognize and remedy the hell these young men feel they inhabit, a social purgatory so inescapable that shooting one's way out appears their only option?

Students who targeted adults for revenge—and 61 percent of them did—don't signal their intentions; only 17 percent threatened any action before the attacks.

After a desire for revenge, students who target their schools for violence are impelled by two key motives: they want attention and recognition (24 percent), and they feel desperate or suicidal (27 percent). In a world where every new television show offers another version of "reality," why wouldn't adolescents hunger for their fifteen minutes of fame, their chance to express their feelings, however homicidal, before a national network audience?

Students regularly face gun violence, or its potential. A national survey of 15,877 middle and high school students, taken in 2000, found that one in three (39 percent of middle schoolers and 36 percent of high schoolers) say they feel unsafe in school. One in five high-school-age boys took a weapon to school.[6]

Even before the rash of high school massacres, a dozen young Americans traveled to Washington, D.C., to tell lawmakers on the House of Representatives Subcommittee on Crime and Criminal Justice, Committee on the Judiciary, how they felt about the presence of guns in their lives.

On February 3, 1994, they stood before twelve legislators. The hearing, called by New York State representative Charles Schumer (D), began at 10:33 in the morning.

Ruth Leeds, then a thirteen-year-old eighth-grader at the Francis Scott Key Middle School in Fairfax County, Virginia, an upper-middle-class suburb, told committee members a student had brought a loaded gun to her school in a book bag—students were subsequently forbidden from carrying book bags.

"I was frightened, but not shocked in the least," she said. "I wasn't shocked because teenagers see this type of behavior every day, whether it be on TV or outside their front doors. I figured someone in my school was bound to imitate it. Today's young people are faced with the reality of such actions and are very apprehensive when it comes to their personal safety."

Margaret Childers, a seventeen-year-old student at Georgetown Day School, a private K-12 school in D.C., argued for "grassroots education. I would like to see a national curriculum that teaches conflict resolution at a really young age and maybe some handgun safety because it starts young. When their parents are at work and they don't have people at home when they are coming home from school, I think kids need to learn somewhere how to be responsible and how to take care of themselves and that is really important."

Alicia Brown told the group that guns had been a part of her life since she was twelve. "A lot of older people are shocked that kids have to think about guns. It was not as bad when you were growing up, but things have changed. There is a lot of anger inside young people today they don't talk about. Instead they take their anger out on other people. And if they have guns, they use them. . . . Because of guns, kids have to be cautious about everything they do or say. You have to think about the way you look at people. You have to think about how you react to what they say. . . . You just don't—you just don't know what that other person might do. They might have a gun and they might kill you."

Monique Malloy, then a sixteen-year-old sophomore at Eastern High School in D.C., told the committee that her cousin had been killed barely a year before, shot sixteen times. "I knew four other people who have been shot and killed by guns. . . . Kids carry guns because they think they gain respect. And it is not just a male issue anymore. It is teenagers, period. Teenagers, boys and girls both, are carrying guns. . . . I could have been one of the sisters in trouble out there on the streets. I was headed that way but the boys and girls club I belong to helped me with jobs and after-school programs. We need more things like that."[7]

America has faced vicious teen violence before. In 1943, a gang of twelve teenagers raped a seventeen-year-old girl in a crowded movie house in the Bronx, "without one of the patrons moving to interfere."[8] Juvenile delinquency was a rising problem during World War II; in 1944, two girls, eleven and thirteen, killed a nine-year-old in a New York schoolyard at recess, and a teacher was tortured to death in her classroom. "It was this evident readiness to employ deadly force that was the most frightening feature of the youth gangs which sprang up during the war in most big cities."[9]

Another contemporary repercussion—the long, thick lines of students outside many American schools, like John F. Kennedy High School in the Bronx, waiting to clear metal detectors. At the four-thousand-student school, waits in line can take thirty minutes. "We know the process," said Hanna Reyes, a junior. "We know what to take off, what shoes will set off the metal detectors. But you do feel like a prisoner. It's frustrating to us. You kind of dread going to school."[10]

Metal detectors have been used in New York City schools since the 1980s, and some sixty-five city high schools employ them. A photo of the boys' lineup reveals a majority of them wearing thick, puffy jackets and loose, baggy pants; in his 2002 film, *Bowling for Columbine*, filmmaker Michael Moore showed a young man, similarly dressed, nonchalantly pulling out more than fifteen handguns, and a rifle, easily concealed beneath his loose jeans.

In the Los Angeles Unified School District, school security guards are required to conduct random searches in at least one classroom every day in middle and high schools. Philadelphia put large metal detectors in all city high schools in 1997.[11]

Yet for some teens, guns offer a benign way to learn skills, make friends, and develop athletic competence. Thousands of young men and women enjoy the growing confidence that sport and target shooting provide. Many young women I spoke to say they especially treasure a chance to connect easily with their fathers and brothers, to gain their respect and spend time with the people they love. For these youngsters, gun use is a family value.

For Michiaela Marshall, a blond, blue-eyed fifteen-year-old from Lincoln, Nebraska, trapshooting offers her a new sport and the admiration of her peers. She had already shot at three competitions in her home state when we met in August 2002 at the Grand American, an annual national competition, and had traveled fourteen hours by car from her home to compete. "I wouldn't do it if my brother and dad didn't do it, too. But my girlfriends think I'm buff and tough."

"I never realized how hard this could be and how much fun I could have," says Holly Ward, a sixteen-year-old sophomore on the ROTC air rifle team of MacArthur High School in San Antonio, Texas. She had had no previous firearms experience but found shooting "really cool." Ward's team had, in 2002, recently received $10,400 from the South Texas Friends of the NRA.[12]

The Olympic-style competition requires students to fire air

rifles in standing, kneeling, and prone positions at tiny bull's-eyes on each target. In 2001, the school's team placed first in statewide competition against students from about 120 schools. Each team member practices at least an hour and a half each weekday and some on weekends as well, said their coach, First Sergeant Steve Chavan. "A lot of kids who have never shot anything before take for granted that this will be easy," he said. "But to be competitive, you have to shoot scores of 288 to 290 out of 300. That's pretty tough."

Thanks to the national Scholastic Clay Targets Program, whose enrollment jumped from 750 in 2001 to 3,100 in 2002, thousands of teenagers enjoy sport shooting. There were 197 female shooters and at least twenty-five women coaches. At the annual Grand American competition, held every year in Vandalia, Ohio, there were 41 youth teams in 2001—and 105 in 2002. With the average age of the competitors at the annual Grand American competition now a portly, white-haired fifty-two, the sport needs to find and keep a younger crowd.

Becky Groves, a tall, freckled, blond thirteen-year-old from Kettering, Ohio, at the Grand American wore a white T-shirt that read "Smokin' Clays—I Love This Sport!" She had already shot a Beretta 391 shotgun and a Remington 1100 and had seen her brother shoot. She plays basketball and field hockey and shoots. "Everyone does it. They're cool with it."

The day's top woman competitor was Whitney Ruesch, Alaska's top female shooter, a sixteen-year-old who had traveled alone all the way from Chugiak, a town of ten thousand about twenty miles northeast of Anchorage. She wore silver 4-H earrings, a white vest, and khakis—and on the hot and humid August day I watched her easily shoot 24/25 clays in a row, essential to competing seriously at a national event. Ruesch said she had no natural talent for the sport. "I just kept at it! My coach said, 'You'll be the best female shooter in Alaska, or the U.S.,' and I said, 'Yeah, right, whatever.'" After she hit a hundred clays in a row, she started thinking about the Olympics.

For eighteen-year-old Jeanette Nielsen, of Pleasant Grove, a town thirteen miles north of Provo, Utah, shooting was already old hat, a sport she had taken up at fifteen. She shoots skeet, clays, and trap, has hunted pheasant and deer, and said she was looking forward to hunting elk.

"Trapshooting is fun. I like the challenge. You have to have your mind clear and concentrate really hard, just think about getting that one bird, not all twenty-five. You do the task at hand, then keep progressing." Nielsen says the guys she dates are initially surprised that she shoots—"because I'm a girl"—but then think it's cool. Her high school graduation gift? A $200 Beretta 390 12-gauge shotgun.

While New York City remains one of the toughest places in America to obtain a pistol permit, New York State boasts the nation's largest group of teen shooters, ten thousand, thanks to the twenty-six-year-old Shooting Sports program run by 4-H, a mostly rural group (the four *H*s are Heart, Head, Hands, and Health). A family can enroll in the program to learn together. The program is paid for through fund-raising and donations from groups such as the National Rifle Association. All staff are volunteer, and the group receives no government funds. Nationally, 110,000 youngsters participate.

Youth between twelve and nineteen can participate in 4-H shooting programs; in New York, most of those are between thirteen and fifteen. To maintain safety—New York's program has never had an accident—the youngsters don't bring their own guns but use those owned by 4-H itself and annually inspected by a licensed gunsmith. The group also gives out new ammunition (while many shooters privately save money by using reloaded cartridges, 4-H does not for safety reasons). It costs $15 per child and $7.50 per accompanying adult for a ten-week class.

"I teach our instructors that the first 'accident' will probably be the last as the program will fold," says Bill Schwerd, who runs the New York State 4-H program. As a result, says Schwerd, "our insurance rates are the same as for general 4-H projects and less than those for horse programs."

He says the program is hugely popular and has received no

protest or negative press. "What is done is legal, safe, ethically and morally correct. It is a lifetime activity, a family activity." One reason 4-H is gaining so many young shooters is the result of decades of social change. There are simply few other places to learn. "Once you could go out the back door and shoot in an informal setting. You didn't have to belong to a club or 4-H group. And everyone was a shooter—or so it seemed. Fathers, uncles, grandfathers, and the like were all involved. A high percentage of homes had firearms. . . . People want to shoot, to see what happens and, as importantly, to learn about the environment."

Nationally, more than 30 percent of those attending 4-H shooting programs are female; 35 percent of the coaches are women. In addition, 350,000 youth take hunter education courses each year.

College

By the time young American women head off to college, they're veterans of violence, if not in their own school or district, then on television, in film, on the Internet.

"Today's college freshmen like to feel sheltered and they trust authority figures to take care of them," say Neil Howe and William Strauss, authors of the 2003 book *Millennials Go to College*. Today's incoming students demand a "secure, regulated environment. . . . Campus security is a key concern for millennial students, many of whom became accustomed to metal detectors and a visible police presence in their high schools. Security for the first time is being actively marketed by campuses."[13]

Australia is enjoying a boom in foreign-student enrollment, partly for this reason. Twenty percent of postsecondary students there come from other countries; only Switzerland has more. (In the United States, that figure is 6.4 percent.) Australian universities "have long emphasized their country's relatively low rates of gun-related violence, particularly in comparison with the United States. . . . We're still seen as a tranquil international haven," says

Jennie Lang, an international recruitment executive at New South Wales University."[14]

Every year since 1966, the Higher Education Research Institute at the University of California at Los Angeles has surveyed nearly twenty-five thousand freshmen at 109 four-year colleges. The survey, since 1989, has asked, "Should the federal government do more to control the sale of handguns?" The answer, in 2002, was a resounding yes: 80 percent of those attending all baccalaureate institutions, 81.2 percent at all four-year colleges, 80.1 percent at all universities, and 90.1 percent at all-black colleges. Students attending public black colleges agreed 89.3 percent, and at private black colleges 91.9 percent—by far the highest percentage of all students surveyed.

Yet guns do show up on campus, to the dismay of students, teachers, and administrators. Four-year schools with the most weapons arrests in 2000 were the University of Colorado Health Sciences Center (22); Michigan State University (19); State University of New York Upstate Medical University (17); East Carolina University (17); the University of South Carolina at Columbia (15); and the University of Washington Harborview Medical Center (14).[15]

About 450,000, or 4.3 percent, of college students own guns, according to a Harvard University survey. An antigun group, the Alliance for Justice, surveyed 150 colleges and universities in 2002 and found a "broad array" of policies on gun use. The group found that eighty-two schools strictly prohibited firearms; twenty-seven restricted them to members of the ROTC or a specific school activity; twenty-five only allowed guns if stored in a university-sanctioned facility.

In states such as Utah and Virginia, however, students used more lenient state laws to challenge school officials. Like most other colleges, the University of Utah in Salt Lake City has long banned students, professors, and staff members from possessing firearms on its campus, but the policy is at odds with a nine-year-old state law allowing those with permits to carry concealed weapons. "The college campus is unlike almost any other public area of our society," said university president J. Bernard Machen, who wants guns banned to allow heated debate. Rancor over poor grades is a more likely predictor of violence; in January 2002, a student suspended from the Appalachian School of Law in Virginia used a handgun to kill a dean, a professor, and a student.

"You have very driven individuals trying to get A's so they can get the perfect job," said Darren Bush, a visiting associate professor of law at the University of Utah. "If they get something less than that, you can get very heated discussions, and you're all alone. In those moments, you want to be thinking on the merits. You don't want to be thinking, 'Gee, is this person packing heat?' "[16]

It's a fair question and one that should have been asked of Robert Flores, a forty-one-year-old Gulf War veteran whose scholastic frustrations erupted in a murderous spree of revenge. Flores was studying nursing at the University of Arizona at Tucson but was failing his courses, which required him to start repaying his student loans. Already behind on his other bills, Flores shot dead three of his nursing instructors, all women: Robin Rogers, fifty; Cheryl McGaffic, forty-four; and Barbara Monroe, forty-five; before shooting himself.

While Texas is a concealed-carry state, and his job is protecting a 120-acre campus, John Erwin, a genial, gray-haired, broad-shouldered former police officer, takes it in stride. He's spent thirty years protecting college-age women as campus security officer for Texas Woman's University in Denton, an hour's drive northwest of Dallas. (TWU has five campuses, three in Dallas, one in Houston, and one in Denton, a middle-class town of eighty thousand with a murder rate of fifteen to twenty per year.)

His staff of fifteen officers and two guards are responsible for safeguarding eight thousand students on a lush, green campus in the heart of a small city. Yet the quality of campus safety, he says, depends on a number of variables. "It's the campus, it's the age of the students. In Dallas and Houston, the students are much more serious, often grad students. Up here, we've got younger students, so there's more dating, drinking, and drugs."

Erwin is proud of his safety record, "If we're not the lowest for assaultive-type crimes [among American colleges], we're number two."

He and his all-male team cover a large campus. "We try to be very, very visible, talking to people or the students to make folks aware that we see them. People see we're out here." Officers are on patrol twenty-four hours a day, inside and outdoors, with five on bicycles, designed to make them approachable, accessible, and silent. "We've snuck up on people who didn't know we were there," he says. Officers carry a variety of guns, including a .45, 9mm, .38 special, and shotguns.

Erwin firmly believes in self-defense; since 1996, fifty students a year have learned these techniques on campus. The idea is to get away, he says. "The survival rate is much better. Most women won't be able to overcome most men. If you try for retribution, you'll forget about trying to get away. We want you to survive—and leave the retribution to people like me. The idea we teach is to stun or surprise someone to the point you can get away. The outcome is not to hurt someone, but to get away and survive."

But persuading well-raised Southern women to shout or even raise their voice is tough, Erwin says. "We're slower here, less aggressive. They're taught that being less aggressive is the way to do things. We have a culture that is more sedate."

Carrying or using a gun is a poor choice, he says. "Most women will not train their skills to a sufficient level. Choosing within a second who is a threat to you, or not, is an awesome choice and the only way to make it well is through training."

Anyone wanting to determine the safety of a college campus can log on to www.campussafety.org, a Department of Education website that, under federal law, the Campus Security Act, reveals individual campus crime statistics that must be updated every year. Yet a national survey of 2,438 institutions, released in October 2002, found that fewer than 40 percent of colleges were in full compliance.[17] The two-year study found that numerous colleges and universities didn't provide students with information about preventing sexual assaults. Failure to report all required crime data was common among the universities surveyed, as were problems related to investigating sexual-assault cases.

Underreporting of rape and assault is a significant problem among students. "One of the most serious factors that prevents student victims from reporting the crime is that they do not recognize they have been criminally violated, particularly when they know their perpetrator," said Heather M. Karjane, the study's principal investigator.

But the onus also lies with campus administrators, who "need to openly acknowledge that sexual assault occurs within the student population. It is not typically the stranger-rapist intruders breaking into an otherwise-safe campus community." The study found that 75 percent of colleges do not undertake an investigation to collect evidence once a report of rape or sexual assault is made.

While campus crime rarely involves the student use of guns, police discovered in the fall of 2002 that students from New York City attending Southern colleges had found a lucrative new revenue stream—gunrunning. Students at colleges in Alabama, Georgia, Texas, and other states had brought at least eight hundred cheap firearms to New York in the prior two years. Forty were used in attempted robberies and other crimes, and by tracing the serial numbers, within six months fourteen students were arrested for gun trafficking. According to the Bureau of Alcohol, Tobacco, and Firearms (which tracks gun sales), three students at Georgia Southern University transported forty-five guns to New York.

"This is a low-start-up-cost venture," said David Fields, supervisory agent for the ATF office in Atlanta. A $100 gun in Georgia can sell for six times that in New York City. "I needed book money," one student told investigators.[18]

Shooting also offers college students a way to have fun and earn some tuition. It's the only coed sport in the National Collegiate Athletic Association, with almost fifty schools across the country participating in small-bore rifle and air rifle. University of Alaska, Fairbanks; the University of Kentucky, Lexington; and Xavier University in Cincinnati are the top three teams, all coed. It's no surprise, given the popularity of guns in the rural South, to find teams at colleges in Alabama, Tennessee, and Texas, yet MIT also has a riflery team, as does the University of San Francisco.

Men and women shoot equally well, says Gary deBoy, chair of the NCAA riflery committee and a coach at Jacksonville State University in Alabama since 1990. "But the best shooters I ever had were girls. I've had all-Americans in both disciplines. The majority of my award winners are females." Why? He laughs long and hard before replying. "The males are macho. They get upset if they fail. They bang things and throw things if they don't perform well. In shooting you have to be calm, keep your heart rate down, control your breathing. I think the woman shooter is able to control her emotions better because she doesn't feel she has to win at all costs."

DeBoy says shooting is much safer than any other collegiate sport. His athletes have never had an accident. "I don't believe any other sport can claim that."

Shooting gave Kari Baldwin, from Verbena, Alabama, a town of twenty-five hundred, a college scholarship at Jacksonville State University worth $1,700 a year for four years. "I was about four or five when I got my first BB gun. I was overjoyed because I could go hunting just like my parents. Both were real active during the hunting season. I just wanted to be involved. My dad is the one who would hand me the rifle or shotgun and would go with me to try it out. My mother is the one who got me to practice and signed me up for a shooting program in 4-H. This is where I met my coach, who led me all the way through high school."

For Candace Emory, a black twenty-one-year-old senior at a small Lutheran college in Pennsylvania, shooting is "a leisure activity. My life isn't guns, but I think if someone is scared, she should have the right to defend herself." She loves target shooting, an activity she was introduced to at eighteen by her mother, who took her to the range and taught her how to shoot a Ruger .22 pistol.

Initially scared to pull the trigger—most fearful of being burned by hot flying brass—Emory found she loved it. "I had a blast!"

"I'd never paid attention to guns. I never paid attention to gun laws. I didn't want to go shoot at first. I was kind of anxious, but when I saw my mother shoot and saw how good she was, even as a beginner, the anxiety went away." Emory has only shot the (small-caliber) .22 and a .357 Magnum, admitting she preferred not to try shooting a .45: "That was huge and scary-looking."

Her friends and boyfriend had no problem with her new enthusiasm. Her boyfriend thought it "cool," she says. "After the first shot, I kept the target to show him."

Emory's hometown is Baltimore, in 2002 the nation's most violent city. Guns there are as unremarkable a possession as telephones, she says. "Everyone in Baltimore has a gun and knows how to shoot one." She says a dozen of her male friends have shot one—although fewer than five of them did so legally.

She says she doesn't worry about other students who might misuse guns or fear a bloody campus rampage. Nor did she worry while attending high school. "There are so many other things for me to worry about right now that I can't focus on it. I wouldn't say it's unlikely," she admits. Pressed, she thinks it's probably too frightening to think much about—more a matter of denial than improbability.

Girls with guns are scary, and never scarier than when horrified adults just can't figure out the attraction. Gun enthusiasts at an elite Northeastern liberal arts college even merited a visit from a *New York Times* columnist. Under the dismissive headline "Chicks with Guns," the women of Mount Holyoke, a traditionally liberal, 137-year-old, all-female college of 2,100 (which cost $35,808 a year in 2002), came under dismayed, disbelieving scrutiny from

Nicholas Kristof for their decision to found the first collegiate chapter of Second Amendment Sisters, a national gun rights group. About fifty girls joined.

In March 2002, I sat down with five of them to learn what had prompted them to start shooting—a mix of passion and pride, ambivalence and ambition.

Their campus is gorgeous, filled with five- and six-story red-brick Gothic buildings scattered behind imposing wrought-iron gates, set in the center of South Hadley, a sleepy 250-year-old town. The college is a genteel world apart, with a greenhouse and its own large pond. One evening, after dinner, we sat in a dorm common room with soft lighting and deep sofas. The women were welcoming, extremely friendly, and media-savvy; one had been the focus of the *Times* column, another had that morning been the subject of a nationally televised interview with Paula Zahn.

They included Alexandra D'Urso, twenty-one, a political science major, a junior from Cohasset, Massachuetts, slight and serious with a fringe of dark bangs and wire-rim glasses; Sabrina Clarke, a twenty-year-old international relations major with shoulder-length blond hair, a pale velvet shirt, and jeans, from a town in western Massachusetts; Elizabeth Abbate, a lively twenty-year-old theater and art history major, her long red hair tucked up beneath a cap; twenty-one-year-old Christie Caywood, a pale, chunky, wildly gesticulating native of Christiansburg, Virginia; and Simone Cornielle Irizarry, thirty-six, a heavyset, Hispanic, New York City–born neuroscience major.

Caywood is the founder and president of the group.

For Clarke, attending on financial aid, Mount Holyoke was a clear step up; both her parents attended two-year colleges. D'Urso radiated pride in her choice of school and her hopes for the future: "There are no limits to us." Added Irizarry, "We know who we are. Even the first years have a sense of this." The women described an atmosphere of intellectual challenge, cooperation, and camaraderie. "The niceness is a big factor here," said Caywood. "Lots of spirit," added Abbate. "Courtesy," said Irizarry.

No wonder Kristof and others couldn't quite reconcile a school that unembarrassedly enjoys the nightly nine-o'clock tradition of "milk and cookies," where girls gather to munch, sip, and chat, with the nation's first collegiate chapter of a national group advocating firearms ownership.

For Sabrina Clarke, shooting had simply, always, been a part of her life—and a major source of parental approval and acceptance. "My father hunted. I remember the first time I ever shot a shotgun. I was so proud! I was twelve and we shot clay pigeons. That was the happiest moment of that year for me. He called me Annie Oakley."

With her long, pale blond curls, her hands tucked deep into her sleeves, Clarke resembled a pre-Raphaelite heroine, lighting up at the happy memory. She described shooting her grandfather's 16-gauge shotgun. "It's a pathetic little gun, but I love it to death." Shooting showed her, and her family, that she was smart, capable, competent, one of them. She loved that recognition from her father, brother, and uncle. "It was a powerful experience."

Abbate took her first shot with her father's pellet gun, hitting a tin can. She felt a similar sense of exultation. "I ran around the yard!" she recalls. For Irizarry, acceptance was also key to her enjoyment of guns. "I was my father's son. I'd gone fishing with him, done archery, rode sidesaddle." She attended an all-girls Catholic school but saw no dichotomy in wanting to handle a gun and handle it well.

Of the five women, she was the most experienced hunter, shooting and gutting her own deer at the age of eighteen. "I was the first one to take out a buck," she proudly recalled, even pausing to drink some of the deer's blood from an aluminum cup, a sign of respect for the life she had just taken. "It was very somber, respectful, honorable. It was also a feeling of 'This is *mine!*' This is my dinner. I love wildlife and I think it should be respected—but it tastes good, too!"

Caywood started the Second Amendment Sisters group after inviting NRA executive vice president and CEO Wayne LaPierre to speak on campus. "It was my first time shooting," she said of their visit to the nearby Smith & Wesson Academy, a range and school that teaches law enforcement officers from all over the world. Of the six women who initially joined her group, four had never before touched a gun. "I got on-line to see what [SAS] were about, liked their name, and loved their website. My goal in founding this group was to raise awareness about this issue of firearms and self-defense." While MIT has a riflery team with its own guns, the women of Mount Holyoke do not have guns on campus.

Theirs is an individual, unofficial passion.

Abbate was eager to buy her first gun, a 9mm, sharing the cost with her father. "My dad is leaving the decision in my hands. But he told me, 'I want you to get something that will last a long, long time.' I want to get a carry permit. I have friends who were rape victims." No stranger to vulnerability, Abbate herself has spoken on national television about her own experience of being video-taped naked by a former boyfriend who then passed the tape around to his friends. "I've been afraid to get out of my car at one or two in the morning in a snowstorm," she said.

Irizarry, whose home state of New York does not allow carry permits, has also felt the taste of fear. She said she keeps a wood-and-steel letter opener in her car for self-defense. (She also carries the scars of someone's teeth on her right hand from a right hook she once threw.)

When, if ever, would these young women shoot to kill? For Alexandra D'Urso, never. "I'm interested in skeet shooting, not self-defense. I'd rather trust my physical skills. I'd put that decision in God's hands."

Abbate said she enjoyed target shooting. "I take a lot of pleasure in it, and I'm good at it. I have a choice of what to do with that skill within my complete control. I'm an extremely religious person. Something will tell me, 'Okay, this is serious enough [to shoot someone].' " Yet, Abbate, a third-generation Mount Holyoke student, when pressed to describe what that provocation might be, admitted, "I'd rather hit the person on the head with the gun or throw it at them."

"I don't know if I could ever shoot someone," said Clarke. "I would like to get my carry permit, but I can't imagine a scenario where I would use it." At which point an older, wiser Irizarry cautioned her fellow students, "If you're going to carry a gun loaded, you have to be prepared to use it."

For Clarke and Irizarry, shooting complicated their romantic relationships. "My last boyfriend wasn't cool with it!" said Clarke. "He also didn't know I was Republican. I don't know if I told him or he saw my targets from the last time I'd been shooting." They discussed her love of guns about three months into dating. "I worry sometimes what would have happened if I pressed the issue. . . . There's such a block there!" she said, slamming her fist into her palm for emphasis. "Other guys have felt this way, too."

For Irizarry, calmly and confidently awaiting the arrival of her "two-carat, six-prong, platinum" engagement ring, guns are a nonnegotiable part of her married future. "I told him, 'This is not a passing thing!' He knows for the most part I'm a rational, thoughtful person. But I told him, 'I need to teach you how to shoot, too, so our kids will understand it.' It's not going to be just me and my Chihuahuas—for the home, I want a double-barreled shotgun. It's much more impressive. It also works when you're nervous or scared. It's security."

For these confident, poised, polite young women, shooting is as much a part of their lives as mascara or midterms. "It's like meditating. It's like a minivacation," says Irizarry. "It's so clean, so clear."

Adds Clarke, "It's therapeutic. That's why we go during finals!"

The distance between the nurturing refuge of Mount Holyoke and the grimy, noisy midtown Manhattan corner of Eighth Avenue and Thirty-fifth Street is measured in more than miles. Here, on the twelfth floor of a nondescript, faded office building, a small group of adults devote their attention each year to four hundred troubled teenagers aged ten to twenty-one. The clients of Friends of Island Academy, a social service organization that

provides educational, vocational, leadership, and life-skills training, are overwhelmingly poor, more than 80 percent. Sixty percent are black and 39 percent Hispanic. Almost all arrive at FOIA
after being imprisoned at Rikers Island.

Some of the young women, a hundred of whom pass through
FOIA's doors each year (now on Thirty-eighth Street), are as passionate about guns as their collegiate counterparts. They, too, recognize the respect and fear that guns command. They, too, crave
the delicious and elusive sensation of power a loaded weapon con-
veys. Both groups of women use similar weapons and want the
men they know to respect their competence with firearms, to play
equally on the same field.

While guns are a common interest, their paths quickly diverge.
The well-educated young women of Mount Holyoke and other
schools confidently look forward to the helping hands of alumni
networks, internships, study abroad, a welcoming world where
their résumés are read and telephone calls returned. Media interest in Mount Holyoke's groundbreaking Second Amendment
Sisters collegiate chapter was intense, with dismayed reporters
from the *New York Times, Los Angeles Times,* and *Boston* magazine
wondering how such bright, groomed-for-success young women
could even consider gun ownership.

One young student, bemused by the fuss, shrugged and said,
"If we were men, you wouldn't be reading about us."

Few seem interested in the choices made by the young women at
FOIA, who live in tough, crime-plagued neighborhoods such as
Bedford-Stuyvesant or Harlem or the South Bronx. For these young
girls, many of them high school dropouts from splintered families,
owning a gun and letting others know it is one of few ways they can
feel powerful. Doors open. Suddenly, cocky and disdainful men
speak to them politely, even fearfully. Rich white folks cower and
offer their wallets. At gunpoint, even the most dominant residents of
their neighborhoods—drug dealers—hand over their profits.

Normally, in their world, women are powerless, their grip on
esteem tenuous at best, they say. Have sex with too many men,
you're a slut. You can't get your hands on serious money without

committing some serious crimes. It's a long way from hand-wringing national media attention or the soothing nightly ritual of "milk and cookies."

One cold January afternoon, I sat in a small room around a central table at FOIA with Esta, Recoil, Rachel, and Pamela, three of them convicted felons. The oldest, Recoil (a nickname she chose), was twenty-four. Like the students I met at Mount Holyoke, these young women were bright, funny, passionate, articulate, and clear-eyed about the choices they had made and the costs of having made them.[19]

Esta dropped out of school in ninth grade and, when we met, had recently attained her GED, hoping to study hospitality management or become a chef. Recoil was studying at Staten Island College, deciding between philosophy and political science. Rachel was facing two to four years in prison. They nodded their heads in agreement as each recounted lives saturated with guns and gun violence: friends shot, bystanders killed, getting one, owning one, using one, being threatened with one. At Rikers, each was mocked with the corrections officers' singsong "See you later! See you next year!"

Lean and elegant in a red angora Kangol fedora, red Coach leather belt, and boots, her fingernails matching in narrow red and white stripes, Rachel spent much of the interview staring into her lap. At nineteen, she had recently been arrested for the first time for soliciting a minor into prostitution. She was terrified. She had gone to a friend's house, hungry for some adult attention, already the black sheep of her deeply religious family: "They don't want to have anything to do with me."

The friend, a man of fifty, told her to hand out flyers for his "escort service"—and waved his revolver to press his point. "This is what I'll use if you defy me," he said. Rachel noted, "I've seen guns on TV, but I'd never seen one in real life." She saw no choice but to obey. Her family wouldn't help, nor could her friends. "If I'd gone to the police, he would have found out and killed me."

A cop saw her hand a flyer to a girl of thirteen, and Rachel was arrested.

Esta is Hispanic, light-skinned, a curvaceously pretty girl with sleek hair pulled back into a ponytail. She wore a peasant blouse and clingy beige pants. "I'm the type of female who wants respect from males," she began. "I'm a female with a male's mentality." The challenge, she said, was how, without money or an education, to win that respect as a woman. It came quickly and easily after she acquired a .25 pistol she wore every day, tucked into the waist of her long johns. She wore gloves every time she touched it to make sure she left no fingerprints.

The world looked different, then. Better. "You feel like God. I felt in control when I had it. Everyone I was with felt uncomfortable when they knew I had it." What she won, though, was not respect but fear. "If you have a reputation for taking no shit, and you have a gun and people know you have a gun, they'll talk to you differently. They'll behave with you differently."

She faced a new stress throughout the two and a half months she owned it, that of protecting her weapon, and her life. "I had to watch out for my back all the time. Not only was I now scared of people on the streets, but of the police."

Esta knew well the risks of accepting an illegal gun: "If the gun has bodies on it, they're your bodies. There's a lot of pros and cons to having a gun, but mostly cons." ("Bodies," the girls explained, are murders already committed by a weapon's previous users; whoever owns the gun when it's recovered by police can be charged with every murder previously committed with it. Or turn in the person they bought or stole it from.)[20]

Arrested at a friend's funeral for possession of an illegal weapon, Esta did six months in Rikers and came out facing an additional five years on probation. "It's changed my perspective on life, on society, and on the government. I feel like I can't get a chance. I think about it all the time." She had already applied unsuccessfully for five jobs; each time she had been honest about her felony conviction.

I asked her what she would rather have had than that gun. Her answer was urgent and instant.

"Education! The mind to talk to people in government and in

business. You can speak out politically if you have education. You're seen differently in the eyes of society because you have an education."

"This time last year I would have been out robbing," said Recoil, a tall, dark-skinned black woman with dreadlocks. She weighs at least two hundred pounds and wore a cotton turtleneck in a tiny blue floral print and dangling, delicate, gold, flower-shaped earrings. "I've been around guns all my life. I've seen someone get shot quite a few times."

She first saw a gun during a video arcade robbery. "I was young as hell. I was scared!" The next time was during the robbery of a corner toystore. She was standing outside at the bus stop, "just minding my business." She was ten. By sixth grade, she saw a gun for the third time when her friend Michael showed one off to her. The next day it went off accidentally, killing him.

"You can't escape guns in the hood. Guns, guns everywhere. There's no escaping it. Legal or not legal, you're going to have one for protection." Home was a hell of domestic violence. "Every damn day was a fight." Her older brother was useless to protect her or her mother. "He was fat and he was scared. He was a punk!"

At twelve, she started carrying drugs for local dealers, earning $500 every week for two years. At fourteen, she got a .22 which, before the era of metal detectors in schools, she kept in her purse or book bag. After school, she'd head to midtown Manhattan to commit armed robberies or to con men staying at midtown hotels. She never needed her gun; after using her bulk to knock someone to the sidewalk, they'd hand over their valuables. One day the tables were suddenly turned—a man she was trying to scam for money shoved a gun in her face. "I almost pissed on myself. No one was around to help me. I was crying." She stopped carrying a gun after that.

Arrested at sixteen for assault and battery, she served eight months on Rikers Island.

"Jail was like open-heart surgery. It saved my life."

Pamela, a twenty-one-year-old who wore a Burberry, checked

wool scarf and a dazzling pair of cubic zirconium stud earrings, has beautiful almond-shaped eyes and a quiet, shy manner. She, too, weighs at least two hundred pounds. When a neighbor raped her in the unlit hallway of the Brooklyn project where she lived with her mother, twelve-year-old brother, and seventeen-year-old sister, she told only a few friends. "Who would have believed me?"

Despite a life surrounded by violence, it was the first time she considered getting a gun.

"The thought of not being armed then was tough, but my family stopped me. I was worried that my little brother would get ahold of it. I sometimes thought of getting one, but I chickened out. It would have been easy to get one, but I can't see myself killing anyone. Taking someone's life would really bother me."

What needs to change? I asked. Only Recoil, the most voluble, answered.

"Loose laws! If we had one set of certain guidelines, you wouldn't have the majority of guns out there [illegally] that you now have. A lot of them are coming in from other states," flooding neighborhoods already crime-ridden. "You can't have one set of laws here and others there. Things fall apart!"

Chapter 12
What to Do?

WHAT, THEN, WILL IT TAKE FOR AMERICANS WHO DISLIKE GUNS to feel safe around those who legally own them? Is anything enough? *Are* new gun controls or laws needed? Will they be effectively enforced? In an era when many Americans are most worried about unemployment or national security and terrorist threat, can gun safety ever dominate the political agenda?

I believe change is possible, but achieving it demands less dogma and more dialogue. For now, that seems unlikely.

Gun owners, especially those who don't belong to the NRA, need to appreciate the perspective of those who view the organization's timing and tactics with despair, even rage. Like it or not, the NRA has become the predominant public face of gun ownership, and its positions and politics are often seen, erroneously, as representing those of *all* gun owners. I met many American gun owners, male and female, whose stance is considerably less doctrinaire than that of the NRA.

While some gun control advocates are as unyielding in their positions as the NRA, others tell me they believe there is room for compromise. But for useful dialogue to occur between gun owners and gun opponents, the faces and voices of gun-owning moderates need to be as visible, recognizable, and credible as those of former NRA spokesman Charlton Heston or NRA executive vice president and CEO Wayne LaPierre. Not all gun owners maintain an arsenal of weaponry in their basement—although those ignorant about gun ownership fear that this may be true. And too often, it's the fervor of the frenzied that makes headlines about gun rights, not the many gun owners who are moderate, quiet, and largely invisible. It's no secret that many journalists feed on controversy and conflict, and gentler voices make poor sound bites.

I've seen, and felt, the hostile and disrespectful divide between those who enjoy owning guns and those who abhor them. Mutual ignorance is not bliss. It perpetuates stereotypes and forestalls workable political progress.

Those opposed to private weapons ownership need to consider a wider set of choices, choices currently perpetuated by law. If you don't like these choices, work to change them. Many who vehemently oppose gun ownership simply choose to ignore others' sense of vulnerability to crime. They dismiss the popular, intergenerational, growing, and widespread pleasures of sport shooting. A woman who has been or fears becoming a victim of violent crime lacks meaningful connection to those who remain convinced that buying a handgun for protection will only hurt her or her children.

Bottom line? Neither woman wants to be raped, robbed, or murdered. While arguments rage over methodology, what is being done to address the violence both women fear?

And self-righteous finger-wagging—the predominant trope of both sides—serves us poorly.

Those who argue blindly for the individual right to own firearms say less about their responsibility to do so safely, slamming head-on into collective frustration with what others perceive as nonstop gun-related mayhem. Isolated deaths, whether a teenager committing suicide, the woman blown away by a vengeful ex-spouse, the two-year-old killed by a drug dealer's stray bullet, or the individual killings that, when finally added up, proved that snipers John Muhammad and Lee Malvo had actually been hunting humans across America for months, collectively cost this country every year thousands of needless losses.

Yet heading to the courts or pressuring federal politicians who seek reelection and to do so must work with colleagues with very different views on gun control doesn't work especially well either. Gun control activists, clamoring for "sensible" gun laws, bring tremendous passion to the table—where they consistently encounter the intransigence, however justified, of law-abiding and responsible gun owners. Nor does suing the gun industry fix the problem, because the reasons for ongoing gun-related carnage, whether those guns are used legally or illegally, are persistent, complex, and not easily resolved.

Jamilah Clark, who runs the women's program for the Friends of Island Academy, a New York City–based agency serving teenagers who have served time at Rikers Island, says her clients, many of whom drop out of school, would be less likely to pick up a gun if they could envision a future without one.

"What would motivate a young person to *stay* in school?" she asks. "Future aspirations and goals, receiving a quality education, a positive peer group. A majority of the young people we work with don't have those things. To say that a life of crime is an attractive choice to these girls is to say that eating out of the garbage can is an attractive option for the homeless. From their perspective it seems as though it is the only choice.

"The majority of young people in Rikers Island are from eight neighborhoods: Harlem, South Bronx, East New York, Bedford-Stuyvesant, Washington Heights, Brownsville, the Lower East Side, and South Jamaica. These neighborhoods have the highest unemployment rates, the lowest-performing schools, often dilapidated housing, and consequently high crime rates. There is a logical correlation between crime and poverty. When you withhold basic needs from people—adequate food, proper housing, a family-sustaining wage, community resources, safe neighborhoods, quality education—often a person regresses to survival mode," says Clark. "At that point they do whatever is necessary to make it through the day."

"Many [violent deaths] involve social issues that aren't the responsibility of the police department. It becomes the responsibility of the entire community," says Inspector Craig Schwartz, chief of Detroit's homicide division. "These things are very hard to prevent."[1]

In his Oscar-winning 2002 documentary, *Bowling for Columbine,* filmmaker Michael Moore made much of the fact that Canada enjoys a lower murder rate than the United States. What he omitted was how differently it views the social contract with its citizens. Social and economic disparities are softened by higher federal and provincial taxes that pay for government-supplied, cradle-to-grave health care and heavily subsidize excellent, affordable, exclusively public postsecondary education. There is always a gap between rich and poor, but it's not a yawning, heartless chasm—one that criminal gun violence in America reminds us is not diminishing.

The average annual salary in America, expressed in 1998 dollars, went from $35,522 in 1970 to $35,864 in 1999. In the same period, according to *Fortune* magazine, the average real annual compensation of the top one hundred CEOs went from $1.3 million—forty times the pay of an average worker—to $37.5 million, or over a thousand times the average worker's pay.

Add to this growing Grand Canyon between the haves and have-nots a swelling army of the never-will-haves.

"In the last twenty-five years, a large segment of society has become more vulnerable," says Robert Perrucci, a sociologist at Purdue University and coauthor of *The New Class Society: Goodbye American Dream.*

According to Perrucci, four measures determine where one lands on the class scale: social capital (whom you know); credential capital (where you received your degree[s]); income or consumption capital; and investment capital (stocks and bonds). Minorities are far less likely than white men to amass elite educational credentials and social capital. Although the black middle class roughly doubled in the last twenty years, about 30 percent of blacks—versus 8 percent of whites—are poor by government standards.[2]

Whatever their skin color, the number of Americans who remain poor and powerless is growing. A 2003 report from Northeastern University, *Left Behind in the Labor Market*, showed that joblessness among out-of-school youths between sixteen and twenty-four had jumped 12 percent since the year 2000. The study estimated there are *5.5 million* such youths wandering the streets in hopeless search of a job or the first steps toward one.[3]

Will the playing field ever level? If not, the rage of those demanding redress through firepower will continue to interrupt leisurely or politically motivated debate on what, if any, social assistance to offer those in need.

We can pay now or pay later.

Law-abiding Americans cherish their individual rights and mobility more fiercely than perhaps any other citizenry on earth. When political movement stalls, they typically use the courts—a cumbersome, slow, and costly reach for resolution. The civilian warrior culture of armed resistance to authority and to foreign threat is not about to die anytime soon; in an era of persistent terrorist warnings, it may even increase. The popular culture—whether "reality" shows, cop shows, nightly local newscasts, film, videos, or television—feeds us an unabated, poorly regulated stream of glorified violence, faux and real. This both distorts our sense of fear and falsely glamorizes shoot-'em-up solutions.

A health-care system divided between public and private entities, among state and government agencies and HMOs, and Americans' persistent distrust of centralized government oversight also ensures a persistent myopia on gun violence. It has never been viewed—like AIDS, syphilis, or any other epidemic threat to public welfare—as a matter of public health. Gun violence needs well-funded, undivided attention and accumulated expertise from many local or regional authorities on crime, violence, and suicide. Instead, gun-related information has remained scattered, unshared, and unanalyzed throughout the databases of coroners and hospitals, law enforcement agencies, and statisticians.

Finally, in the fall of 2002, a new national system, the National Violent Death Program, was begun, a joint project of the Harvard School of Public Health and the Centers for Disease Control and Prevention. Six states—Maryland, New Jersey, Massachusetts, Oregon, South Carolina, and Virginia—agreed to collect more than one hundred pieces of information about each violent death. Suicides account for 57 percent and homicides for 33 percent. The study will receive about $20 million a year—the same annual budget as the National Rifle Association.

Said Dr. Leonora Olson, one of many researchers participating, "This is part of a paradigm shift that lets us look at violent deaths with an epidemiological approach, not just as accidents that can happen to anyone. By finding out the who, how, where, and why, we realize that there are patterns. If we can predict them, then we can intervene."

We need solutions to the pandemic of gun violence, and we need them now. Some gun control groups say the solution is to get rid of privately owned firearms—an approach that denies the many complex and interrelated root causes of gun violence: poverty, substance abuse, drug addiction, rage. Pro-gun groups disingenuously insist that licensed gun owners are de facto responsible gun *users*. Overly simplistic answers cost both sides credibility.

And those with the power to effect change often don't or can't. Politicians pick their gunfights carefully. Gun and ammunition manufacturers stay away from the fray, already bleeding financially from the many lawsuits they're still fighting. Those working within the criminal justice system say they face their own structural battles.

Two areas demand immediate attention. When individuals sell firearms privately—i.e., at flea markets, gun shows, garage sales—they can legally do so without performing a background check of the buyer. Restricting use of the NICS background check to only those guns sold by federally licensed firearms dealers means bolting only half the barn door.

The federal government, and the states, must also commit to financing and policing a more detailed, timely, interconnected collection of data on criminals who have obtained firearms. Snipers John Muhammad and Lee Malvo were able to operate for months killing men and women across America, unlinked and undetected, as a direct result of this failure.[4]

That 17 million American women now own guns, many of them for self-defense, speaks to larger, quieter questions that resonate deeply: a hunger for personal power, the fervent wish to feel safe, the right to fully enjoy the hard-won gains of feminism such as the right to travel solo far and wide, to live alone, at any age, and do both *safely*—untethered from the reach of a 911 response.

No matter how much discomfort this choice of a gun causes, and it does, American women want what we all do: to feel safe, respected, admired, and when necessary, feared. Many women also crave the excitement and sense of competence that recreational shooting provides. James William Gibson argues in his book *Warrior Dreams* that men are pushed into the dark world of paramilitary culture by a wish for adventure and experience of community. Some women want these, too.

Just as men crave external validation, a chance to test themselves physically and mentally, and hunger to bond with others far from the routine concerns of work and family, so do some women. The failure of such publications as *Condé Nast Sports for Women* and *Sports Illustrated for Women* showed, some said, how little women are interested in sports and in testing their limits. I disagree; competing for limited advertising revenue, the magazines could not sustain themselves financially. Women who remain hungry at any age for adventure and experience, to learn and test challenging new skills, can just as easily reach for a Glock or a Remington as a snowboard or a motorcycle. And so they do.

Whether you are an avid gun owner, determined to fight for your right to bear arms, or someone horrified by, and determined to fight against, personal weaponry, common ground exists. Individually, there remains much to be done.

Make Women's Safety a Priority

If you're horrified that American women are choosing to arm themselves, remember their reasons. Three-quarters will become the victim of crime. Every day, three will be killed, overwhelmingly by male intimates. More than a third will be violently assaulted, raped, or robbed in their lifetime.

What can you do?

Individual action can only mitigate institutional reform moving at glacial speed. Thousands of rapists escape prosecution entirely because there are no systematic procedures to collect and process DNA evidence.

Police, district attorneys, criminal defense lawyers, and domestic violence workers told me the same thing—they feel overwhelmed by a popular culture that persistently and profitably glorifies violence against girls and women, minimizes the many effects of domestic violence, and pushes women who fight back against it into a judicial system still overwhelmingly run by men. They lament the frustration of working, no matter with what sense of mission, within a system where 87 percent of law enforcement officers are still male and some of whom still lack effective training in handling domestic violence, 95 percent of which is men attacking women. They decry ineffectual restraining orders, plea bargains for assault and rape, laughably short sentences.

A General Accounting Office report found that nearly three thousand domestic abusers bought firearms between 1998 and 2001, despite laws designed to prevent such purchases, because the FBI could not complete criminal background checks before the sales went through.[5]

Women of all ages need, and deserve, effective legal protections, and they need and deserve to stay safe.

If guns seem a poor choice, girls and women must adopt other options: studying self-defense, learning basic safety measures, paying close attention to their surroundings, trusting their gut instincts. If someone, no matter how polished or suave, feels threatening, women need to learn to get away from him fast.

" 'No' is a complete sentence," points out security expert Gavin de Becker. "The predatory criminal of every variety is looking for someone, a vulnerable someone, who will allow him to be in control, and just as he constantly gives signals, so does he read them."[6]

"Since fear is so central to our experience, understanding when it is a gift—and when it is a curse—is well worth the effort," adds de Becker, who argues strongly that women, especially, must shake off the cozy mantle of denial to develop and use their life-saving skills, acknowledging danger as soon as they sense it.[7] "We deny because we're built to see what we want to see," he adds. Who among us really wants to honestly consider, or address, the American pandemic of male violence?[8]

"Girls think it's cute when their boyfriends are possessive and cut them off from their friends," says Cambridge filmmaker Margaret Lazarus, whose documentary about domestic violence won a 1994 Academy Award. "We're so tuned in to being into relationships and *not* tuned in to the warning signs of a man who can become abusive."

Women also need to ensure that their home, even one they share, protects their personal safety—brighten a poorly lit hallway, trim thick, house-hugging shrubbery that can hide an intruder. Away from home, women need to play it much smarter and safer.

"We've trained and turned out many female black belts," said David Weiss, editor of *American Karate* magazine. "But how to avoid your attacker—not to be stupid and blind when you walk on the streets—that is more important and easier to learn."[9]

Many women still face a major internal obstacle. *They can't imagine fighting back.* In a situation of potential danger, women who feel socially compelled to be polite, congenial, and tolerant place themselves at great risk, less scared of male violence than of confronting it, either verbally or physically.

As feminist writer Martha McCaughey points out, "We have been so busy analyzing women's victimization by men's aggression that we have almost reified men's power to coerce women physically, failing to highlight women's potential for fighting back."[10]

"Women's inability to fight is a cultural matter of sexual politics, not a natural matter of hormones, brawn, or life-affirming biological programming. The feminine demeanor . . . is precisely what makes us terrible fighters. . . . For most women, the decision to learn to defend oneself is life-altering. It goes against what we've been taught from birth. We experience our bodies as fragile encumbrances rather than as tools with which to get something done."[11]

"Women no longer have to ride sidesaddle, work in long skirts, or cavort in corsets. How is it that so many of us still don't know how to hit?"[12]

Girls and women need to feel completely comfortable saying *"No!"*

And men need to listen.

With date rape at an all-time high on U.S. college campuses, much of it going unreported *because women don't even consider it a crime,* young women, especially, need to develop a much clearer sense of their boundaries—and how to enforce them. Women's binge drinking, also epidemic on college campuses, even to the point of unconsciousness, betrays serious ambivalence about taking personal safety seriously.[13]

Women of all ages, and college-age women especially, need to decide what they are willing to do to stay safe. What steps will they take to foresee, forestall, or halt, if possible, situations that can escalate into rape, injury, or death?

Thinking through some of these scenarios, no matter how unpleasant or unlikely, is a powerful, responsible first step.

Parents also need to educate themselves. How safe *is* your child's grammar/middle/high school/college/graduate school? Are there metal detectors? What is their weapons policy? What is the nature of campus security? Under federal law, every college must make available their crime statistics on sexual assault.

Protest Depictions of Violence against Girls and Women

Every day, Americans see women treated as objects of submission and violence—on television, in film, in videos and video games, on the Internet. Someone, a few years ago, decided to start emailing me access to scenes of violent graphic rape; filtering it out does nothing to stop its production or consumption. There's clearly an unregulated market for such material, no matter how nauseating.

"The country as a whole behaves as though there is no real-world price to pay for a culture that has so thoroughly desensitized us to violence that it takes a terror attack or a series of suburban sniper killings to really get our attention," wrote *New York Times* columnist Bob Herbert in a column lamenting popular violent games and toys. "The building blocks of violent behavior are dehumanization and desensitization."[14]

The culture consistently seems to reward misogynistic violence or ignore it; when women lined up to compete for the attentions of Rick Rockwell on the 2000 Fox television show *Who Wants to Marry a Multi-Millionaire?* they didn't learn until later that he'd been the subject of two restraining orders from women he had dated.

"The legal process requires specific targets against which to litigate," writes film critic Andrew Sarris. "No one can sue a social atmosphere or collective state of mind. So what is at stake is not this movie or that one, this video game or another, this outrageously costumed rock act or its rhetorically raging rap rival for the top spot on the charts. It's all of them put together as continuous noise and tumult."[15]

"When I channel surf late at night, I keep finding one hellhole after another, with people torturing and killing each other as slowly and tauntingly as possible . . . the most jaded quasi pornography . . . a steady stream of relentless, malignant sounds and images, a virtual continuum of malice and murder."[16]

Living in a sea of images and messages that degrade women and minimize their power, we simply stop noticing, even on a public university campus.

In 1984, a mural went up on a wall at Iowa State University. Located on a men-only floor in a coed dorm, it featured three camouflage-clad soldiers, all armed, one holding a beer keg, one a scantily clad woman under his arm. Over the years, the mural gained additions: *date raper extraordinaire* appeared on one bandanna, the word *roofies* (referring to Rohypnol, aka the date-rape drug) on the keg. In 2002, students in a women's studies course, emboldened by a university ban on pro-alcohol or sexually embarrassing images in public places, asked for, and received, its prompt removal.[17]

Why did it take *nineteen years?* What message did so large, public, and accepted a mural send to male students living daily with this image?

Speak up. If such depictions disturb you, let producers, manufacturers, and distributors know. Boycott such products and urge others to do the same. Publicize your concern in local, regional, and national mass media.

Address Domestic Violence

One-quarter of American women are in abusive relationships. The abuse may be sexual, physical, emotional, or financial, but it must be stopped early or, as abused women and those who try to help them know, it will escalate.

"We need to start earlier to prevent the escalation to broken bones and to dead bodies," says Casey Gwinn, director of the Family Justice Center in San Diego, a new and innovative alternative to traditional battered women's shelters. Not only are women injured and killed by domestic violence, he says, but so are police officers, coworkers, neighbors, and children, who are "caught in the crossfire."[18]

The Tubman Family Alliance Center in Minneapolis and the Family Justice Center in San Diego use the same principles: intervene early; help both men and women halt the cycle of abuse through counseling; remove children from a dangerous environment; help women find paid employment.

The Tubman center offers child care, computer classes, and even a meditation room. Women in San Diego seeking help to flee domestic violence formerly visited thirty-two different city agencies; the three-story Family Justice Center, which receives two hundred cases a week, offers "one-stop shopping," with legal advice, clothing, and even on-site physicians specially trained to document physical signs of abuse. "Victims couldn't make it through the system before," says Gwinn.[19]

In 1985, thirty women died in San Diego from domestic violence; in 2002, there were nine such deaths.

Filmmaker Margaret Lazarus urges parents to talk to their children about violence, and choosing not to use it. "We really have to be talking about intergender relationships, to let people really know what domestic violence *is.*" She wants the subject openly discussed in schools, church groups, youth groups, and other forums. "It's absolutely critical to show this to younger women."

Educating police, district attorneys, prosecutors, and judges is equally crucial, she says. One judge, sentencing a woman who killed her husband in self-defense, said, 'If I don't come down on her, it will be open season on husbands.' People don't give up power willingly, and if you give women more power in their relationships, it's at the expense of men who want to [abuse them] with impunity. Who are you aligned with in this struggle?"

Address Youth Violence

American boys are still learning—whether from their family, friends, or culture—that violent solutions work best. Students who bully with impunity, and those who are bullied without adult protection or intervention, create a significant risk pool for the future.

A national survey of 15,877 middle and high school students, taken in 2000, found that one in three of the boys (39 percent of middle schoolers and 36 percent of high schoolers) took a weapon to school.

More disturbing, 43 percent of high school and 37 percent of middle school boys said they believe it's okay to hit or threaten a person who makes them angry; only 19 percent of girls agreed. An even higher percentage actually resorted to violence: 75 percent of boys and more than 60 percent of girls surveyed said they had hit someone in the past twelve months because they were angry.[20]

A 2001 survey of 477 teens found that more than two-thirds of fourteen- to seventeen-year-olds report a group of students in their school sometimes or frequently intimidates others, often with few or no consequences. Only 16 percent of teens said they would intervene if they saw someone being intimidated or embarrassed, saying they simply didn't know what to do.[21]

While two cases were recently tried, and won, in Canada against young female bullies (one's behavior helped push a male fellow student to suicide), it is virtually impossible in the United States to sue a child or adolescent for such harassment. What you *can* do, in only fifteen states—California, Colorado, Connecticut, Georgia, Illinois, Louisiana, New Hampshire, New Jersey, New

York, Oklahoma, Oregon, Rhode Island, Vermont, Washington, and West Virginia—is sue local school authorities for failing to adequately protect your child from such harassment. Typically, the law varies considerably state by state: California's fails to define bullying, while in Georgia, a student who has bullied another three times in one school year is reassigned to an alternative school.

Schools need to do a better job of keeping students safe, not just by adding surveillance cameras, ID cards, and metal detectors they hope will prevent another shoot-out, but from the persistent low-grade emotional torment that unleashes such fury.

A national study released November 30, 2000, of ten thousand black, white, and Hispanic students in grades seven through twelve at 134 schools across the country, found that one in four students surveyed said they had carried a gun or a knife in the last year—a total of 5 million students.[22]

In 1998–99, 3,523 students across the country were expelled for bringing a firearm to school—down from 5,724 in 1996–97; of that number, 57 percent of expulsions were from high school, 33 percent from junior high, and 10 percent from elementary school. Fifty-nine percent had brought handguns to school, and 12 percent rifles or shotguns.[23]

A 1996 analysis of juvenile homicides found that six states—California, Texas, Illinois, New York, Michigan, and Florida—accounted for 56 percent of the country's juvenile homicide arrests. Four cities—Chicago, Los Angeles, New York, and Detroit—accounted for 30 percent of the nation's juvenile homicide arrests, although these cities contain only 5.3 percent of the nation's juvenile population.[24]

"You will always be fighting the influences of the media and popular entertainment that glorify guns and violence," says Margaret Childers, a twenty-seven-year-old schoolteacher. Childers, a white woman whose friend Alain Colaco was shot point-blank on his front lawn by a stranger when both were in high school, spent several years while still in high school organizing fellow students, distributing petitions, and even speaking at press conferences, to help pass the Brady Bill. "The primary responsibility belongs to the parents, parents who allow their children to play violent games and watch violent movies.

"The next battle line is the classroom. Teachers have an enormous power to effect change in children's lives, especially when children are still young. Conflict resolution education gives children the skills to solve their problems without resorting to violence."

Determine Your Child's Access to Weapons

When *USA Weekend, Teen People,* and Channel One television, a TV news program produced for schools, surveyed 129,593 students in grades six through twelve, almost 50 percent said they had a gun in the home, and more than half of those said they could get their hands on it. Forty percent said they could get a gun within their community within a day.[25]

Do you know which of your child's friends have a gun in the home?

Consider the following checklist:

- Are they handguns or long guns?
- Do you know how many there are and what caliber?
- Does each weapon carry a gun lock or are they kept in a gun safe?
- Who has the key?
- Where is ammunition kept and who has access to it?
- Has your child's friend been taught safe gun-handling? By whom?
- What are that family's rules about access to weapons?
- Are you comfortable knowing your child may be around guns with other adults? Under what circumstances?

- Do you know which of your child's friends' parents or siblings work in law enforcement and may have a handgun in the home?
- What about weekend homes, hunting camps, cottages, a car's glove compartment, or a truck's gun rack?

If you are not a gun owner, has your child ever seen or handled a firearm? Especially for teenage boys, statistically those most likely to kill themselves or others with a gun, ignorance can equal death. No matter how much guns may horrify you, consider, especially, a frank conversation with your son(s) about them.

Do you know your local and state gun laws? Even if you're viscerally opposed to gun ownership, consider finding out how close your child may come to touching or handling one *without your knowledge*.

Ask your child directly what s/he knows about guns and how to make one safe; many children have only seen one on television or in the movies and have no idea how much they weigh or how they function.

Have you talked through with them what they would, and should, do if they find a gun or are offered a chance to handle one? Gun owners are, naturally, private about their possessions. But relying on others isn't enough. Before you let your child play, certainly unsupervised, in another home, determine how safe that environment is. You'd ask the same about access to drugs or alcohol, wouldn't you?

When Depression Enters, Remove Guns (and Alcohol) from the Home

If someone you love may be considering suicide using a firearm, your best ally is their physician—someone whose concern and expertise they trust, someone they will listen to; some patients will turn over their firearms directly to a doctor or mental health care worker.

Suicidal adolescents are *75 times more likely* to commit suicide when a gun is kept in their home.[26] The recent rise in the adolescent suicide rate is also associated with increased alcohol and substance abuse in this group. A 1987 study found a 46 percent increase between 1978 and 1983 in the proportion of youths committing suicide while intoxicated, a time when adolescents are more likely to employ firearms than any other means of suicide attempt.[27] "Even if the desire to die is instantaneous and fleeting, the likelihood that a suicide attempt will result in a fatality increases dramatically when firearms are present in the home."[28]

Suicide by young adults aged five to nineteen by all means other than guns increased 175 percent between 1960 and 1980—over the same period, the percentage increase by the same age group using firearms was 299 percent.

Commit to Knowing Your Gun Intimately

What struck me throughout research for this book was the carelessness of some female gun owners. I'm not offended by any woman's decision to own a gun, or several; those who have bought a handgun for self-defense have made a significant decision with serious consequences—when, how, and where they are willing to take a life.

But gun ownership is a major responsibility, not one to be taken lightly. *It is a purchase like no other.* While the smooth, gleaming metal of a new gun may carry the material appeal of the latest cell phone, digital camera, or SUV, it is not simply another sexy accoutrement to make you feel cool.

Store it safely. Tell those who share your home that you own a gun, and make sure they have no access to it, or to ammunition. Set aside a budget to buy practice ammunition and for some classes. Commit to the many hours it will take you to become proficient as a shooter.

Practice often, at least once a week—the only way to rely on your gun to save your life is to know exactly what it will do. Clean it regularly. If you need adjustments to the grip, stock, trigger, sights, or other areas, make them and get used to using them. Take classes in defensive shooting to prepare both mentally and physically for shooting at night, outdoors, in small spaces. Learn ballistics and choose your ammunition accordingly. Know the law.

Your gun can only save your life if you can get to it quickly, use it unhesitatingly, and shoot it efficiently.

Speak Out for Safer Gun Use

Many Americans want to see safer gun use by legal gun owners, and much stronger enforcement of current gun laws, but don't know how to achieve it. Some want tougher gun controls or laws. Whether you own a gun or never wish to touch one, this is an issue both sides can support.

Raise your voice.

In addition to supporting gun control groups such as the Brady Campaign, Americans for Gun Safety, or Women Against Gun Violence, share your concerns with your elected officials at every level—municipal, county, state, and federal. Let them know how you feel and why. If you have a personal gun story to share, tell them about it. Write letters to the editor, opinion pieces, and editorials.

Since most new gun legislation will be passed at the state level, focus your energies there.

In thinking about women and violence, about vulnerability and fear, observing national apathy, ignorance, and denial, I wonder, What will American women do to claim their own safety in this violent culture? Can they reasonably expect succor from neighbors and colleagues, friends and family? The kindness of strangers?

Have women *ever* enjoyed it? Should they?

Forty years ago, on March 13, 1964, a twenty-eight-year-old manager of a bar in Hollis, Queens, headed home at 3 A.M. after parking her red Fiat. A man pursued her and stabbed her. She screamed, he fled, and she hid in the back of an apartment building. He came back and stabbed her to death. On a quiet street in a decent New York City working-class neighborhood, thirty-eight witnesses ignored her screams. Not one person called the police. Kitty Genovese's name became a national byword for civic callousness and indifference.

Yet is the world any safer for women today? How can we make it so, for gun owners and non–gun owners alike?

"The self-protective shells in which we live are determined not only by the difference between big cities and small," wrote A. M. Rosenthal, then a young reporter who covered that story for, and who later became executive editor of, the *New York Times*. "They are determined by economics and social class, by caste and by color, and by religion, and by politics."[29]

Little has changed.

There are, he writes, "only two logical ways to look at the story of Catherine Genovese." The first, to forget it. "The other is to recognize that the bell tolls on each man's individual island, to recognize that every man must fear the witness in himself who whispers to close the window."

Let's keep the windows open.

Notes

Chapter 1: A Moving Target

1. Monica Rhor, *The Miami Herald,* July 14, 2002.
2. *Tales of the Gun: Women and Guns,* documentary, History Channel, 1998.
3. Personal interview with author, July 2002.
4. Ivor Peterson, *New York Times,* July 13, 2002, B10.
5. Jonathan Green, "Graveyard Shift," *Financial Times Magazine,* September 15, 2001.
6. Max and Rice, "Shooting in the Dark: Estimating the Cost of Firearm Injuries," *Health Affairs* 12 (1993): 171–85. A 1994 study, reported in the *Journal of the American Medical Association,* whose lead author was Dr. Philip J. Cook of Duke University, estimated that figure *at only $2.3 billion* annually. This much lower figure excluded other costs such as mental health treatment for victims and lost days of work. Such enormous disparities in statistics regarding gun violence are not unusual and, I would offer, should suggest some caution to readers, and legislators, who rely exclusively on statistical data when proposing gun policy.

7. Bureau of Alcohol, Tobacco & Firearms, "1998 Annual Manufacturers Excise Tax Report."

8. U.S. Fish & Wildlife Service, "1996 National Survey of Fishing, Hunting, and Wildlife Associated Recreation."

9. Susan Straight, "Love Me, Love My Guns," Salon.com, October 21, 1999.

10. Elizabeth Marchak, *Cleveland Plain Dealer,* February 14, 1994, 6A.

11. Bill Finley, *New York Times,* July 6, 2002, D3.

12. Sallie Tisdale, Salon.com, May 6, 1999.

13. Paxton Quigley, *Armed and Female* (St. Martin's Press, 1989), 93.

14. Carol K. Oyster and Mary Zeiss Stange, *Gun Women* (New York University Press, 2000), 85–86.

15. *New York Post,* June 4, 2002, 10.

16. Melissa Chessher, *Health,* July 2002, 130–36.

17. Ibid.

18. Ibid.

19. Denise Caignon and Gail Groves, eds., *Her Wits About Her: Self-Defense Success Stories by Women* (Perennial, 1987).

20. Frederic Storaska, *How to Say No to a Rapist and Survive* (Random House, 1975), 147.

21. Pat Moore with Charles Paul, *Disguised, a True Story* (World Publishing, 1985).

22. Nicole Hahn Rafter, editor in chief, *Encyclopedia of Women and Crime* (Oryx Press, 2000), 60.

23. Elizabeth Marchak, *Cleveland Plain Dealer,* March 16, 2000, 7.

24. Oyster and Stange, *Gun Women,* 85–86.

25. Ann Jones, "Is This Power Feminism?" *Ms.,* June 1994, 36–44.

Chapter 2: Annie, Get Your Gun

1. T. J. Stiles, ed., *In Their Own Words: The Colonizers* (Perigee, 1998).

2. Joan McCullough, *First of All: Significant Firsts by American Women* (Henry Holt & Company, 1980).

3. William W. Fowler, *Woman on the American Frontier* (Hartford, Conn.: S. S. Scranton & Co., 1886), 179.

4. DeAnne Blanton and Lauren M. Cook, *They Fought Like Demons: Women Soldiers in the American Civil War* (Louisiana State University Press, 2002), 31, 33.

5. Ibid., 4.

6. Ibid., 8.

7. Ibid., 28.

8. Ibid., 57.

9. Ibid., 85.

10. Ibid., 148.

11. Ibid., 189.

12. *Tales of the Gun: Women and Guns,* documentary, History Channel, 1998.

13. Matthew Page Andrews, comp., *Women of the South in War Times* (Norman Remington Company, 1927).

14. Cathy Lee Luchetti and Carol Olwell, *Women of the West* (Antelope Island Press, 1982).

15. Glenda Riley, *A Place to Grow: Women in the American West* (Harlan Davidson, 1992), 214.

16. Julie Roy Jeffrey, *Frontier Women, "Civilizing" the West, 1840–1880* (Hill and Wang, 1998).

17. Ann Fears Crawford and Crystal Sasse Ragsdale, *Texas Women, Frontier to Future* (Ragsdale, 1998).

18. Sandra L. Myres, *Westering Women and the Frontier Experience, 1800–1915* (University of New Mexico Press, 1982).

19. Duncan Aikman, *Calamity Jane and the Lady Wildcats* (Henry Holt and Company, 1926).

20. Ibid.

21. Ibid., 194.

22. Ibid.

23. Tristram Potter Coffin, *The Female Hero in Folklore and Legend* (Seabury Press, 1975), 138.

24. Aikman, *Calamity Jane.*

25. Ibid., 271.

26. Ibid., 271–72.

27. Glenda Riley, *The Life and Legacy of Annie Oakley* (University of Oklahoma Press, 1994), 11.

28. Ibid., 141.

29. Ibid., 140–41.

30. Ibid., 14.

31. Ibid., xv–xvi.

32. Nicole Rafter Hahn, *Encyclopedia of Women and Crime* (Oryx Press, 2000), 162.

33. Ibid.

34. Women Airforce Service Pilots, The Woman's Collection, Texas Woman's University.

35. Joyce Thompson, *Marking a Trail* (Texas Woman's University Press, 1982).

36. Geoffrey Perrett, *Days of Sadness, Years of Triumph: The American People, 1939–1945* (University of Wisconsin Press, 1985).

37. The American Rifleman, June 1956, 17.

38. Rosa Parks with Jim Haskins, *Rosa Parks, My Story* (Puffin Books, 1992), 30–31.

39. Ibid., 67.

40. Kay Mills, *This Little Light of Mine: The Life of Fannie Lou Hamer* (Dutton 1993), 46.

41. Ibid., 108.

42. Howell Raines, *My Soul Is Rested: Movement Days in the Deep South Remembered* (G. P. Putnam's Sons, New York, 1977), 251–52.

43. Ibid., 271.

44. Timothy B. Tyson, *Radio Free Dixie: Robert F. Williams and the Roots of Black Power* (University of North Carolina Press, 1999), 91.

45. Ibid., 159.
46. Ibid., 91.

Chapter 3: Thelma, Velma, and the Fembots

1. Molly Haskell, *From Reverence to Rape*, 2d ed. (University of Chicago Press, 1987), 4.
2. Ibid., 3.
3. Martha McCaughey and Neal King, eds, *Reel Knockouts: Violent Women in the Movies* (University of Texas Press, 2001), 2.
4. Ibid., 5.
5. Ibid., 95.
6. Ibid., 98.
7. Andrew Sarris, *New York Observer*, June 21, 1999, 27.
8. Jamie Diamond, *Glamour*, July 2002, 139–40, 214.
9. Marjorie Rosen, *Popcorn Venus: Women, Movies and the American Dream* (Coward, McCann & Geoghegan, 1973), 133.
10. *Sunday Times*, March 10, 2002.
11. Richard Corliss, "Girls Just Wanna Have Guns," *Time*, April 22, 2002.
12. *New York Times*, December 22, 2002, AR5.
13. *Studio 360* radio broadcast, WNYC, January 18, 2003.
14. *New York Times*, January 5, 2003, AR35.
15. Patrick McMahon, *USA Today*, April 5, 1999.
16. Bob Herbert, "The Gift of Mayhem," *New York Times*, November 28, 2002, A35.
17. NPD press release, January 27, 2003.
18. Hoover's Online, March 5, 2003.
19. Michel Marriott, *New York Times*, May 15, 2003, G1.
20. *Washington Informer*, January 9, 2002, 6.
21. Trina Robbins, *The Great Women Superheroes* (Kitchen Sink Press, 1996), 50.
22. Trina Robbins, *A Century of Women Cartoonists* (Kitchen Sink Press, 1993), 78.

23. Gordon Russell, *Times-Picayune,* July 6, 2003, 1.

24. Vanessa E. Jones, *Boston Globe,* March 1, 2003, D4.

25. PR Newswire, January 14, 2003.

26. Rick Bragg, *New York Times,* September 6, 1996, A12.

27. *New York Times,* January 23, 2002.

28. Charlotte McKenzie, *Woman's Outlook,* February 2003, 33, 59.

Chapter 4: The Decision to Arm

1. David P. Barash, *Chronicle of Higher Education,* May 24, 2002, B7–B9.

2. Elizabeth Dermody Leonard, *Convicted Survivors: The Imprisonment of Battered Women Who Kill* (State University of New York Press, 2002), 3.

3. M. Elizabeth Blair and Eva M. Hyatt, "The Marketing of Guns to Women: Factors Influencing Gun-Related Attitudes and Gun Ownership by Women," *Journal of Public Policy & Marketing,* spring 1995, 121.

4. *New York Post,* December 25, 2002, 3.

5. Karen MacNutt, *Ladies Legal Companion* (MacNutt Art Trust, 1993), 13.

6. Adam Miller, Philip Messing, and Marsha Kranes, *New York Post,* January 24, 2003, 3.

7. Steve Berry, "Armed and Anonymous," *The Los Angeles Times Magazine,* November 18, 2001, 12–19.

8. *New York Times,* May 9, 2002, quoting from the introduction to *Every Tongue Got to Confess: Negro Folk Tales from the Gulf States.*

9. A pseudonym.

10. *New York Times,* September 8, 2002.

11. Karen MacNutt, *Ladies Legal Companion* (MacNutt Art Trust, 1993), 15.

12. Ibid., 14.

13. Elizabeth Dermody Leonard, *Convicted Survivors: The Imprisonment of Battered Women Who Kill* (State University of New York Press, 2002), 37.

14. Ibid., 15.

15. Ibid.

16. Ibid., 26.

17. Ibid., 91.

18. MacNutt, 17–18.

19. Leonard, 108–09.

Chapter 5: The Dark Side

1. Anita Rodger's name and state have been changed at her request.

2. Elizabeth Dermody Leonard, *Convicted Survivors: The Imprisonment of Battered Women Who Kill* (State University of New York Press, 2002), 3.

3. Ibid.

4. Violence Policy Center.

5. Maria Luisa Arredondo, *La Opinión,* March 18, 2001.

6. Ibid.

7. Arthur Bovino, *New York Times,* December 26, 2002, B6.

8. Jonathan van Meter, *Vogue,* December 2002, 269.

9. Leonard, *Convicted Survivors,* 3.

10. Elizabeth Richardson Vigdor and James A. Mercy, *Disarming Batterers: The Impact of Domestic Violence Firearm Laws* (The Brookings Institution, 2003), 159.

11. Ibid., 190.

12. Daisy Hernandez, *New York Times,* December 21, 2002, B2.

13. Ibid.

14. Mary Ann Dutton, *Empowering and Healing the Battered Woman* (Springer Publishing Company, 1992), 47.

15. Angela Browne, *When Battered Women Kill,* (Free Press, 1989), 20.

16. Ibid.

17. Donald Alexander, *More Than Victims: Battered Women, the Syndrome and the Law* (University of Chicago Press, 1996).

18. Eric Brown, www.caller2.com, March 31, 1996.

19. Ibid.

20. Ibid.

21. Coramae Richey Mann, *When Women Kill* (State University of New York Press, 1996).

22. Dominick Dunne, *Vanity Fair,* October 2002, 192.

23. Walter Isaacson, *Time,* March 9, 1981, 20.

24. Elizabeth Peer, *Newsweek,* March 2, 1981, 38.

25. Associated Press in *New York Times,* January 29, 2003, A21.

26. Nicole Hahn Rafter, editor in chief, *Encyclopedia of Women and Crime* (Oryx Press, 2000), 44.

27. *The Unspoken Tragedy: Firearm Suicide in the United States* (The Educational Fund to End Handgun Violence and The Coalition to Stop Gun Violence, May 31, 1995).

28. Adam Miller, Clemente Lisi, and Marsha Kranes, *New York Post,* December 31, 2001, 21.

29. *The Unspoken Tragedy.*

30. Ibid.

31. Katharine Graham, *Personal History* (Knopf, 1997), 330.

32. Ibid.

33. Ibid., 332.

34. Bill Bryan, *St. Louis Post-Dispatch,* STLToday website, February 19, 2003.

35. Jonathan Green, "Graveyard Shift," *The Financial Times Magazine,* September 15, 2001.

36. Jodi Wilgoren, *New York Times,* January 1, 2003, A11.

37. Amy Wilson, *Orange County Register,* April 25, 1999, A1.

38. Michael Granberry, *Los Angeles Times,* January 19, 1989, Metro section, pt. 2. p. 1.

39. Personal interview with author.

Chapter 6: A Member of the Family

1. Maureen Orth, *Vanity Fair,* December 2002, 220.
2. Nanette Varian, *Glamour,* October 2002, 290, 319.
3. *FBI Law Enforcement Bulletin,* November 1995, 12–16.
4. Susan Straight, "Love Me, Love My Guns," Salon.com, October 21, 1999.
5. M. Elizabeth Blair and Eva M. Hyatt, "The Marketing of Guns to Women: Factors Influencing Gun-Related Attitudes and Gun Ownership by Women," *Journal of Public Policy & Marketing,* spring 1995, 122.
6. *Washington Post National Weekly Edition,* July 29–August 4, 2002.
7. Paxton Quigley, *Armed and Female* (St. Martin's Press, 1989), 139–40.

Chapter 7: A Gun for Fun

1. *Woman's Outlook,* February 2003, 31.
2. National Shooting Sports Foundation.
3. Ibid.
4. Ibid.
5. Ibid.
6. Karen Mehall and Ann Y. Smith, *Woman's Outlook,* January 2003, 37.
7. James Fallon, *Women's Wear Daily,* July 6, 1989, 2.
8. Marion Maneker, *New York,* October 11, 1999, 19.
9. Alba Gaggioli, *Italia, Life in Style,* fall 2002, 84–85.
10. Tom Henderson, *New York Post,* February 3, 2003, 33.
11. ICan website, March 4, 2002.
12. National Shooting Sports Foundation.
13. Ibid.
14. James Barron, *New York Times,* November 26, 1997, B1.

15. Mary Zeiss Stange, *Woman the Hunter* (Beacon Press, 1997), 2.

16. Francis X. Clines, *New York Times,* September 29, 2002, A28.

17. Ibid.

18. Devin Rose, *Chicago Tribune,* February 20, 2002.

19. Barron, *New York Times,* B1.

20. Ibid., B5.

21. Stange, *Woman the Hunter,* 103.

Chapter 8: In the Line of Fire

1. Joseph P. Fried, "Police Hero in 1994 Is Now a Bitter Retiree," *New York Times,* June 30, 2002.

2. Donna St. George, *Washington Post National Weekly Edition,* May 6–12, 2002, 6–7.

3. Jodi Wilgoren, *New York Times,* March 28, 2003, B1.

4. Ibid., B11.

5. Nicole Hahn Rafter, editor in chief, *Encyclopedia of Women and Crime* (Oryx Press, 2000), p. 34.

6. Philip H. Melanson with Peter F. Stevens, *The Secret Service: The Hidden History of an Enigmatic Agency* (Carroll & Graf, 2002), 113.

Chapter 9: Guns Mean Business

1. Dolores Tropiano, ArizonaRepublic.com, March 11, 2002.

2. Shooting Sportsman, November/December 2002, 28–36.

3. Personal interview with author.

Chapter 10: Both Sides of the Aisle

1. Personal interview with author, December 2002.

2. Sarah Brady with Merrill McLoughlin, *A Good Fight* (Public Affairs, 2002), 102.

3. Ibid., 103.

4. Ibid., 124.

5. Ibid., 166.

6. Ibid., 104–05.

7. Tom Diaz, *Making a Killing* (The New Press, 1999), 8.

8. Ibid., 14.

9. Ibid., 146.

10. Ibid., 21.

11. Jens Ludwig and Philip J. Cook, eds., *Evaluating Gun Policy: Effects on Crime and Violence* (Brookings Institution Press, 2003), 442.

12. Endnote, Census, 2001.

13. Ludwig and Cook, *Evaluating Gun Policy*, 449.

14. Ibid., 447.

15. Diaz, *Making a Killing*, 66.

16. Ibid., 67–68.

17. Ludwig and Cook, *Evaluating Gun Policy*, 442.

18. Michael Janofsky, *New York Times*, February 14, 2003, A20.

19. Associated Press in *New York Times*, February 14, 2003, A28.

20. Katherine Q. Seelye, *New York Times*, October 20, 2002.

21. *New York Post*, December 13, 2002, 4.

22. Ibid.

23. Chris Cobb, *Calgary Herald*, September 28, 1998, A3.

24. Dan Barry, *New York Times*, November 7, 1996, A1.

25. Peter J. Boyer, *The New Yorker*, May 17, 1999, 65.

26. Personal interview with author.

27. Guy Coates, Associated Press, June 3, 1999.

28. Personal interview with author.

29. *New York Times*, October 5, 2002, B1.

30. Thomas B. Edsall, *Washington Post Weekly National Edition,* January 6–12, 2003, 12.

31. Ibid., 13.

Chapter 11: The Next Generation

1. Linda Deutsch, AP special correspondent, Associated Press, April 18, 2001.

2. Lorna Hughes, *Sunday Mail,* April 22, 2001, 18.

3. B. Vossekuil, R. Fein, M. Reddy, R. Borum, and W. Modzeleski, *The Final Report and Findings of the Safe School Initiative: Implications for the Prevention of School Attacks in the United States* (U.S. Department of Education, Office of Elementary and Secondary School Education, Safe and Drug-Free Schools Program and U.S. Secret Service, National Threat Assessment Center, Washington, D.C., May 2002), 36.

4. Ibid.

5. Frank Rich, *New York Times Magazine,* November 3, 2002, 56.

6. *Report Card on the Ethics of American Youth 2000, Report #1: Violence, Guns and Alcohol* (Josephson Institute of Ethics).

7. *Hearing Before the Subcommittee on Crime and Criminal Justice, of the Committee on the Judiciary, House of Representatives,* 103d Cong., 2d sess., ser. no. 82.

8. Geoffrey Perrett, *Days of Sadness, Years of Triumph: The American People, 1939–1945* (University of Wisconsin Press, 1985).

9. Ibid.

10. Jennifer Medina, *New York Times,* November 6, 2002, A25.

11. Ibid.

12. Ralph Winingham, *San Antonio Express-News,* April 9, 2002, 1B, 3B.

13. Jeffrey R. Young, *Chronicle of Higher Education,* January 31, 2003, A37.

14. David Cohen, *Chronicle of Higher Education,* January 31, 2003, A41.

15. *Chronicle of Higher Education,* February 1, 2002.

16. Ben Gose, *Chronicle of Higher Education,* September 20, 2002, A26.

17. *Chronicle of Higher Education,* November 1, 2002, A33.

18. Patrice O'Shaughnessy, *New York Daily News,* September 29, 2002, 4.

19. The girls requested that I use only their first names; two of these are pseudonyms.

20. Possession of a stolen weapon is a felony. Despite the girls' firm belief to the contrary, however, the prosecution cannot automatically charge a gun's current illegal owner with murder for mere possession of a weapon responsible for unsolved murders, but must collect evidence clearly connecting the owner to the previous crimes and indict them on these separate charges.

Chapter 12: What to Do?

1. Jodi Wilgoren, *New York Times,* January 1, 2003, A11.

2. *New York Times,* January 18, 2003, B9.

3. Bob Herbert, *New York Times,* February 6, 2003, A39.

4. David Tuller, *New York Times,* January 14, 2003, F7.

5. Dan Eggen, *Washington Post National Weekly Edition,* July 1–4, 2002.

6. Gavin de Becker, *The Gift of Fear: Survival Signals That Protect Us from Violence* (Little, Brown and Company, 1997), 63.

7. Ibid., 11.

8. Ibid., 32.

9. Jeffrey Cohen, *Adweek,* November 21, 1988.

10. Martha McCaughey, *Real Knockouts: The Physical Feminism of Women's Self-Defense* (New York University Press, 1997), 12.

11. Ibid., 90–92.

12. Ibid., 18.

13. Karjane, Fisher, and Cullen, *Campus Sexual Assault: How*

America's Institutions of Higher Education Respond (2002), Education Development Center, viii.

14. Bob Herbert, *New York Times*, November 28, 2002, A35.

15. Andrew Sarris, *New York Observer*, June 21, 1999, 27.

16. Ibid.

17. *Chronicle of Higher Education*, January 17, 2003, A7.

18. *Oprah*, ABC, January 30, 2003.

19. Ibid.

20. *Report Card on the Ethics of American Youth 2000, Report #1: Violence, Guns and Alcohol* (Josephson Institute of Ethics).

21. The Empower Program, www.empowered.org.

22. "*Protecting Teens: Beyond Race, Income and Family Structure:* The National Longitudinal Study of Adolescent Health," *American Journal of Public Health*, December 2000.

23. *2000 Annual Report on Safety* (U.S. Department of Education and the U.S. Department of Justice).

24. Vincent Schiraldi, Eric Lotke, *An Analysis of Juvenile Homicides: Where They Occur and the Effectiveness of Adult Court Intervention*, Center on Juvenile and Criminal Justice, Washington, D.C., 1996.

25. *USA Weekend*, 13th annual Teen Survey, 1999.

26. *The Unspoken Tragedy: Firearm Suicide in the United States* (The Educational Fund to End Handgun Violence and The Coalition to Stop Gun Violence, May 31, 1995).

27. Ibid.

28. Ibid.

29. A. M. Rosenthal, *Thirty-eight Witnesses* (University of California Press, 1999), 76–77.

Bibliography

———◆•※•◆———

Newspapers and Magazines

Maria Luisa Arredondo, *La Opinión*, March 18, 2001.

James Barron, *New York Times*, November 26, 1997, B1.

Dan Barry, *New York Times*, November 7, 1996, A1.

Steve Berry, "Armed and Anonymous," *The Los Angeles Times Magazine*, November 18, 2001, 12–19.

Arthur Bovino, *New York Times*, December 26, 2002, B6.

Peter J. Boyer, *The New Yorker*, May 17, 1999, 65.

Rick Bragg, *New York Times*, September 6, 1996, A12.

Fox Butterfield, *New York Times*, February 27, 2002, A16.

Calgary Herald, September 28, 1998, A3.

Melissa Chessher, *Health*, July 2002, 130–36.

Chronicle of Higher Education, February 1, 2002; November 1, 2002, A33.

Francis X. Clines, *New York Times*, September 29, 2002, A28.

Guy Coates, Associated Press, June 3, 1999.

David Cohen, *Chronicle of Higher Education*, January 31, 2003, A41.

Jeffrey Cohen, *Adweek,* November 21, 1988.

Richard Corliss, *Time,* April 14, 2002.

Jamie Diamond, *Glamour,* July 2002, 139–40, 214.

Dominick Dunne, *Vanity Fair,* October 2002, 192.

Thomas B. Edsall, *Washington Post National Weekly Edition,* January 6–12, 2003, 12.

Dan Eggen, *Washington Post National Weekly Edition,* July 1–4, 2002.

James Fallon, *Women's Wear Daily,* July 6, 1989, 2.

FBI Law Enforcement Bulletin, November 1995.

Alba Gaggioli, *Italia, Life in Style,* fall 2002, 84–85.

Anita Gates, *New York Times,* June 5, 2002, E4.

Sarah Gilbert, *New York Post,* February 3, 2003, 33.

Ben Gose, *Chronicle of Higher Education,* September 20, 2002, A26.

Michael Granberry, *Los Angeles Times,* January 19, 1989, Metro section, pt. 2, p. 1.

Jonathan Green, "Graveyard Shift," *Financial Times Magazine,* September 15, 2001.

Bob Herbert, "The Gift of Mayhem," *New York Times,* November 28, 2002, A35.

Daisy Hernandez, *New York Times,* December 17, 2002.

Spencer S. Hsu, *Washington Post National Weekly Edition,* September 2–8, 2002, 30.

Lorna Hughes, *Sunday Mail,* April 22, 2001, 18.

Walter Isaacson, *Time,* March 9, 1981, 20.

Michael Janofsky, *New York Times,* February 14, 2003, A20.

Ann Jones, "Is This Power Feminism?," *Ms.,* May/June 1994, 36–44.

Marion Maneker, *New York,* October 11, 1999, 19.

Elizabeth Marchak, *The Cleveland Plain Dealer,* February 14, 1994; March 16, 2000.

Charlotte McKenzie, *Woman's Outlook,* February 2003, 33, 59.

Patrick McMahon, *USA Today,* April 5, 1999.

Jennifer Medina, *New York Times,* November 6, 2002, A25.

Karen Mehall and Ann Y. Smith, *Woman's Outlook,* January 2003, 37.

Adam Miller, Clemente Lisi, and Marsha Kranes, *New York Post,* December 31, 2001, 21.

New York, March 18, 2002.

New York Times, October 5, 2002, B1.

Maureen Orth, *Vanity Fair,* December 2002, 220.

Elizabeth Peer, *Newsweek,* March 2, 1981, 38.

Ivor Peterson, *New York Times,* July 13, 2002.

Monica Rhor, *Miami Herald,* July 14, 2002.

Frank Rich, *The New York Times Magazine,* November 3, 2002, 56.

Devin Rose, *Chicago Tribune,* February 20, 2002.

Andrew Sarris, *New York Observer,* June 21, 1999, 27.

Katherine Q. Seelye, *New York Times,* October 20, 2002.

Shooting Sportsman, November/December 2002, 28–36.

Terry Teachout, *New York Times,* December 22, 2002, AR5.

David Tuller, *New York Times,* January 14, 2003, F7.

USA Weekend, 13th annual Teen Survey, 1999.

Jonathan van Meter, *Vogue,* December 2002, 269.

Nanette Varian, *Glamour,* October 2002, 290, 319.

Washington Informer, January 9, 2002, 6.

Jodi Wilgoren, *New York Times,* January 1, 2003, A11; March 28, 2003, B1.

Amy Wilson, *Orange County Register,* April 25, 1999, A1.

Woman's Outlook, February 2003, 31.

Women Airforce Service Pilots, The Woman's Collection, Texas Woman's University.

Jeffrey R. Young, *Chronicle of Higher Education,* January 31, 2003, A37.

Books

Duncan Aikman. *Calamity Jane and the Lady Wildcats.* New York: Henry Holt and Company, 1926.

Donald Alexander. *More Than Victims: Battered Women, the Syndrome and the Law.* University of Chicago Press, 1996.

Matthew Page Andrews, comp. *Women of the South in War Times.* Norman Remington Company, 1927.

Daisy Bates. *The Long Shadow of Little Rock.* New York: David McKay Company Inc., 1962.

DeAnne Blanton and Lauren M. Cook. *They Fought Like Demons: Women Soldiers in the American Civil War.* Baton Rouge: Louisiana State University Press, 2002.

Sarah Brady with Merrill McLoughlin. *A Good Fight.* Public Affairs, 2002.

Angela Browne. *When Battered Women Kill.* Free Press, 1989.

Christopher M. Byron. *Martha, Inc.: The Incredible Story of Martha Stewart Living Omnimedia.* John Wiley & Sons, 2002.

Denise Caignon and Gail Groves, eds. *Her Wits About Her: Self-Defense Success Stories by Women.* Perennial, 1987.

Tristram Potter Coffin. *The Female Hero in Folklore and Legend.* New York: Seabury Press, 1975.

Cynthia B. Costello, Shari Miles, and Anne J. Stone, eds. *The American Woman, 1999–2000.* Women's Research and Education Institute, 2001.

Ann Fears Crawford and Crystal Sasse Ragsdale. *Texas Women, Frontier to Future.* Ragsdale, 1998.

Gavin de Becker. *The Gift of Fear: Survival Signals That Protect Us from Violence.* Little, Brown and Company, 1997.

Tom Diaz. *Making a Killing.* The New Press, 1999.

Mary Ann Dutton. *Empowering and Healing the Battered Woman.* Springer Publishing Company, 1992.

William W. Fowler. *Woman on the American Frontier.* Hartford, Conn.: S. S. Scranton & Co., 1886.

James William Gibson. *Warrior Dreams: Violence and Manhood in Post-Vietnam America.* Hill and Wang, 1994.

Margaret T. Gordon and Stephanie Rieger. *The Female Fear.* Free Press, 1988.

Katharine Graham. *A Personal History.* Knopf, 1997.

Molly Haskell. *From Reverence to Rape.* 2d ed., University of Chicago Press, 1987.

Deborah Homsher. *Women & Guns: Politics and the Culture of Firearms in America*. Armonk, N.Y., and London, England: M. E. Sharpe, Inc., 2001.

Julie Roy Jeffrey. *Frontier Women, "Civilizing" the West, 1840–1880*. Hill and Wang, 1998.

Elizabeth Dermody Leonard. *Convicted Survivors: The Imprisonment of Battered Women Who Kill*. State University of New York Press, 2002.

Cathy Lee Luchetti and Carol Olwell. *Women of the West*. Antelope Island Press, 1982.

Jens Ludwig and Philip J. Cook, eds. *Evaluating Gun Policy: Effects on Crime and Violence*. Washington, D.C.: Brookings Institution Press, 2003.

Karen L. MacNutt. *Ladies Legal Companion*. Boston, Mass.: MacNutt Art Trust, 1993.

Coramae Richey Mann. *When Women Kill*. State University of New York Press, 1996.

Robert Markel, Susan Waggoner, and Marcella Smith, eds. *The Women's Sports Encyclopedia*. Henry Holt & Co., 1998.

Mitford Mathews. *American Words*. World Publishing Company, 1959.

Martha McCaughey. *Real Knockouts: The Physical Feminism of Women's Self-Defense*. New York University Press, 1997.

Martha McCaughey and Neal King, eds. *Reel Knockouts: Violent Women in the Movies*. University of Texas Press, 2001.

Joan McCullough. *First of All: Significant Firsts by American Women*. Holt & Company, 1980

Philip Melanson with Peter F. Stevens. *The Secret Service: The Hidden History of an Enigmatic Agency*. Carroll & Graff, 2002.

Ronald Dean Miller. *Shady Ladies of the West*. Los Angeles: Westernlore Press, 1964.

Kay Mills. *This Little Light of Mine: The Life of Fannie Lou Hamer*. Dutton, 1993.

Pat Moore with Charles Paul. *Disguised: A True Story*. World Publishing, 1985.

Sandra L. Myres. *Westering Women and the Frontier Experience, 1800–1915*. University of New Mexico Press, 1982.

Rosa Parks with Jim Haskins. *Rosa Parks: My Story*. Puffin Books, 1992.

Geoffrey Perrett. *Days of Sadness, Years of Triumph: The American People, 1939–1945*. University of Wisconsin Press, 1985.

Paxton Quigley. *Armed and Female*. St. Martin's Press, 1989.

Nicole Hahn Rafter, editor in chief. *Encyclopedia of Women and Crime*. Oryx Press, 2000.

Howell Raines. *My Soul Is Rested: Movement Days in the Deep South Remembered*. New York: G.P. Putnam's Sons, 1977.

Glenda Riley. *The Life and Legacy of Annie Oakley*. University of Oklahoma Press, 1994.

———. *A Place to Grow: Women in the American West*. Harlan Davidson, 1992.

Trina Robbins. *A Century of Women Cartoonists*. Kitchen Sink Press, 1993.

———. *From Girls to Grrrlz: A History of Female Comics from Teens to Zines*. Chronicle Books, 1999.

———. *The Great Women Superheroes*. Kitchen Sink Press, 1996.

Marjorie Rosen. *Popcorn Venus: Women Movies and the American Dream*. Coward, McCann & Geoghegan, 1973.

A. M. Rosenthal. *Thirty-Eight Witnesses*. Los Angeles, London: University of California Press, Berkeley, 1999.

Victoria Sherrow. *Encyclopedia of Women and Sports*. ABC-CLIO, 1996.

Mary Zeiss Stange. *Woman the Hunter*. Beacon Press, 1997.

Mary Zeiss Stange and Carol K. Oyster. *Gun Women: Firearms and Feminism in Contemporary America*. New York University Press, 2000.

T. J. Stiles, ed. *In Their Own Words: The Colonizers*. Perigee, 1998.

Frederic Storaska. *How to Say No to a Rapist and Survive*. Random House, 1975.

Joyce Thompson. *Marking a Trail*. Texas Woman's University Press, 1982.

Timothy B. Tyson. *Radio Free Dixie: Robert F. Williams and the Roots of Black Power.* Chapel Hill and London: University of North Carolina Press, 1999.

Reports

Vincent Schiraldi, Eric Lotke, *An Analysis of Juvenile Homicides: Where They Occur and the Effectiveness of Adult Court Intervention*, Center on Juvenile and Criminal Justice, Washington, D.C., 1996.

M. Elizabeth Blair and Eva M. Hyatt. "The Marketing of Guns to Women: Factors Influencing Gun-Related Attitudes and Gun Ownership by Women." *Journal of Public Policy & Marketing*, spring 1995.

Bureau of Alcohol, Tobacco, and Firearms. *1998 Annual Manufacturers Excise Tax Report.*

Max and Rice, "Shooting in the Dark: Estimating the Cost of Firearm Injuries." *Health Affairs* 12 (1993): 171–85.

Mark H. Moore, Carol V. Petrie, Anthony A. Braga, and Brenda L. McLaughlin, eds. *Deadly Lessons: Understanding Lethal School Violence.* National Research Council and Institute of Medicine, Division of Behavioral and Social Sciences and Education. Washington, D.C: National Academy Press, 2002.

"*Protecting Teens; Beyond Race, Income and Family Structure:* The National Longitudinal Study of Adolescent Health." *American Journal of Public Health*, December, 2000.

Report Card on the Ethics of American Youth 2000, Report #1: Violence, Guns and Alcohol. Josephson Institute of Ethics.

United States Congress House Committee on the Judiciary, Subcommittee on Crime and Criminal Justice. *Caught in the Crossfire: Kids Talk about Guns.* February 3, 1994. Government document Y4.J 89/1:103/82.

United States Fishing and Wildlife Service. *1996 National Survey of Fishing, Hunting and Wildife Associated Recreation.*

The Unspoken Tragedy: Firearm Suicide in the United States. The

Educational Fund to End Handgun Violence and The Coalition to Stop Gun Violence, May 31, 1995.

U.S. Department of Education and the U.S. Department of Justice. *2000 Annual Report on Safety*.

B.Vossekuil, R. Fein, M. Reddy, R. Borum, and W. Modzeleski. *The Final Report and Findings of the Safe School Initiative: Implications for the Prevention of School Attacks in the United States*. U.S. Department of Education, Office of Elementary and Secondary School Education, Safe and Drug-Free Schools Program, and U.S. Secret Service, National Threat Assessment Center, Washington, D.C., May 2002.

Websites

ArizonaRepublic.com, Dolores Tropiano, March 11, 2002

bangbangyouredead.com

BJS.gov

BradyCampaign.com

campussafety.org

CDC.gov

empowered.org

Fec.gov

Hoover's Online

Ican.com

MillionMomMarch.com

NRA.com

Opensecrets.org

Salon.com, May 6, 1999; October 21, 1999

SecondAmendmentSisters.com

St. Louis Post-Dispatch, STLToday website

VPC.com

Television, Film, and Radio

Margaret Lazarus. *Defending Our Lives*. Cambridge Documentary Films, 1993.

Michael Moore. *Bowling for Columbine*. 2002, film.

Oprah. ABC, January 30, 2003, television show.

Thom Powers. *Guns and Mothers*. Sugar Pictures, 2003.

Wendy Rowland. *Packing Heat: Does Safety Come from the Barrel of a Gun?* National Film Board, 1996.

Studio 360. WNYC, January 18, 2003, radio show.

Tales of the Gun: Women and Guns. History Channel, 1998, film.

Index